Happy return!
to dear from

[signature]

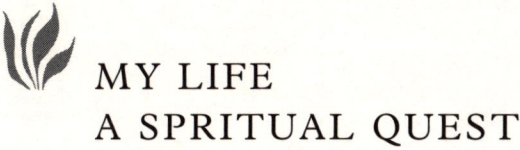

MY LIFE
A SPRITUAL QUEST

This book is dedicated to Marjorie Marston Von Harten, my dearly beloved sister and constant companion, who initiated so many of the travels that we were able to undertake and who introduced me to so many of the spiritual teachers we met

Also to my dear and kindly friend, Mrs Jill Redford, who has helped me at every turn and has been so interested in the progress of this book. She has helped me so loyally throughout.

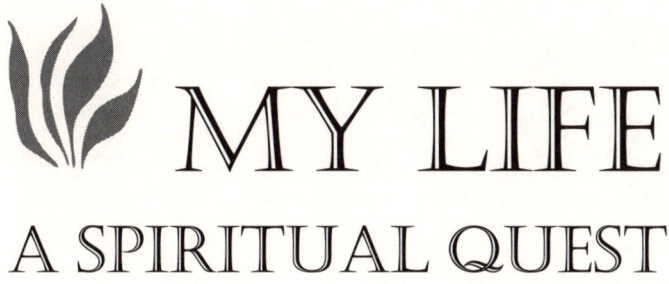

MY LIFE
A SPIRITUAL QUEST

Melissa Marston Macleod

Published by
Major J. Keith Macleod, M.B.E.
"Marylands"
Snowdenham Links Road
Bramley Guildford
Surrey GU5 OBX

ISBN 0-9538263-0-9

Designed and typeset by
John Saunders Design and Production, Reading

Printed in Great Britain by
Biddles Ltd., Guildford and King's Lynn

CONTENTS

CHAPTER 1

Introduction

I came into this world on April 17th, 1908 and it is now almost April 17th, 1998. So I am able to look back over a long, stimulating and adventurous life. I was born in a time of changes. I remember many of the events in World War I and I took an active part in World War II. It was a time when one could no longer rely on the conventional support of Church and State or our social environment to see us through life. We had either to search and find out for ourselves or run the risk of finding that change had overtaken us un-prepared. To search for an answer to life's problems becomes an obligation that we all must face rather than a whim in which a few eccentrics can be allowed to indulge. Those who search and find an answer, even an imperfect answer, to their question and will test this question in practise, have an obligation to share their experience with others. This is not easy to do, and very few people give a written account that will be of real help to those who are still seeking.

With these thoughts in mind, Mr. Bennett* invited my sister, Marjorie, to write an account of her own search for a way of life and together we wrote two small books for the Coombe Springs Press, the first entitled "A Way of Living" and the second one about our travels, and entitled "Walking in the World", and I hope to quote freely from these two books which are now out of print.

I will also quote from extracts taken from the book "Man of Wolverhampton" written by my sister and me in memory of our father, with other books mentioned.

My father, the late Sir Charles Marston, was himself a seeker as

---

* Our teacher and friend with whom we worked from 1949 to his death in 1974.

I

well as being a successful businessman and was one of the pioneers in promoting research into the truths of the Christian and Jewish scriptures. He imparted the thirst for a better understanding of life to his two daughters, and he also taught us to be impartial and open minded. This has helped us to make friends with the followers of different spiritual paths. At this time, when new ideas are entering the world through the labours of a few remarkable men, it is not enough to describe the few remarkable men and their impact on individual teachers nor is it so necessary to recall personal impressions of their teaching, for this is done by books. We need, in addition, to understand how they worked and how the events took place.

This can be done only by those who are present and have a gift for writing. We cannot grasp Gurdjieff's Science of Idiotism unless we can enter the situation in which he created it in order to talk about it. The Shivapuri Baba's words "Think of God alone" mean little unless one can picture the authority with which they were uttered. Both my sister Marjorie and I have been privileged to meet and work with many of the great spiritual leaders of our time, and I wish to record my account of some of these meetings as well as the contact of like-minded groups throughout the world where we were privileged to travel.

CHAPTER 2

Family Background

My father, Charles Marston, was the eldest son of John Marston, founder of the Sunbeam cycles, cars, etc. in Wolverhampton, West Midlands. Charles was a devout student of the Bible, a prominent Conservative politician, and, like his father, an industrialist by profession. My mother, Louise Isobel Johnson, was one of the first Americans to marry into a Midland business family. They had met in 1890 when my father was crossing to the States on a business trip sponsored by the Iron and Steel Institute in collaboration with the Verein Deutschen Institute. They were promoting tours around the industrial states of eastern United States and Canada on the new railroads covering the country. It was therefore a very convenient moment for a young English Commercial traveller to take over the newly developed bicycles and other wares. Finally, as John Marston could not obtain a good quality pedal for his bicycles, he instructed his son to discuss pedal production with the engineering firm of Pratt and Witney of Hartford, Connecticut and to return not only with a high class pedal, but also the machinery for making it.

Consequently, Charles, aged 23, sailed with a select collection of his wares in the hold of the ship on August 23rd, 1890 in Cunard liner S.S. Servia" sailing from Liverpool to New York via Queenstown (now Cobh) in Ireland. After some rough weather leaving Queenstown, Charles appears to have made contact with an American, Mrs. Johnson, and her young fifteen year old daughter, Louise, who was travelling back with her mother after visiting England and Germany. Charles comments in his diary: "They were much more friendly and approachable than English girls."

Louise and her mother were from Ithaca, New York and as Louise was already showing promise as a pianist, they had been to Bayreuth in Germany for the Wagner Festival. They were travelling with their cousins, Dr. and Mrs. Northrup with whom they lived in New York City. This friendship between Charles and Louise was to blossom in the years to come when my father, on further trips to the States, stayed in New York City with the hospitable Northrups and Johnsons, and Charles found there an affection, stimulation and freedom which his own somewhat staid and confining background in the Midlands had not provided. Louise's father, William Gordon Johnson, lived in Ithaca, New York and was a good friend of Ezra Cornell, founder of the University. He was an extremely artistic, sensitive and loveable man and was, by profession, a landscape architect. But in those pioneering times, there was no place for one who could not find his work in one of the learned white collar professions or in business. Accordingly, Mrs. Johnson had accepted an invitation from her cousins in New York and had taken up work herself with Associated Artists Inc. the grandmother of all interior decorating firms, which were to follow in order to give her daughter a sound education.

In spite of all the usual difficulties of a new venture, Charles made good headway in getting orders for bicycles in U.S.A. and Canada where the demand for them was far greater than the supply, and this necessitated his return to consolidate his contacts and increase the number of his customers. He made several further trips, when he made his headquarters in 79th Street with the kind family of Northrup, and finally, in 1895, he married "little Louise", now aged nineteen, a tall, slender young lady and already an accomplished pianist.

It was hoped that some of the Marston family could be persuaded to come to the wedding of Charles and Louise at "All Souls Episcopal Church" in New York City on January 30th, 1895. In the event no-one came. John and Ellen Marston and Charles' brothers and sisters had already met their future sister-in-law when she had visited England previously and they had all written to her welcoming her into the family – but they could not be persuaded to cross the Atlantic at that time.

4

CHAPTER 3

Homecoming

Charles and Louise made their first home in Penn Fields on the outskirts of Wolverhampton, a comparatively small country town with a large marketplace and a very ancient church. Factories were already in being and streets of houses were being built for workers, some of which had already degenerated into slums. But the house in Penn Fields called "Highfields" was a pleasant two storied Victorian house standing on high ground above a country road leading out of the town, and near the "Sunbeam" factory. The home had been decorated down to the smallest detail by Charles for his bride. His own Works supplied all the pots and pans for cooking and the rest of the house was under the care of Mrs. Johnson and her United Artists Inc. So Louise had little to do but approve or disapprove their work. She was, however, quick to make friends and Auntie Annie (Mrs. Horace William Bayliss) the first American to marry into an English industrial family, and a Southern Belle from Richmond, Virginia, became her greatest ally and companion.

Three years after their marriage, a daughter was born. They named her Marjorie, which was decided upon just before the christening ceremony, a compromise, since they could not agree upon their first choice.

In the 1900's, the family moved to a new and more modern house with beautiful views and a large garden with greenhouses, central heating and electric light and three bathrooms. The family inherited a gardener named Wall, who had "green fingers" and was very independent in his views on life and he stayed with us until his death at a ripe old age. The kitchen was ruled over by an impressive cook, Jane, two maids Jasper and Emma. There was also William, who looked after the pony and trap and later the "Sunbeam" car.

Marjorie had her Nanny, who took entire charge of her, including making her clothes. Nannie also taught her lessons and was the centre of her small life, and when Nannie took time off, Marjorie was often in the kitchen with Jane or out in the garden with Wall. Marjorie admired her mother tremendously. She was very lovely – she looked like a being apart in her black velvet dress and big black hat with the white feather. Marjorie was happiest when her mother glided into her room to kiss her "good night" in her shining evening dress. She loved it too when her mother, during the day, made lovely music on her piano for hours and she was able to sit and listen.

There were many visitors to the new home, both from home and abroad, for those were the days when entertaining on a large scale was possible and lavish. Charles' brothers and sisters were growing up and getting married and so there were many dinner parties and garden fetes and some were political meetings.

Charles went again to the States in 1905 to sell bicycles in the South, Middle West and Canada and Louise went with him to see her own friends and relatives, while Marjorie went to stay with her family of cousins in Birmingham and was ecstatically happy with them.

CHAPTER 4

Enter Melissa

Several years later, Marjorie, on her birthday, received her largest and most important present with the arrival of her sister, the real Melissa Mary, a cheerful, noisy baby. Both Charles and Marjorie were disappointed. They had hoped for a boy.

Melissa was born just a few years prior to her mother's illness, diagnosed as Multiple Schlerosis. In those days, little was known of remedial methods of massage, etc., and my beautiful mother grew quickly more confined in her movements and the joy of playing the piano was curtailed. The household was more and more geared toward helping my mother face her life of hardship and my father's increasingly busy industrial life. My sister, Marjorie, became a mother figure to me as well as to my Nannie and the other staff in the house. I was allowed few companions of my own age, with one exception, since my father felt they might bring infection into the house which might further exacerbate my mother's illness. Ruth Lathbury, the daughter of our groom, and his Welsh wife, our parlour maid, was living nearby and was always welcome at our house.

My father spent much of his spare time with Marjorie and me. When he came into my bedroom to say goodnight to me he would read me tales from the Bible, mostly from the Old Testament. One story about the three holy youths, Shadrach, Mesach and Abed-nego who were ordered by King Nebuchadnezzar to be cast into a burning fiery furnace to test their faith in God made a deep impression on me, and when my bedroom light was out and I saw through the window the furnaces spewing flames in the night air, it became too much for me and I felt nervous that I, too, might have to face such a fate. This led me to wonder about God and how He came into being.

Sundays were always "special" days when we were expected to walk to church, kneel very uncomfortably for long periods through the litany, and I resented being called a "miserable sinner". After such services, we joined forces with our uncles, aunts and cousins and went to our grandparents' Victorian house for a family lunch party. My grandfather, John Marston and his wife Ellen presided over a long dining room table. John was in charge of the joint and sat at one end and his wife served the pudding or sweets at the other end. A story which was told when I was small was of a young and rather nervous lady sitting next to my grandfather. He asked her what she would like to eat for a sweet, and when she said: "some gooseberry fool" my grandfather called loudly: "Mother, Mother, serve the fool!"

My grandfather was a very imposing, but kindly old man with a grey-white short beard, and he would always call me "his little maid". My grandmother, Ellen, had a companion known simply as "Patter". She was Miss Paterson and very Scottish. We were great friends.

Like my sister, I had a Nannie from my earliest days and she was the centre of my life. I slept in the same room with her, but when I was five or six she was replaced by a nursery governess who began to teach me the three "R's" and I joined with a small group of cousins and friends for nursery classes with my governess in charge.

At home and in the garden, I owned the usual collection of small animals, rabbits, etc. but almost my earliest recollection were some of the clothes I was supposed to wear. I remember a sheepskin cape and a cotton bonnet very well. I hated that cape and threw it off in anger whenever I could and I delighted in wearing my bonnet back to front, so that the gathered part usually at the back, dangled over my forehead. I'm sure I looked very droll!

As my Sister Marjorie was at boarding school, I saw very little of her except in the holidays but very soon, it was considered by my parents and sister that I should follow in her footsteps and I was packed off to my sister's school. She had been a very successful scholar there and had become head girl. I was very homesick from the start, and unable to cope with my fellow companions. Although my sister had officially left school, she was asked to help me to become more adjusted to my school mates and staff. For four long years, I stayed at the school, but perhaps because my sister was so highly regarded, I tried every trick in the trade of naughty behaviour.

The first world war was upon us, and my father, in response to my Mother's failing health and desire to be in her home country, decided to take her back to the States. He planned to take me, too, together with two nurses for mother and our lovely, fat, companionable cook, Jane. Since Marjorie had left school, she had lived at home, as she felt a responsibility to help my father, both as his hostess and a real desire to try and help get my mother better. My parents were constantly moving from one rented house to another, and everything was done to help my mother face her illness: faith healers came and went, even osteopaths thought that they might help, but were of no avail. I would return for holidays and when Mother was most depressed, I would get into bed with her and just hugged her and told her funny stories until she roared with laughter.

My first trip to the States was an unforgettable experience. I was just 13 – we sailed on the Cunard Line R.M.S. "Carmania" and like the ill fated "Lusitania", we sailed north to Cape Wrath and were amongst the icebergs, before coming South and entering the fine harbour of New York City. We all stayed in 42nd Street in a massive hotel opposite Grand Central Station, and I loved the comfort of it all. Our bedroom with bathroom("en suite" as they say now) and the elevators – with a uniformed usher on the ground floor, who kept repeating: "Ground floor please" to all and sundry.

My sister had already preceeded us and was at Vassar College in New York State. She joined us when she could for the vacations. Many of Father's friends, especially the Northrups and his banker friends the Haydocks, came and went. My Father rented a house in Ithaca, New York, so that my Mother could be amongst her relatives. After some months in Ithaca, it was decided to put Mother in a nearby nursing home. Her English nurses and Jane wished to return home, so this was a necessary next step. She was happy to be back amongst her own friends, but in the following year, she died quite suddenly. I had already been introduced to a boarding school in New Jersey opposite New York City and the Hudson River. I enjoyed it very much. I had a nice American room mate who took me home with her to a lovely house on the Palisades for weekends. My Father, who insisted upon returning to England with my Mother's body, soon came back, and in 1922 married an old friend also from Ithaca, Ruth Miller Bayne. She had been married before and had one daughter, Margaret, five years my junior, an only child, rather assertive, as so many children in the States can be, in my eyes!!

My sister Marjorie, still at college, insisted that we should join my Father and his new wife at vacation times, and we went by train each time overnight to Miami to the Brickell Apartments at Cocoanut Grove, where we joined Ruth and her relatives and bathed in the sea nearby. It was a difficult period of readjustment for my sister and myself, but I believe that it was right and paid dividends in the future. After so many years of enforced loneliness and futile hopes with his first wife, my Father wished just to settle down again to a steady, normal life, and it took sometime for him to adjust to it. He had been offered a seat in parliament in England, for Wolverhampton West, but he refused it, quoting the well-known Bible saying: "I have married a wife, and therefore I cannot come". In due course, Charles and Ruth returned to England and I was again sent to yet another boarding school, this time, a classic church school in Harrogate, Yorkshire, high church, emphasis on sport and a staff which I felt were intimidating for a girl of my age of fifteen. The school curriculum was limited – no good science courses and the mathematics teacher frightened me. I excelled at English, History and philosophy, but languages were not good, so I did not do well in the final exams.

Ruth, my new stepmother, introduced a Ford "Flivver", a type that she had been driving previously in the U.S.A. This was much criticised by some in Wolverhampton, as they felt it was disloyal to the family business, and in this I, too, felt rather deeply. We had always had a Sunbeam and we would again have one in the future.

When my father was knighted in the New Year's Honours List of 1926, and went to the Palace with Ruth, a new era was dawning for us all. Already an established leader in Industry and Politics, the Marstons were in a position to give their three daughters a more social life. We were all presented at Court, although I rather resented the artificiality of it all at the time. I was just beginning to mature, a frightening process I thought, and not explained to me in any way. My stepmother insisted that I should give and go to balls at home, and of course I began to have boy friends, but my Father was over-protective of me. Finally, he agreed to send me on a year's course of Domestic Science in Eastbourne, where I had the time of my life with many friends, interesting studies and very beautiful surroundings. Marjorie had meanwhile graduated from college and was living and working in New York City. I was allowed by my Father to join her with the understanding that I should continue my home economic courses in New York City, but my stepmother insisted that I should "come out" there and asked a friend of hers living nearby and with a daughter to present, to shepherd me as well. I was frankly bored with the elaborate and very costly parties and to salve my conscience, I joined the Charity Organisation Society and part of each day went on visits to the Bronx and other downtown areas on family visits for them.

We would frequently return to England during the long summer recess and on one of these returns from England, after the summer holidays when my sister was still at college at Vassar and I was at school in Englewood, New Jersey, we had a funny experience.

The U.S. customs official came aboard as usual, and when my sister and I presented our passports we were asked to wait behind. Nothing was said, but our customs man was busy chain smoking. Finally, my sister went up to him and asked him what was the matter with our passports? We expected two very old frields of my Father's to meet us and so we did not want to be delayed. My sister persuaded the customs official to stamp our passports provided we agreed to appear at Ellis Island before a special board of inquiry when called upon. My sister found out that the customs thought she was bringing me to U.S.A. as slave labour or for prostitution. The customs officer had only to telephone Vassar or my school to find out that we were registered there, but he preferred to send us to a higher authority.

So Dr. Northrup, Mr. Haydock, Marjorie and I set off for Ellis Island one morning in a ferry for that notorious Island, which was frequently in the news as the place from where unwanted immigrants were forced to return to their land of origin. Our two friends were put into another room while my sister and I were interrogated about our reasons for coming to the U.S.A. and my sister had to answer numerous questions about her previous visits. Finally, the board realized that we were bona fide students, apologised profusely to us and let us go.

Since the above episode, I have always been a little nervous of entering the United States on my many trips there.

CHAPTER 5

My Sister

Marjorie had found Vassar College a wonderful relief after the First World War and coping with her Mother's illness. It was also a chance to go beyond our Father's mental world and to explore new sides of life. Christianity was left alone, but she studied other faiths, Buddhism, Hinduism, all of which our Father had considered to be "heathen", whatever that meant!! From the very first her historical sense, inherited from her Father, asserted itself and she became fascinated with the many great empires, civilizations and faiths which had occurred in the world, and she longed to visit some of their places of origin and see them for herself. In studying Philosophy, Marjorie found that it seemed to take up the great problems of Universe. Why were there always two substances: mind and matter, body and spirit, etc? Her Philosophy teacher, realizing that she was deeply interested, gave her generously of his time and attention. She studied science as well – physics – but she was not interested in writing out precise scientific statements. What struck her was the mystery of it all. For instance, in the experiments with electricity, she was told about "positive" and "negative" forces and how they arose, but nothing about electricity itself and *what it really was*.

After graduating from college in 1924, my sister was able to take her first world trip, accompanied by her Father's cousin, Mrs. Marguerite Milward, who was by profession a sculptress and Christian Scientist. "Daisy", as she was called, was a much older companion, who had the same feeling for adventure and for getting at the essential quality of things as had my sister. Daisy's career was in wood carving and sculpture in an age when practically no woman seriously attempted such a feat. She had been married to a tea planter who had been killed in the First World War, but before that she had lived in Ceylon and East Africa and so had considerable experience of heat, travelling problems and, most important, the natives themselves. She had far more emotional understanding than my sister, who was "All up in her head."

Conditions were favourable in 1925-6 for two adventurous ladies embarking for the east: most of the world was still in the British, French and Dutch empires, although even then the British Raj had become somewhat shaky in India. Egypt, Ceylon and Burma were practically under British control, so were Singapore and the Malay Peninsula.

After French Indo-China, they approached Hongkong and Shanghai, the international ports. Beyond stretched the great chaos of China. The Emperor and the Manchus had fled, and generals with their private armies rampaged around fighting each other. Fortunately no-one was touching foreigners just then; there was quite a considerable British Army and other European troops in the treaty ports. But Peking was isolated, its "Blue International Train" from Nanking had been stopped. Our Father insisted that the travellers should not go there, and tried to make them promise but they managed to slip out of giving a direct assurance.

It is hard nowadays to realize that not a single plane was flying anywhere in the world for travellers – all their trips were made by boat, railroad, car, rickshaw, horse or mule, or even bullock wagon and camel!! They also had excellent credentials and there were few tourists in those days, only people returning to their jobs or going home on leave.

From the welter of experiences in the nine months of travel, some impressions stood out as though coming from a different world: the wonderful intellectualized art of ancient Egypt, with its amazing statues, and in particular, the great pyramids and Sphinx. What did the latter represent, and why did one get the impression of living in a different time in the King's Chamber, or looking at the Sphinx?

The emotional intensity of the Indian art and, above all, the wonderful three-headed bust of the Trimurti or Indian Trinity, Brahma, Vishnu and Shiva – or the three aspects of Shiva some said – in the Elephanta Caves near Bombay. This trinity seemed to be one of the most profound visions of reality these visitors had ever seen and appeared to symbolise all the principles of philosophy that they had read and thought about; creation and destruction, mind and matter, man and woman, good and evil, etc. But what was the third aspect represented? This they would, only much later begin to understand. Then when the visitors travelled in Cambodia – then part of Indo-China, they noticed the almost incredible harmony of Angkor with its combination of Egypt and India and something else: all the temples in Egypt give the impression of enormous intelligence, while those in India are bursting with life and emotion.

Angkor Vat has perfect balance, heart and emotion controlled by head and intelligence, but losing none of their power – all Egypt and India seemed to have been leading up to this – the travellers felt.

Other great moments in India were their meetings with the Tagore family and above all, with Sir Jagadis Chandra Bose, the great plant scientist and his assistant Boshi Sen, a considerable scientist on his own account, and a member of the Rama Krishna Vivekananda sect. Bose was one of the greatest botanists in his time, and his special subjects included experimenting with living and non-living matter. He had invented marvellously delicate instruments, so sensitive that variations in the root of the growth of plants so minute as one fifteenth millionth of an inch per second had been detected.

He had ascertained through these just how plants live, breathe and grow, and believed that the essentials of plant life are just the same as those of human life. More astonishing still, he had been working also with metals and had discovered that they, too, are under many of the same laws.

He was convinced by all these discoveries of the thinness of the partition between organic and inorganic matter and, to quote his own words, it was when I perceived in them (the result of his own experiments) one phase of the fading unity that bears within it all things – the mote that quivers within ripples of light, the teeming life upon the earth and the radiant sun that shines above us. It was then that I understood for the first time a little of that message that came from our ancestors on the banks of the Ganges thirty centuries ago: "They who see but one in all the changing manifoldness of this universe, unto them belongs eternal truth, unto none else." (from the Vidanta).

Boshi Sen, a much younger man than Bose, became Marjorie's own very good friend for a number of years. He practised meditation, which Marjorie did not understand at all, and seemed to have a deeper point of view of life than the intellectual, as you call it. He laughed, too, in a kindly way, about Marjorie's enthusiasm for international affairs and her insistence on "stopping wars".

After the World trip, Marjorie returned to New York to a flat of her own and threw herself with much enthusiasm into an international job dealing with young university people from all over the world. Surely, the young intellectuals could understand each other and work to prevent wars. The movement was most idealistic.

CHAPTER 6

Threads of an Ancient Teaching

The first thread appeared out of the blue and neither my sister nor I can exactly remember its place or date, although we think it was at a well known hotel in New York City. Somebody gave us tickets for a *show of dancing*. Little was said about it and we presumed it was some sort of ballet. The dancers, men and women, came in silently and formed themselves into seven rows, two or three in depth. They were dressed in simple white costumes, trousers and shirts for men and trousers and tunics for women with different coloured sashes for each row.

Our first reaction was of derision. How homely the costumes looked and what a poor ballet they seemed to be. Also, the music that accompanied them was played on a very second rate piano. Then the dancers started a curious series of odd jerks and rather wild movements which seemed to have no relation to each other. The rows of people were all doing different things. The music,too, was quite unlike any we had heard before. It all went on and on, but when a solo dancer stood up alone and began doing a continuous turning movement, we both realised that we had never seen anything like this before. We came away quite stunned and spoke to nobody at the time, and had no idea who was the originator of this performance.

A second thread to appear was a letter from Marjorie's cousin, Daisy Milward, who was living then in Paris. She wrote enthusiastically of a new book by P.D. Ouspensky entitled "Tertium Organum." Moreover, she had been introduced to it by some French friends. The author, who was a well known pre-Revolutionary Russian, was completely unknown to the West.

Nicholas Bessarabov, had brought a copy of this book to a distinguished American author, Claud Bragdon, a student of the

Philosophical Conception of the Fourth Dimension, and together, realising the excellence of its contents, they had translated the work into English and had published it. The book was a great success, but the author had disappeared into the holocaust of the Russian Revolution and only turned up in Constantinople, having escaped with a party of other distinguished people from Russia. The said French family knew all about this as their daughter was engaged to Charles Bragdon, the son of the American translator.

Marjorie adds: "This led to a most delightful experience for me. I not only read the book in question. It's first sentence: "The most difficult thing to know – what we do know and what we do not know sent me on a non stop journey to its end." But the little French fiancee came over to stay with me in New York. One evening, she invited to my flat her father- in-law-to-be, Claud Bragdon, who sat in my armchair looking like a Buddha and told me many more things about Ouspensky and his own work on this book. To begin with, the importance of its title. In naming his book "Tertium Organum", Ouspensky reveals at a stroke an astonishing audacity which characterises his thought throughout. Such a title says, in effect, here is a book which will re-organise all knowledge. The Organum of Aristotle, formulated laws under which the subject thinks. The Novum Organum of Bacon, the laws under which the object may be known; but the third Canon of Thought existed before these two, and ignorance of its laws does not justify their violation. "Tertium Organum" shall guide and govern human thought henceforth."* How passing strange in this era of negative thinking, of timid philisophising does such a challenge sound!

The third thread, like the first two, seemed to come again from a different source. As I have already mentioned, Marjorie was taking some writing courses and she was recommended to get in touch with Mr. A.R. Orage, former editor of a well known English journal. And one day while discussing the manuscript she had submitted, a student friend mentioned something about Mr. Orage's 'other' groups. When my sister enquired what they were, she was told something about philosophy or psychology of John Watson of "behaviourist" fame, which she had studied at college – man being motivated by stimuli inside and outside of himself. He then pressed us relentlessly down into being automatons in every respect with his usual wit and clarity. There was a pause, and then he added: "But there is something in us which can watch *all this*. It seemed a vast

* Claud Bragdon's Introduction to the English Translation

illumination to Marjorie who began to see her path lit up and clear to follow.

And lastly, there was a visit to New York of the Master himself, Mr. Gurdjieff. There was a certain amount of discussion within Orage's groups about him. He had visited New York earlier and had brought with him his "movement" pupils. He was spoken of as undoubtedly a magician or man of power. His general appearance was that of a riding master or dancing master. He had recently suffered a very serious motor accident which would probably have killed anyone else, although he himself had recovered from it.

But when one day in 1929 he came into the studio where the groups took place, Marjorie felt that here was essentially a great and good man. Her friend from England thought otherwise and warned my sister against him. Later that same year, my sister brought 10 dollars and was given a mimeograph translation of "Beelzebub", the book she had already had some tantalising glimpses of. This was the first version of an objectively impartial criticism of the life of man or Beelzebub's tales to his grandson published twenty years later in a very similar form as "All and Everything."

CHAPTER 7

Our Life Together in New York City

From 1928 onwards I shared my sister's flat with her in New York City. We entertained a great deal international students and friends from India that my sister had met on her world trip as well as some cousins who had come to live in the States and friends and colleagues from the National Federation of Students where she worked.

Early in 1928 we learnt that a new Junior College was to be founded at Bronxville, New York, a residential town about an hour's ride from the city. This new college, named Sarah Lawrence and built in the lovely grounds of the Lawrence home "Westlands" was to offer a two year course, very experimental, and we already knew well some of the members who were to be on its board. I applied to become a "charter" member, took various so-called "intelligence" tests and was accepted.

Nearly two hundred girls were brought together in October, 1928. The dormitory halls were almost complete, but the main dining hall and studios were still not finished. The students were recruited from those who did not wish to attend a four year course offered at regular universities and colleges. Many of those who came had special interests which they hoped to develop, and some like myself were already older than the normal college age.

A highly intelligent and original staff of young women and men graduates were engaged to guide and tutor us (my sister had been asked if she would participate). We had been told that large classes were not to be the order of the day, but rather small lecture and discussion groups and individual tutorials were to be included so that each pupil could follow her own interests and contribute her own independent thesis on particular aspects of her subject.

My particular interests were the social sciences and piano music. It was difficult for me to see which would take priority.

As we were, indeed, "Charter" members, we were asked to undertake all the proceedings which are necessary to create an active student community. There were no traditions or student government, so some of us signed up to participate in both by studying the principles and actually putting them into practise. Ours was the task of drawing up a constitution for the college. Another group supervised the publication of the college magazine "The Keynote" as well as other publishing work. There were also groups studying music, health, drama and religious subjects. Each group contributed in their own particular way to the entertainment and wellbeing of the community and, at the same time, they were studying different sides of these activities with faculty advisers.

I found a renewal of purpose and a deep joy in study organized in this way.

I had been almost a year away from study of any kind and this had strengthened my resolve to work harder and my experiences of life in New York had deepened this resolve. The college was near enough to New York and this enabled staff to commute from there, and also for students to use it freely for their field work.

While busy with my studies during the week, I was free to spend weekends with my sister. In vacation time, we travelled across America from New Orleans in the South, and through the southern states to California. It was my first contact with the American Indians and I was deeply impressed by them, especially the Pueblo tribes, and I sensed a very old tradition. I witnessed with my sister their mysterious "snake" dance and felt for the first time the strength of group worship and the change of consciousness which that could evoke.

When I returned to college, I wrote a thesis about them: their history and their customs. In history, too, I began to read about the ancient world: Mesopotamia and Egypt. Also I was fascinated by the latest discoveries of the death chamber at Ur of the Caldees. During my second year there, I was able to study modern history and took a very real interest in the founding of the Soviet State, Karl Marx and Communism. I used my study of Economics to help me to understand the "finer" arts of banking and investment and my letters to my Father were full of the more practical aspects of this study. I delved into the foundations of "cell" biology and a study of the anatomy of some primitive forms of life.

There was also a very real contact with Vassar College. We could drive there in two hours and often went there on field trips. So when I was nearing the end of my two years at Sarah Lawrence, I felt a need to try to enter Vassar and get my B.A. degree.

As Henry MacKracken was President of Vassar College as well as being a Trustee of Sarah Lawrence College and my sister had been a graduate of that same College in 1924, I felt that I had a good chance of continuing on to that College to gain my B.A.

Accordingly, two of us went up for interviews to Vassar and were accepted for a trial year on condition that we did extra work and were able to keep up with the other students.

Note I'm afraid I was regarded as rather a prig by my fellow students at Sarah Lawrence College. Students in the States tend to go around in gangs. I was unaware of this and picked my own friends, a room mate and others that I liked. One day, I came into my bedsitter to find that it had been turned upside down. Sticky marmalade was spattered on the walls and there were watermarks all over the place. My feeling of anger at what I saw was quickly succeeded by one of British "fair play". I wanted to find out what I was guilty of. So I invited all the student members of that particular house to come and share a pot of tea with me, so that we could talk face to face. The ringleader was a certain Narcissa Swift from Chicago, a wealthy girl who was used to having her own way, and we became great friends after this episode!

Another of my adventures at College was organising dances on Saturday evenings. This was done really to keep students happy over the weekends. Many of my friends came out from the city, and then they would invite us back for evenings in New York City. I remember one particular evening when my girl friend and I were asked to that popular English play 'Journey's End', and afterwards we were taken to a 'speak-easy' nightclub, a wonderful golden domed affair presided over by Rudi Vallee and called 'The Villa Viennese'. One of our escorts, a friend of mine, and a young student, was considerably embarrassed because it was all so expensive, and I never forgave myself for allowing this to happen!! This was, of course, during prohibition time in the States when these nightclubs would outdo themselves in their charges for prohibited liquor.

I returned to the States in the autumn of 1930 to spend a year at Vassar College. I was already familiar with the campus, Maine building, the library and now I was to live in one of the dormitories called Raymond Hall. I had an ambitious course of study to follow, musical appreciation with Professor Dickinson, baby (beginning) philosophy with Professor Drake, history with Miss Ellery, a course in heredity and a continuation of my biology course taken the previous year. Another course in comparative religions and also beginners' German. I was not good at languages, but my new friends, the German exchange students, did all they could to help me and I did the best I could to try and learn it.

The method of learning was, of course, different here than it was at Sarah Lawrence College. At Vassar, there were large classes to be lectured to and tests were held every few weeks and examinations at the end of each seminar, but I managed to keep up fairly well, and I found myself able to adapt to all that was required of me. Here, I was a member of a much larger community with well tried traditions - but there was also a great deal of freedom to come and go as one pleased.

My German student friends who were third year students, were always having their friends to visit them, and in general I found that these students and some of the staff from Europe were drawn closer together by their older tradition although our fellow American students were delighted to share our activities. And the weekends were full of social activities. In the winter there were skating and skiing parties and in the summer boating and picnicking. I remember one such occasion when a wealthy American student whose Father owned a yacht which was then cruising up and down the Hudson River, invited me to come along. Their car came to fetch us, and we transferred at the riverside to a fast speeding motor launch which took us out to their yacht, which was very luxurious with a Captain and crew, wide decks and several beautifully equipped cabins, complete with their private showers etc. We spent the day sunbathing and returned in the evening the same way we had come.

In the spring of 1931, I had to try and make some decisions about my future. Two different courses of action seemed possible. I was prepared to stay at Vassar another year, and work through the summer if the Vassar authorities would allow me to graduate in the class of 1932. I had proved to them that I could keep up with a heavy scholastic schedule, but I was rather older than the average student and had already three years of college life behind me. Alternatively, I was prepared to return with my friend to Germany and continue with my education with her there. This might help me to overcome this weakness of mine in languages.

But in actual fact, I did neither of these things. Vassar insisted that I should go through the full four years to graduate and my Father, backed up by my sister, put paid to the idea of my going to Germany to study. My Father knew that I admired German students and was fearful that these attachments might become stronger, and when my sister joined him I reluctantly agreed to return to England. To this day, I have wondered whether I should have defied them all. I did, of course, visit Germany many times, but as my friends could all speak English I was never able to improve my German as I had wished.

My sister, who had been in England, came over for a further summer vacation which we spent on a ranch in Wyoming and a trip to the Yellowstone Park. We explored by muleback the Grand Canyon, staying the night at Phantom Ranch in the hollow of the Canyon before returning together to Europe.

My sister's colleagues at the National Student Federation were Miss May Hermes and Miss Martha Biehle - (May being English by nationality and Martha being a distinguished member of Wellesly College). Part of their work was to promote and organize international student travel. They had already brought over from South Africa a large student group to meet American students in the States and Canada and in 1930 I signed up to go with American Women Students to the Baltic States where we would be entertained by Norwegian, Danish and Swedish students, and then to Finland, Estonia, Latvia and Lithuania, before continuing on to Germany.

It was quite an unusual thing in those days for a group of women students to be entertained by their opposite number, even in "modern" Scandinavia. American women students had a reputation even in those days of being 'high flyers', and the Scandinavian men students felt equal to their task. We were entertained most lavishly, and when we wished to have a little extra sleep, we were told: "Now it is the summer, and you can do that all winter! So on we danced or drank, as the case might be, and we would also be expected to view their wonderful modern churches, museums and civic halls. I enjoyed so much the 'freshness' of it all and the lovely scenery in the fjords and waterways.

I was impressed by the lovely architecture I saw everywhere, really the first of the modern buildings in honey coloured stone. Helsinki, too, was very modern, especially its railway station, and I had my first experience of Finnish 'sauna' baths. Some of us spent a whole day there in various degrees of heat, beating ourselves with birch twigs to improve our circulation, with frequent showers and massage. Then a long swim in a full-sized pool for as long as we liked. The final act was a light meal and then a long sleep in our comfortable cubicles. Certainly one of the most refreshing experiences of a very strenuous trip.

From Helsinki, we crossed the Gulf of Finland to Tallinn and were met there by our new 'student guides'. It was wonderful the number of languages spoken there. Their schools and universities were far more able to teach, and students more adroit at learning languages than we are. German and Russian were the languages in common use, by the Baltic students, but they were adept at English and French as well.

After the Scandinavian countries, there was a marked difference observable here between the peasants living on the land and the more cultural ruling group. American students were not often seen here and therefore the student group were anxious to make a good impression.

In Kaunas, Lithuania, the students outdid themselves by hiring a government launch for our entertainment. One afternoon, we were taken for a short spin on the river, but when we heard that the students were hoping later to take us on an all night excursion, we felt this might be a little too much. The boat had no proper sleeping accommodation - only an open lounge and decks and our escorts were very attentive. So at the risk of an international incident, our leader arranged for another afternoon trip instead and it all passed off peacefully. My particular pal was an opera singer by profession and I fell in love with his wonderful tenor voice. How, I wondered, did the man in him measure up to his voice? I was tempted to try and see, but my more conservative feelings overcame this temptation.

Throughout this whole trip, I had felt a deep sense of responsibility for the reputation of my fellow travellers. Our leader was not, in my opinion, very alert to the care of the younger students, and so I tried to assume this role myself.

If we kept together as a group, all was well, and this we succeeded in doing.

At the end of this tour, we took a train to Germany and I met my sister by arrangement in Munich and we both stayed together at the Bayrischerhof Hotel. What a joy to be in more luxurious surroundings, and to be free to indulge one's whims again, sleeping, shopping etc. before moving on to Oberammergau and the 1930 version of the Passion Play.

Although we were, at this time, going through a rather anti-religious phase following years of indoctrination by our Father, nevertheless we were deeply impressed with the atmosphere of Oberammergau and the sincerity of the actors in the play. It brought the drama of Christ's life alive for us, and we actually felt that we were participating in it. It had something of the force of the early Christian 'mystery' plays and the Greek drama - when all who took part shared in something on a higher level.

We had been invited to spend a few days at Schloss Kopernick on the banks of the River Spree by Dr. Morsbach who was in charge of German Students exchange with the United States. The students who were returning from a year in the States were meeting and exchanging views with those Germans who were setting off for the States to study. The students were an exceptional group and of course spoke a good deal of English already.

Marjorie and I were introduced to the students by De Horsbach and were given a great welcome. I was just about to go to Vassar College and was introduced to the two German girls chosen to go there. One of them, Amelie von Behr, became my best friend in years to come. The men students acted as our guides and dancing partners, and were avid for all the news we could give them. There was a feeling of camaraderie amongst us, as though the past had never been and the future was to be altogether different.

I made up my mind seriously to learn German, so that I might be on more intimate terms with some of these friendly and intelligent young people.

Afterwards, we rented a flat on the Bayswater Road near Marble Arch and I resumed my social work, visiting in South London with the Charity Organisation Society.

CHAPTER 8

Our Return to England

My sister asked Mr. Orage to give her an introduction to Mr. Ouspensky in London and it was suggested that she write to him directly. She was asked by his secretary to come to a small house in Gwendwr Road in Barons Court where he, at that time, interviewed people. He himself answered her ring at the doorbell. A square, vigorous and rather squat looking man, very near sighted. He courteously ushered her into a small room with a fire, offered her a chair and sat down opposite and said: "Well?" My sister had been eagerly looking forward to this meeting and had prepared many things to say, but not one single thing could she remember of it. They sat in silence for a few minutes and then Mr. O. suggested that he should read something. After that, mutual conversation appeared more possible.

Marjorie asked if she might join his groups and he agreed on one condition, that she should not mention to any of the people that she met there her previous connection with Mr. Orage's group. Mr. O. explained that he was now separated from Mr. Gurdjieff, explaining that from his point of view something had gone wrong with Mr. Gurdjieff's work. He also pointed out to my sister that there would be certain rules for those in his groups. As he explained it, no games could be played without rules. She should hear from his secretary when a group for her would be possible. So ended their interview.

About the same time, Marjorie's cousin, Daisy Milward, left Paris and came to live in Hampstead, London. She, too, applied to go to Mr. Ouspensky's groups and for the next few years Marjorie and Daisy did many things together. There was nothing permanent about these groups. Sometimes there was only one meeting, sometimes a few; occasionally they lasted longer.

Much depended upon whether one rang and asked, indeed the initiative was always placed on the newcomer to ask, ask, ask. One could not sit down and read books about it, because there were no books about " it" to read! Ouspensky had published a further book after "Tertium Organum" with the title of "A New Model of the Universe", but work was never mentioned in it except for a very slight reference at the end of his chapter on "What is Yoga", something about "Fragments of an Unknown Teaching". In the same way as in the Orage groups, the initiative was mainly on the pupil to ask questions. Sometimes very simple questions got most enlightening replies, purely intellectual ones got nothing, or very little. At intervals large chunks of material (later published in "In Search of the Miraculous") were read out, which often left us breathless. Mr. Ouspensky used to say they should listen and take in what they could.

At the beginning of the meeting Mr. Ouspensky would enter abruptly with a large sheet of paper in his hand. After sitting down he removed his glasses, and put the paper right up to his eyes for reading. They never knew what was on it, but always presumed it was a list of people who wished to see him! If only a period of dead silence greeted his "well", he would say: "Talk a little", and he would get up and rush out of the room. Then his understudy for that particular meeting, chosen from a half dozen or so of men who were nearest to him, took over. Usually the atmosphere relaxed somewhat and questions came more easily. In due course, Mr. Ouspensky would return.

Marjorie found that she was to be under considerably more rules than the particular one that he had made for her. No-one was to speak about meetings or what they heard there without permission from him. Various people objected to this on the grounds that it was like a secret society! They were also to be known to each other by their surnames only and sometimes when they were put into small groups, they should only meet members of their own group! This did not mean that no new people entered the work with him. There were special meetings for people who for one reason or another wanted to join. On looking back years later, Marjorie saw how necessary were many of his "rules." They were to have a different relationship to each other than just the usual personal one. Who was this Mr. Mrs or Miss inside oneself? They had so little knowledge on how to handle situations in life. The teaching was such a new and tender plant.

The Ouspenskys had a house in the country, South of London, and one Sunday Daisy and Marjorie were invited down there and told to take a certain train from London. They were both looking forward to it very much, until Marjorie spied in the train an old lady whose questions in the groups had always irritated her. She talked all the time and, to Marjorie, sounded idiotic, although she sometimes got remarkable replies. She was in despair, her day was ruined!

They arrived at their destination and there seemed to be a great many more people there than the Ouspenskys! Everyone was working either in the house or in the large garden. Marjorie remembers making a rather condescending remark: "Oh, you do housework here?" to a lady who was showing them where to put their coats. A simply delicious luncheon was served. Madame Ouspensky, a dark and very distinguished looking lady, was sitting at one end of a long table with the ladies, Mr. Ouspensky and the men at the other end of the table. Afterwards, they all assembled in a spacious drawing room, Madame Ouspensky asked them – the old lady and her daughter, Daisy and Marjorie – to sit in front of her, and all the assembled company crowded silently around them. They were to be the guinea pigs now!

The old lady started to ask questions, all of which Madame Ouspensky answered with the greatest courtesy. Daisy remained silent, but Marjorie, when she got the chance, and feeling the electric atmosphere, launched into some vast question about economics. Madame then turned her attention to Marjorie. She saw her as a squirrel going round and round in a cage. She said my sister was very critical, and to be critical was vulgar and so on and so forth. All she said was true, and my sister realised this. Madame saw her very clearly, but somehow without a bit of personal dislike, as usually happens when people express criticism of another . Madame had a particular gift of insight into people as they really were, and this must have been very hard for her, for many people would not have understood, or been badly hurt by her remarks. To Daisy she said nothing, thinking, Marjorie was sure, that she was too sensitive.

The old lady continued to talk, and Madame to answer courteously. Somehow now Marjorie felt differently towards the old lady. It was a relief to go on talking. She really liked her. Marjorie never saw Madame Ouspensky again, but she remembered most vividly her answer to a perennial question, as to what was the use of trying to work when we realised how feeble we were and we realised how little we could accomplish in ourselves. She said most emphatically that we should remember the enormous size of the stalactites or stalagmites which were composed of only myriads of tiny drops. *

* Taken from "A Way of Living by Marjorie von Harten, Ch.2.

The next major event in Marjorie's life was her marriage in 1933 to Georg Von Harten, a young Baltic concert pianist and a member of Mr. Ouspensky's group. From their first meeting she knew that she would marry him, although she quailed at the differences between them. She comforted herself that their work would hold them together. This is exactly what did not happen. Georg left the work to promote his own music, feeling that he could not manage two immense subjects at the same time. He agreed that Marjorie should stay, but after a time became jealous of its influence. This was her real emotional trial, not even for a beloved husband could she leave our work. It had already become too much a part of herself. When this difficulty arose, she rushed to Mr. Ouspensky for advice. As usual, this was most practical. Would her marriage be better if she gave up the connection with the work? She saw at once that this would not be so. Georg and Marjorie were going through a turbulent phase. If she added to this turbulence with more mechanical behaviour, there was no hope for either of them. Another conflict arose in her at this time. If man could not "do" and had only the power to buy his cigarettes, as Mr. Ouspensky put it, what was the use of trying to stop wars, etc. She felt dismally that Ouspensky's work was destroying her faith in international work and, for a time, limited herself to a small job connected with housing in her spare time, as she felt that she could at least believe that as a necessity for man. It was a sour, and somewhat arid period in her life, but immensely stimulating. She had to play a large role at home. Her husband's musical activities were developing very much before the War in 1939 and somehow managed to go to meetings and work periods without causing trouble and strife in her ordinary life, all for something part of her was not sure she believed in.

It was at that time that she received enormous help from Mrs. Maurice Nichol. She and her husband were working with the Ouspensky group at the time and shortly afterwards left to have their own centre of work.

The Second World War swept down on us in 1939 like a great ocean that disrupts everything on the beach which it rushes across. The Ouspenskys left for America, as it was impossible to continue with groups in the chaos of war conditions. Marjorie's husband died suddenly in 1941 of some heart ailment we did not know he had been suffering from, and part of her life disappeared with him. At these great moments of our life, I think one is given a choice; whether to lose one's self in endless self-pity or genuine distress or whether to fight on to something higher. There are moments of incredible opportunity, in a sort of way one can break the barrier into another world, at least for a time. With me, her sister at her side, she had to go out alone and tackle the practical problems of the next few days. It was as if he had simply waved his hand smilingly and left her, saying: "This part of the road we do not go together." She never mourned him or felt anything had gone wrong. There was some deeper and continuous understanding about life, the life one never seems to achieve in normal circumstances. But the most difficult part with this kind of parting comes later when one has lost this "inner" vision and is living in one's ordinary life.

CHAPTER 9

My Life in England 1931–1935

I completed my year at Vassar College in 1931 and returned to the family home at Tunbridge Wells, England with my sister. Our old family home at Wolverhampton had been sold in 1928.

Lady Marston was a charming hostess of the new home, a low lying Edwardian house in a beautiful park. I missed the lovely views we had in Wolverhampton, but this home was pleasant and peaceful and was situated well away from the town. Margaret, Ruth's daughter, was also in residence and for a year or more I enjoyed the social activities. Ruth was very musical and played the harp. Relatives and friends from all parts of the world flocked to see her. My Father had been made President of Shropshire Archaeological Society in 1929 and a fellow of the Society of Antiquarians in 1931. So budding and full-blown archaeologists and churchmen frequently called to ask for his advice and help which was freely given.*

For a year or more I enjoyed a very social life, culminating in my being presented at court in 1932 under the auspices of my Father and Ruth. For some months before the great occasion I went regularly to London to have my elaborate court dress of pale pink material trimmed with diamante crystals, a train to match and feathers fitted to my hair. On the famous day, I wore over it a dark velvet coat trimmed with white fur. The family car, a Sunbeam, was driven to London by our chauffeur, Henry, with our previous driver, William, as footman.

The cars with debutantes lined up in the Mall for some hours before the event. Ruth Marston, who had already presented my sister and Margaret at Court, was similarly attired. She sat with Father on

* My father was knighted in 1929.

the back seat and we waited several hours in the queue. To while away the time, Ruth, who had recently had flu, showed me her silver filigree bottle of sal volatile – I was admiring the filigree work when the top flew off and some of the ammonia went into my eye. Ruth was very distressed, as she thought she had blinded me. A kindly policeman went to get us some cold water in which to bathe my eye and it gradually eased off. Then Father's rather fussy secretary arrived and he and my Father walked up and down beside the car talking business.

Finally, the cars moved forward in stately procession and we entered the courtyard of Buckingham Palace where the court ushers took charge of us for the great occasion of my presentation; but I regret, even to this day, that I was not able to entirely remember it all, as I was still in pain from my accident.

Later, we were given tickets for the Royal Garden Party and had excellent views of the royal party headed by King George V and Queen Mary, with many of the royal princes in attendance. I was very impressed at the spaciousness of the royal gardens – one has little idea of this from outside the massive stone walls which surround it.

Another event of my social "fling" was a visit to Lord's Cricket Ground with my Father and Ruth. Father called cricket a "game of "anticipation" – I knew what he meant, but I wasn't patient enough to enjoy it and wandered off to a nearby pavilion to watch a game of old fashioned tennis, which was much more to my liking.

My Father had also booked for Margaret and myself to spend a day at Ascot, but unfortunately I had contracted measles and so was unable to take part.

From Tunbridge Wells there were many social events such as the Aldershot Tattoo and one year, the whole family were called upon to act in a church pageant in which scenes from the lives of some of the English kings, Henry VIII and Charles II, were portrayed with great success by local ladies and gentlemen; Lady Marston was a graceful court lady of the cavalier period carried in a sedan chair by her chauffeur and gardener – of course suitably costumed! I portrayed a Cavalier lady with golden ringlets and Margaret was a most elegant Nell Gwynn.

Unfortunately, my step-mother Ruth was not physically strong and although she went with my Father for several trips to the Holy Land where he was actively engaged in archaeology of the early sites of Jericho and Lachish, which was possible then because Palestine was under British Mandate.

I was to inherit a lovely home in the Weald of Kent. Originally, Father had planned to live there with Ruth and as she was an architect's daughter, they hoped to design it themselves, but as it became obvious that Ruth was not well, Father asked me if I would like it. Of course, I accepted it with much joy and alacrity.

The house was built on five acres of land with every convenience for me and my dogs and with a glorious view over the Weald of Kent south to the sea. I engaged an excellent cook-housekeeper and later an efficient kennel maid, who accompanied me to dog shows.

Meanwhile, my Father and Ruth went on several trips to Israel. My Father, a devout Bible scholar and a lay reader had been elected a member of the House of Laity of the Church Assembly in 1925. Since then, he and Ruth had taken a great interest in Biblical archaeology. He was already a life member of the Palestine Exploration Fund – which had been set up for the purpose of surveying and exploring that country, and since his retirement from business, he had become increasingly interested in excavating there and contributed financially to the Jerusalem excavation funds.

Marjorie and I were able to join my Father and Ruth on one such expedition to Jericho, Lackish and Gaza. which were being excavated at that time. Marjorie began by introducing me to Greece, Egypt and Turkey, and after these great civilizations, Israel seemed rather poor and shoddy. Jericho was being excavated by Professor John Garstang and Lackish by Professor James Starkey.

We all went, too, to Gaza, where Sir Flinders and Lady Petrie were working with a band of students. Both Marjorie and I were a little constrained by Father's approach to religion there – there was Christianity and all the rest was "heathen". We wanted to know much more about the subject of world religions.

Unfortunately, Ruth, developed cancer. Once again, Father took an ailing wife back to her homeland where she died in 1934.

Marjorie, Margaret, Georg, Marjorie's husband, and I met together at my home. I wished to offer Father a suite to live in my house, but we very soon heard that Father expected to marry for a third time a Mrs. Mary Bonney, a native of Atlanta, Georgia, then living in New York City after the death of her husband and while her two sons by him were being educated.

She had worked there with the American Women's Association and in particular with Miss Anne Morgan and Mrs. Vanderbilt. The Marstons had known previously in New York City Mary's sister, Adrienne Battey, and probably she had introduced Mary, her sister, to our Father. Margaret was now in the same position as I had been sometime back when my own mother died and I had to quickly adapt to a new wife in the household.

The newlyweds were expected back in England by ship and so my sister and her new husband took Margaret away on holiday to Spain and I was left to welcome my Father and his new bride home. Mary welcomed me with open arms – she had great charm, tact and a sense of humour. She was an attractive and happy addition to our family and seemed pleased to have inherited some daughters since she herself had only sons.

CHAPTER 10

I Go on a A World Trip
1935–1936

In 1935 a new life began for me with my sister and her husband and Margaret away in Spain, my stepmother and my Father were eager to see my new home and to entertain my friends there. They did not care for my new boyfriend and so decided to ask me to go round the world with them on what was to be their "honeymoon" trip. I was uneasy about leaving my dogs in charge of my kennelmaid, but my family asked Marjorie's friend, Mrs. Milward to look after my house and its inhabitants and so I was free to go. The plan was to cross the Atlantic again by ship to New York City and then have a pause to meet mutual friends and relatives and to take a cruise from New York through the Panama Canal to California, continuing on across the Pacific via Honolulu to Japan and China and India, a wonderful opportunity for me to see new areas of this world and especially the far east, which had meant so much to my sister and Mrs. Milward some ten years earlier.

Accordingly, we embarked in November of that year on the Cunard liner RMS "Aquitania" for New York. It was a very rough trip indeed – many portholes were smashed by the giant waves. Nevertheless, the social life on board continued – we were sitting at the Captain's Table for meals and of course the Captain's Cocktail Party was the first social function of the voyage. We attended it, but afterwards my Father said he wanted to speak to me in private. I had learnt from past experience that these little talks were usually a criticism of my social behaviour. I was, after all, thirty years old now and had been living on my own for some time – what had I done wrong now! My Father wished to criticize my drinking habits – I was only to take "sherry" at parties – never cocktails and I was not to "rouge" my lips. I blew up as I usually did – especially as I felt completely sure that I was blameless on both counts. I went to my stepmother in tears – she heard my complaints and comforted me – then told me to do what my Father asked for the time being. The rest of the trip was so rough that we took to our cabins and for the time being the matter was closed.

We stayed again in New York on 42nd Street and were greeted and toasted by our friends and Mary's family – her sister Adrienne and her elder son George and his wife, who were living in Canada. Mary's great friends Miss Anne Morgan and Mrs. W.K. Vanderbilt, came to call and toast the new bride.

My Father was now 68 years old, and although he had visited the United States and Canada many times and Israel of course, to look at the excavations there, he had never been to the far east before, but the atmosphere of New York cheered and stimulated him and he looked forward eagerly to the big trip and even contemplated with equanimity a flight on "Imperial Airways" as it was then called.

Our trip through the Panama Canal was extremely interesting, to watch the complicated mechanism of the Canal, and the various nationalities we met on the voyage – and then the warm sunshine of the Caribbean and Havana. The more leisurely and comfortable existence was greatly appreciated after the rather strenuous time in the States. So when we finally came to San Diego, California, we all felt much refreshed and ready to face the future. My father and Mary wished to cross the American-Mexican border to have a meal at Tijuana. It was very gay and colourful there and the dancing girls who entertained us for lunch at the Hotel quickly fascinated my Father, and when Mary suddenly ordered from the luncheon menu "A Pale Grey Cocktail", I quickly glanced at her, and murmured: "Two Pale Grey Cocktails, please" and Father turned to the attentive wine waiter and said firmly: "Three Pale Grey Cocktails please". Never again did I have to ask for a sherry – in fact whenever Father wanted particularly to please us at meals, he always asked us if we would like cocktails?

After a short visit to San Francisco to see our cousin Dick Deanesly, we sailed out of San Francisco harbour toward our next port of call, Honolulu, and a short stay at the Royal Hawaiian Hotel. Honolulu was still independent and not "taken over" by the States" although many U.S. citizens were there to enjoy the tropical isles. I loved eating the sliced pineapples in our rooms overlooking the beach and later, tried with the help of a surf rider to breast the waves as he did.

Our next sailing on the Empress of Canada was across the Pacific to Japan. We entered the harbour of Yokahama, and we marvelled at the sight of Mt. Fuji, snowcapped on our left. Our visit to Japan had been greatly curtailed on account of a somewhat out-of-date account of the conditions in that country given by an American acquaintance as to its coldness and lack of comfort in midwinter. We actually found the hotels comfortable, warm and very clean and we were impressed by the Japanese as a simple, virile and adaptable people who seemed to work hard and to look happy and contented. My Father particularly noticed the multitudes of bicycles used on their fine modern roads. We were able to see their sacred city of Kyoto where my Father was particularly interested in a lacquer factory which reminded him of the Japanned Tea Trays made by his father's firm in 1885 before bicycles were manufactured there.

The following day we continued our sea voyage from Kobe to Shanghai where my Father spoke to an interested audience about his Palestine excavations. Here we were met by our American Express Guide, an extremely intelligent author of books about China, Peter Goullart – he was to accompany us on a visit to Hangchow, which was very beautifully situated on a lake, but very cold, and our family were carried in sedan chairs to a Taoist Monastery high up in the hills. I remember the Chinese bearers had no socks or shoes on, and ran along on the snowy, icy paths laughing and calling to each other.

The manager of our hotel laid on a Chinese dinner for us with all kinds of small dishes, but my Father took exception to the eggs served. I called them "archaeological" eggs and our very courteous host called instead for a specially cooked steak which my father much enjoyed.

Mary and I had hoped to go to Peking and therefore had not objected earlier to our hurried Japanese visit, but when the question was brought up, Father said that it would be too cold to go there. He did not want to go and he would not be happy if we went without him. To this day, I have not yet been to Peking and always regretted that we did not make it then.

Saying goodbye to Peter in Shanghai, we sailed on to Hong Kong to stay at the Repulse Bay Hotel and my Father was happy there and felt much more at home. Just at that period we heard of the death in England of King George V, and we all felt sad. He had knighted my Father in February, 1926 and I had been to the palace as a debutante and to their Garden Party.

From Hong Kong, our party took a French boat to Saigon – peaceful under the French at that period of history, and hired a car which took us along a straight and wide highway to the ruins of Angkor, a mysterious Khymer City which had been for many centuries hidden in the jungle and only re-discovered in the early years of this century. We were all moved by these glorious and enormous ruins and spent several days examining them – it was here, too, that I met a young American big game hunter, Phillip Crowe. He was suffering from Blackwater Fever and had periods of fever and hallucinations. Mary encouraged our friendship and he was to travel with us most of the way home. He needed careful nursing and this I endeavoured to do.

Meanwhile, my Father was deeply thinking about the men who founded these wonderful temples, and he thought about their meaning – he insisted: "Surely the time had come for ancient religious symbols to be co-ordinated. The marvellous architectural ability and power and imagination stamp them as belonging to the sons of God (Gen.6.2) "And the sons of God saw the daughters of men that they were fair, and they took them wives of all that they chose." (Bible is True: Leviathan p.206).

He mused further: "These Khymers must have been supermen in their day, a civilization alien to our own, more tropical than the Latin, and apparently untouched by Christian influences. But idolatry and licentiousness must have abounded here." We were all very impressed by Angkor and even the native Cambodians were a charming people whom we were very sorry to leave.

Bangkok with its lovely sugar cake Domes and Temples, was our next stop and we paid a visit to a snake farm where they milk the snakes for their vaccine. I felt sorry for these gorgeous creatures being treated thus, but I was told it did not hurt them.

In Burma, I stayed with my cousin and his wife in their home, a lovely city with its temples and beautiful people. Then we moved on to Singapore and took a Dutch passenger ship to Bali in Indonesia. There were many Dutchmen going on business there and I palled up with an Israeli couple who, like us, was bound for Bali. This was my great opportunity to see a relatively unspoilt Island and I wanted to have the chance to explore as much of it as I could. I can't remember how, but we met a little guide who originally came from the "Isle of Man" and therefore spoke excellent English. While my Father and Mary were installed in a lovely tropical hotel, I was allowed to go with the Israeli couple and guide on a tour of the islands. We were privileged to meet musicians and dancers and listened to the Gamelon orchestras until their music, at first alien to our ears, became closer and closer and more and more poignant to us.

Our island tour culminated in a dance of sheer mysticism – when many dancers were together. Our party sat up on a high platform and looked down on the dancers. It went on and on until some of the dancers were "taken over" or something of that sort. I began to wonder whether we might be in danger – then it stopped as suddenly as it began and the "head dancer" came up to us and asked us if we had enjoyed it! And we all came down to earth with a bang. My Father and Mary were happily installed in our bungalow hotel and they, too, had enjoyed the music and dancing, but Father felt a little out of his depth and was muttering about "heathen" influences again. As in Cambodia, the native "boys" were charming and when we left they ran along beside us with tears in their eyes. We sailed back via Singapore and on to India and our friend Phil Crowe was to join us in Delhi. We had wonderful letters of introduction here from Dad's friends and from Marjorie, my sister, who had so much enjoyed India with Daisy Milward in 1924.

Our visit to Sir Jagadas Chandra Bose was another highlight of our trip. Father had rarely met such a distinguished Indian before and, inspired by his aura, they discussed together religious philosophy. Although interested in the Bhagavad Gita, Sir Charles felt that 'Christianity really embraced it all.' I felt we did not make the most of this wonderful opportunity and after their visit I went out walking and met a wandering Sadhu by the banks of the Ganges. We began talking and comparing the different religions, but he insisted: "God is one and omnipresent and all religions are really each in their own way trying to reach Him". But my stepmother Mary interrupted our talk by suddenly coming upon us and saying loudly: "Come on dear, or we will be late for our train"! And we took the overnight train to Benares, three of us in one carriage did not help us to relax or sleep that night!

Early the following morning, we were met at Benares by a friend of my Father, a curate in a Christian Church, and as neither of my family wished to go on the river, I went alone with the Curate to see the extraordinary sites of the burning ghats and the bathing of so many souls in the river. Then I travelled on with my family to Delhi. There we were to dine with the Viceroy (Lord Willingdon) all in mourning dress after the death of the King. 'Behind each of our chairs was a gorgeously attired Indian in scarlet, with turban and ornate dagger at his waist, who served us.'

Later, we attended a polo match where our big game hunter friend joined us and enjoyed it with me.

A visit to Agra for the Taj Mahal and other Mogul Buildings were next and the ruins of Fatehpur Sikri – which my Father felt were just as wonderful as the Taj but different.

We finally set sail from Bombay on the P & O liner "Rajputana" and Phil Crowe came with us. My Father and Mary were to stop off in Jerusalem to see the excavations and so they left the ship at Port Said after passing through the Suez Canal. Sailing through the Mediterranean, our ship weighed anchor at Malta where a group of us went ashore and were so delighted to be together that we nearly missed rejoining the ship. I went as far as Marseilles and flew home to England. I was eager to see my lovely home again and to prepare my staff for some changes. Phil had continued on our ship, but he was rather unwell and I went to meet him when the boat train arrived in London. He was suffering from fever and although he came home with me for a few days it was clear to us that he needed hospital treatment, and I took him to the Hospital for Tropical Medicine in London and from there he flew back to New York.

Daisy, Marjorie and her husband Georg were my frequent visitors at home. Margaret had decided to return to the States to be with her American relatives and friends.

I was eager to hear more about the philosophical work my sister and Daisy were doing and they gave me Mr. Ouspensky's books to read. Some months later I began to attend evening meetings in London.

My sister and her husband had a flat in Cleveland Square, W2 which made it possible for me to stay with them. Georg, being a concert pianist had two grand pianos in their large studio drawing room – this was a time of flowering of concert music in London. Hostesses were eager to attract small groups of players to their London homes and Georg was able to organise musical concerts with many of the young musicians of that time, such as the Barbirollis, Boyd Neal, Eda Kersey, Moura Lympany, Myra Hess, Constant Lambert, Clifford Curzon, Joan Cross and others. I remember particularly two such concerts, one at Mrs. Bruce's lovely home on the Cromwell Road, Kensington and another at Londonderry House, Park Lane, to which royalty came – our friends were called upon to be ushers and Marjorie was an excellent hostess.

CHAPTER 11

In Which I start upon a New Career 1932–1937

On one of my trips to Potsdam in Germany which was the home of my German friend, I became deeply interested in the role of the German Shepherd dog, its intelligence, beauty and ability to be useful especially as "eyes" for the blind and its potential as a guard dog.

When I returned to England where the so-called Alsatian was still regarded as a "newcomer" of rather unknown quality, I decided to try to learn to train these dogs. Through my American connections, I spent some time with the "Seeing Eye" in Switzerland and learnt what I could, in a short space of time, about their work. Then I returned to England and attached myself to a large Alsatian kennels at Hayling Island, Hants. I felt that if I could procure a good working strain I could breed these dogs myself and help to train them.

Actually, the training of a good "blind" dog was too heavy a task for women and more suitable for men. But I still had much to learn, and the kennels I had chosen to go to were one of the best and most enlightened in England. Winning dogs from good working strains were being imported from Germany where the owner of my chosen kennel had excellent connections. I became the proud owner of several well bred and intelligent animals. I was given further instruction on training these animals and spent a year or two competing at the Kennel Club shows. I finally developed a good eye for a well proportioned dog and a practical ability on how to look after them.

When I left Hayling Island, I rented a furnished black and white house nearer home in a small village and brought my new acquisitions with me, together with a pet wire haired terrier. I had no end of visitors to my beautiful house. My German girl friend visited me frequently and brought with her several of our mutual friends – we toured East Anglia in a caravan trailer and made many trips to

Stratford-on-Avon, Oxford and Cambridge. It was more leisurely to drive in those days and accommodation was easier to find.

I had two excellent maids at my house to take care of everything and my parents close by. They were not, however, very happy about my easy going social life. It was unusual then for young ladies to have their own house and the comings and goings of my various friends did, of course, cause a stir in the small village – especially the rather noisy motor bicycle of one of my men friends! They had me "up on the mat" and insisted that I must not entertain my men friends alone overnight. They threatened to withdraw my allowance if I would not promise to do this. I became very angry and frustrated. My life, I felt, was my own and what I did with it was my own business. I knew I would not keep this promise, although I saw there was nothing to do but to pay lip service to it. I carried on with my life as before, but perhaps not quite so openly.

Father was not annoyed with me for long, and I soon learnt that he was considering buying a plot of land near Sevenoaks. Both he and Ruth were always interested in houses and building. From early times, Father would show me all manner of old houses and ask me if I would like to live there. He was very fond of Ludlow, since some of our ancestors came from the borders of Wales and Ludlow Castle was a favourite show piece for visitors when we lived in Wolverhampton. Father had been offered a piece of land on the hill opposite this castle where Milton was supposed to have composed the Masque, "Comus". Ruth was an architect's daughter and therefore took a real interest in house plans etc. But both my sisters and I had shouted this proposed scheme at Ludlow down, but Sevenoaks was another matter. It was nearer to Tunbridge Wells and London and had a beautiful view over the Weald of Kent due south to the sea. A well known architect living close by was engaged and pressed into service, but Ruth was not very strong physically. She was already quite comfortable at Camden Park and so the new house was to become mine with five acres of land. Thus, the first of several "Marylands" was born after many ups and downs and I had the joy and privilege of furnishing it with lovely new modern fittings. The five acres of grassland surrounding it was fenced and across the fields lay Knole Park and other Trust Properties.

Before the house was finished, I had lived for a few months at home – my family had finally come to accept my dogs and my constant visits to dog shows but there was hardly room to expand my kennels until I moved to my new home which was prepared with two rooms especially for dogs with puppies and so forth.

My German college friend was now married and living in London and I had several good men friends. One living in Tunbridge Wells was made of sporting stuff and together we shot rabbits on my new property, allowing my terrier dog to retrieve them. I was also introduced to car, horse and dog racing. In my car we made many expeditions to Brooklands and the Crystal Palace in the days of Freddie Dixon and Prince Bira and I found in this companionship something so wonderful just because I had not the same possibilities when younger and with my family. I had to experiment for myself and I found I loved the excitement of racing and when we went to Wimbledon and Harringay to watch the speedway racing, that was even more exciting. Why, I wondered, could none of my family enjoy these sports. Perhaps I had inherited this interest from my Mother.

In 1935, I took over my new house and after several unsuccessful attempts to find someone to help me with my dogs, I found a capable kennel maid – Ena Cramp and my housekeeper Ellen became good friends. I taught her all I knew about training dogs and she managed them well. We won many prizes for obedience and some for beauty and I was exporting some of my younger stock to the States and the East. But my original objective to breed dogs for teaching the blind did not seem possible and was no nearer attainment. One or two of my puppies had been accepted but they had to be at least a year old, friendly, not shy, able to withstand noise, yet sensitive, big enough but not too big, etc, all characteristics very difficult to find in one dog. With the most careful breeding, this was still imposssible to get except by a fluke. Meanwhile, this was a very expensive hobby and one could not really make it break even financially. The training of guide dogs was now getting under way in England and so my enthusiasm for pioneering a new social aid lost its initial impulse.

CHAPTER 12

War Years
1939–1945

In the summer of 1937 I decided to go on my own to Budapest to see an old friend of mine, Dr. Helmut Koniges. I had been in communication with him since my visit there with my sister in the 1920s and we had visited together several times. I took the Orient Express train and I actually travelled with the King's Messenger, which had not been arranged beforehand and it was very interesting for me. Europe was in turmoil and at each place where the train stopped the Messenger was met by his colleagues and the political position was discussed. I loved Germany and was horrified that it looked as though we were likely to fight her again. I looked at the blue smocked porters – they were so familiar to me, and I could not think of them as my enemies.

I was met at Budapest by my friend and whisked off to the Hotel Gellert where I was to stay. We did some lovely trips together in Budapest and outside in the country, but as my whole trip was secret, I had not told my family about it before I left, only my stepmother. I began to feel uneasy about being so far from England and my friend had to drive me to the airport several times to show me that the passenger planes were running as usual.

At the end of the week I was due to return by train and again I had the company of the King's Messenger. I had hoped that my Hungarian friend might also accompany us, but it was not to be. He was due to be called up for the army and so he explained to me that he could not come, and I never saw him again.

My sister and her husband were planning, if war was declared, to leave London and come to stay with me. Meanwhile, my German friends, Amelie and Guenther Wilmsen had their first baby. They had been working in England and living in Hampstead, and now they returned to Germany, but not before they asked me if I would become a godmother to their first born, named Winifred Amelie Melissa, and of course I accepted.

So in 1938 I registered at the University of London, Bedford College, to take a social studies course, hoping to become a prison visitor. I had already applied for this work and been accepted, but I needed further qualifications.

1939 came and war was declared. I was asked to help with the evacuation of children from London. We were all very uncertain then about what would actually happen. My sister and her husband joined me and we also looked after two little Scandinavian girls, friends of my sister's maid. Our strong and agile gardener quickly joined up for the army, so it was good to have extra "help" in the house.

Then we were given three young children from the East End of London. Their mother and the youngest child were placed in another home in Sevenoaks. Our children were rough and uncared for. All of us tried to adapt them to our home, including the Scandinavian girls, but they became homesick for Mother and the last I saw of them were their rather pathetic little figures firmly marching down our long drive in search of her.

But as we had a spare second floor, it was not long before we were give a number of women 'ATS.' I must explain that my house was on the slope of a hill and the house above us was already requisitioned by the army, so this was a good idea for their women helpers to be so near. There were about six of them and they shared our facilities, i.e. bathroom and kitchen and slept on the floor in sleeping bags as the second floor was unfurnished. My kennel maid had already signed up for the war and I was busy finding homes for some of my dogs. Our house was situated between two airports, West Malling and Biggin Hill and later when the bombing of London was on, we had activity right over our heads. Sometimes when my sister and her husband would go out for walks in the fields nearby – they would hear the drone of engines and would dive under cover of trees or under nearby blackberry bushes.

We had our air raid shelter built into the hill and we quickly got used to the German raids which seemed to have a time pattern, always coming at breakfast, lunch and dinner hours, so we often had to eat in our dugout. Then we couldn't understand how our English Spitfires and Hurricane fighters knew they were coming -radar was new and secret in those early days of the war. Our fighters would fly into the mass of German bombers and split them up. There would be dog fights right over our heads, and the spent cartridge cases would rain down on us. In fact, some of our friends from London found that they could see much more of the actual dog fights at our home, and so came to see us quite often. I remember some friends would go around with wooden seed boxes on their heads, as though that would really protect them!

Once, during these repeated raids, our fighters brought down a German Bomber which landed in the valley near us. The airmen were taken captive and held at the camp above us.

By 1940 my studies at Bedford College became increasingly difficult to go to, so London University evacuated its students to Cambridge for their second year. Marjorie and Georg were happy to housekeep for me and so I established myself in "digs" at Cambridge – a wonderfully restful place after the constant raids we withstood at home.

My Father and Mary were still living in Tunbridge Wells, but Father was becoming increasingly worried by the constant air raids, so Mary, with the help of one of her friends, found a lovely house at Stratford-on-Avon, with a garden running right down to the Avon river. Their home at Tunbridge Wells was commandeered by the Army. In the increasingly difficult years that followed, we found Stratford-on-Avon another peaceful and cultural place to which we could escape from time to time.

I sat for my final exams at Cambridge in 1940 and returned home. My sister and her husband had bought a house at Rickmansworth in Hertfordshire. Georg was becoming very well known as a concert pianist and was frequently asked to play at local concerts.

In 1941 I was recommended for a police job at Scotland Yard. Being an older graduate, it was considered that I might have had the necessary experience to hold down such a job. I was to work in their Headquarters right on the Thames in London in the "Children and Young Persons" Department on a big index there – in which all young people were registered who had already been in police custody. Every young person who was apprehended by the Police was notified to me there under their name, address and description. It was my job to see whether they had already been known to the Police, and if so, to send for their case papers and to tell their present captors what to do with them next. This was a great opportunity for me to meet others working at Scotland Yard and to read all the case papers of young offenders.

As my work was considered useful toward the war effort and because the railway lines between Sevenoaks and London were constantly bombed, I was given petrol coupons to drive my car and I carried three other passengers to and from their work in London. This continued for six months amid the increasing bombing of London when many times after the air raid alarms were sounded I thankfully reached the "safety" of the Police Headquarters and their well sandbagged entrance!

But the job itself became too much for me. The Police Index carried more and more names and the case papers increasingly difficult to read. I told my boss that they needed two people to do my job! This was pooh poohed, but when I left they did engage two people. As my good and faithful cook-housekeeper was also eager to join up, I had to make a decision about my house. Some friends living in London wanted to rent it unfurnished, so that they could bring their valuable furniture out of London, and so I decided to rent it to them for the remainder of the war period.

My housekeeper and I left our home – fortunately, homes had been found for my remaining dogs – and we went to London to stay. I was frequently going out to Rickmansworth to be with my sister or going at weekends to Stratford-on-Avon. But the tensions of this crowded life were catching up on me, and I suffered also, personally, from some distressing love affairs. Fortunately, I had continued to keep in touch with the Ouspensky students, although meetings in London had been discontinued, and one such member, my doctor, was a great help to me. He felt, as I did, that I should be married, and so one of my men friends was invited to our "work". This was not a success, but my doctor recommended that I should leave London and go to live in Surrey, near Mr. Ouspensky's home, Lyne Place, near Virginia Water.

As every 'single' person had to have a job, my doctor recommended me to the local hospital nearby where I became a full time V.A.D. Part of St. Thomas's Hospital had been evacuated to Surrey and we worked in the Nissen Huts put up in a nearby wood. I was straight away put into the Men's Surgical Ward where I was asked to assist sister with the dressings. One of the following days I was asked to assist in the theatre and then I was introduced to the Women's Surgical Ward, where I felt much happier. The patients interested me and I felt I could give of my best, and I was able to look after several very seriously ill people. My early training in the ideas of Mr. Ouspensky to try not to identify and to try to be aware of myself in all that I was doing were, here in the hospital, an absolute necessity.

When previously I had had dogs and I had taken them to the vet for their inoculations I was unable to watch the needle being plunged into their skins. Now at the hospital this was a common occurence and I had to be ready to do it myself when necessary without fainting. I stayed some months in the hospital and then I was asked if I would like to go and live in at Lyne Place and work there full time.

I felt a great affinity for the place and its members. Mr. Ouspensky, who was now in the States with his wife, had interviewed me when I first came to Virginia Water. I told him of my background, about my Father and his religious principles and the way I felt that some things were more important than others, which he told me were the early workings of my "magnetic centre". I felt that I could talk to him and that he understood me like a grandfather – rather different from the impression he gave us when working with him in "groups" in London.

These were the years of increased bombing raids on London and the mechanised bombs or "Doodlebugs". I felt the danger when the sirens sounded, but was always happy to be able to be amongst my comrades at Lyne Place. I felt that I "belonged" there in some remarkable way. The work to look after the house, the garden and farm was physically hard. A timetable was made each day and one was expected to work at whatever one was given silently, as quickly and as well as one could, always being aware of oneself and those around you. Meals were taken in silence, except by those who were appointed to wait, and the silence was only broken by the angry cries of the cat, who was occasionally sharing a chair with one of the grown-ups!

For many days I worked in the garden digging, hoeing and planting. There was a five acre and ten acre field put down in vegetables and this was an opportunity for a number of us to work in close unison. One day I was privileged to work with an older person and we were doing deep digging on a trench in the garden. I soon became tired and wanted to rest, but my friend insisted that I carry on, and work became almost unbearable. My back felt that it would break, and then suddenly, I felt that I had gone through the pain barrier and was able to carry on digging for some hours. It was as though one was tapping a new accumulator which one was rarely able to do for oneself. Some years later when my sister and I worked on the sacred "movements" created by Mr. Gurdjieff, we were able to see more about this inner strength and its working.

I think my sister, in her book entitled "A Way of Living", gives a very clear and accurate picture of Mr. and Mrs. Ouspensky's house. "Lyne Place" was a sturdy, oldish house surrounded by several acres of farm and gardens with a lovely lake and boat house. In a peculiar way, the entrance to it was somehow hidden. However well one knew it, it always seemed hard to find. There was a long drive up to the house and, for some psychological reason, this seemed a very hard way to walk. My sister, for instance, always felt she was going into a nunnery.

On arrival at the house, one was given a job for the day, with general instructions. Sometimes this was outside for hours. I weeded paths, picked fruit or planted potatoes or cabbages in large fields with possibly a dozen other people – or indoors at some ordinary house job – scrubbing floors, cooking and washing up. One was expected to do this work as fast as one could with as little energy wasted as possible. It had, indeed, something of a convent or monastery about it and the silence was hard at first for some people. But if one has ever truly worked like this, one would realize its extraordinary value and never go back to our haphazard way of living.

Both of us found that if we tried hard to follow the routine, we would end the day with overwhelming energy. The odd and almost terrible thing about all this is that although one can see clearly the results of a real effort like this, it is extraordinarily difficult to make one. Voices in one's body seem to shout against it and deceive one by every possible means to go back to the old wasteful and stupid methods and attitudes. "There is a new path clear to follow, but it is one's own self that refuses to take it." *

Yet again, I decided to change my work. I could have stayed at Lyne as a regular market garden employee or, again, a member of the Fire Service – two jobs which were indeed necessary for the war effort, but if I had to have a job, I wanted it to be more social than it was possible to be there. Some years previously I had become a member of the English Speaking Union, and when I went to see them at Dartmouth House,in London, I learnt that I might be considered for two jobs suitable for me with my Anglo American background. For some months I worked with an American Professor who was travelling the country giving lectures on Anglo-American Understanding, and in my spare time I went to their Anglo-American Hospitality Centre, to do work with a group of women attending to the needs of the many American Military personnel going through England.

I continued to go back to Lyne Place for weekends, and the way of working that I had learnt there helped me very much to face the busy office hours I had in London. I also learnt all I could of London and

* "A Way of Living" by Marjorie von Harten, pp.35,36.

48

used to take groups of American men round London to the Tower, Museums, Houses of Parliament, Buckingham Palace and ended by showing them the busy life in the undergrounds in which so many people actually slept as shelter from the bombs. These sightseeing expeditions usually finished with a hearty dinner, during which a good time was had by all!

At this time, many American Administrators came over from the States – ready and competent to take over the civic administration in Europe when the time was ripe. As I was also working for the Anglo-American relations I found the company of some of these soldier-administrators most instructive and I became friends with many of them. During this time I had been a paying guest, living in Park Lane to be near my work, but after the sudden death of my sister's husband in 1941, I moved to Rickmansworth to be with her. My sister was now free to continue with her interests and together we went to Lyne Place or to Stratford for a quiet weekend with Father and Mary and a Shakespeare play.

On our visits to Stratford to see Father and Mary, we were able to tell them more about our visits to Mr. Ouspensky's home in Surrey. Both of them were very interested in our studies and would have liked to join us if that had been possible. My Father understood and saw that he was someone with many "I". He told me that he felt this study of the "Science of Man" as he put it, was indeed right for me and this was a great blessing to me in the years that followed.

The winter of 1946 was an unusually cold one and I returned to London to be near Colet Gardens and our "Work". The manager of my bank found me a warm flat in Rutland Gate, Knightsbridge. This was very comfortable in the winter, as it was on the ground floor and right over the central heating plant, but rather too warm in the summer, and after a few years I rented a small house near the sea at Seaford, Sussex. I had many visitors both at my flat, and, in summer, at Seaford.

It was hoped that the Ouspenskys would return from the States in 1945. They had been living at Franklin Farms, Mendham, New Jersey, U.S.A. on a property similar to Lyne Place, and the same sort of work was in progress there. Our large group in London was preparing for Mr. Ouspensky's return to the best of their ability.

Someone introduced me to Evelyn Northcroft, an English cousin of my Godchild "Winnie" and she was able to give me news of her family. We had been entirely cut off during the war. I learnt that Winnie's Father, Guenther Wilmsen, who had been a war correspondent, had been killed in the war by a direct hit. Winnie now had two brothers and two sisters and they were all living at Marburg/Lahn, Germany and were rather badly off financially. Their Mother, my friend, Amelie, had a teaching job. Evelyn Northcroft herself was hoping to invite some of her family to England when it was possible. Meanwhile, she was living in Harley Street, London and had a string of rather high class P.G.'s living there with her. I still kept in touch with the English Speaking Union, but their work among the American soldiers became less pressing.

CHAPTER 13

My Father's Death – 1946

Mary with her great good nature had gathered around her many new friends and my Father was also enjoying meeting new people, some connected with the theatre and others interested in religion and archaeology. Mary's younger son, Holbrook, came from the States and joined the R.A.F. He was a rather silent young man whom we all felt rather difficult to understand, but we were all loud in our praise for him in his new venture.

My father and Mary continued their home life at Stratford. Mary did her war work with the St. John's Ambulance and Father wrote and lectured about his archaeological work and composed pamphlets.

When Sir Charles gave his 1945 lecture to the Victoria Institute*, he took as his subject 'The Bible and Present Day Developments' and it opened as follows: "There is a prophecy in the Old Testament of a famine, not of bread, nor of water, but of hearing the words of God. (Amos 8-11). We sometimes wonder whether such prophesies have been fulfilled, or whether the time is now ripe for them – the time may be ripe now for anything to happen: our trouble is that we

* In 1942, Sir Charles was elected President of the Victoria Institute in succession to Sir Ambrose Fleming – he had been a member for several years before that.
The Victoria Institute or Philosophical Society of Great Britain, was founded in 1865. Its objects were "to investigate, in a reverent spirit, important questions of philosophy and science, especially those bearing upon Holy Scripture and to arrange for addresses from men who have themselves contributed to progress in Science and Research, and thus to bring the Fellows, Members and Associates of the Institute into line with the latest advances. Also in humble faith in one Eternal God, who created all things good, to combat the unbelief now prevalent by directing attention to the Divine care for man that are supplied by "Science, History and Religion".
Man of Wolverhampton: V. Harten and Marston, p.209.

lack perspective in which to judge. What will future historians have to say about us? We may suspect that there has been a good deal fundamentally at fault. But little light comes upon underlying causes from our Preachers, or from the Press or through radio.

Now everywhere, all through the ages, the sciences of history, archaeology and anthropology tell us, there has practically been a universal belief and recognition of one or more deities. It was left to the last century to develop a belief in no God at all. He implied then that everything just happens. People believe only in natural explanations. Supernatural, ie. deeper ideas are not understood. The strange thing is that our churches either ignore or make ineffectual attempts to combat these ideas. The modern preacher takes for granted that his audience believe in the supernatural as well as the natural as the implications involved in a real belief in the existence of a Deity are shunned! *

My Father quoted some passages from the Bible here: "He that cometh to God must believe that HE IS and that HE IS a rewarder to them that diligently seek after him."(Hebr.XI.6). "In Him we live and move and have our being." (Acts XVII.26); affirming the Transcendent Nature of the Deity and His Imminence to each one of us.

Again: (Matt 10.29 to 30 and Luke XII.6) "Are not two sparrows sold for a farthing? And not one of them is forgotten in the sight of God. But the very hairs of your head are numbered."

My Father felt that these two sentences testified to the Divine Care for all creation – they lift us up as it were into an atmosphere where we would fain dwell, yet small attention is now taken in our conventional lives of the implications such statements carry with them. All this mental capacity began with the materialistic suppositions of this last century. It is imagined that His care for His Creation would involve interference with the assumed uniformity of those supposed laws of Nature, which according to these nineteenth century ideas were sacrosanct. Thus, through assumptions of the last century which were pure speculations, and limited to the finite, God has been denied the control of His own Universe. Why, Sir Charles asked, had the Bible in the past made such a wide appeal to all races educated and uneducated? The Bible appealed to our intuitive faculties as well as to our mental ones.

Organised religion seems reluctant to talk about this wonderful fact and only emphasises our faults. Faults we certainly have, and

* Man of Wolverhampton: V. Harten and Marston, p.198.

each one of us in our learning process must see and correct those faults, but what a wonderful aim we can have in our lives. Paramanhansa Yogananda states in this little book 'that Man has come to earth solely to learn to know God, he is here for no other reason! (p.177).

In his preparatory notes for his 1946 Presidential Address, which was never delivered, my Father was to take as his subject "Human Nature, the World's Fundamental Problem".

In spite of two world wars – peace and plenty are by no means yet in sight – this is in accord with what we were led to expect, not by prophets of today, but by those of thousands of years ago whose writings are preserved in Holy Scripture, having won two great wars against Germany and Japan in order to preserve the very principles of Peace and Freedom, which continue to recede before our eyes. One can only account for these strange phenomena on the assumption that we are presented with false pictures of the causes which operate to bring them about.

My Father continues: "We all pride ourselves on seeking the Truth, but may it not be that we move in an atmosphere of Unreality. That we are actually in the position Shakespeare describes: 'All the world's a stage, and all the men and women, merely players.' These men and women learn their parts at schools and colleges and grow up to advocate different but conventional lines of thought. The Press and the Radio tend to follow the same lines not because they express the truth, but because they pursue the lines of least resistance. So we are confronted with anomalies in the world situation which do not respond to popular treatment, but are actually aggravated by them".

My Father insisted that we should face the realities of life before it is too late, and pay less attention to material things. Too much attention, he felt, was being paid to the study of science of matter and too little to the study of the science of Man. The nineteenth century side-tracked the problem of Sin. It tended to be swept under the carpet by the broom of education, psychology and socialism. We thought it was well within the power of man to eradicate this. All that man had to do was to decide what to do and then do it. But the simple fact is that many people know perfectly well what they ought to do but do not do it. It is quietly overlooked. My Father felt that Human Nature is the real problem: (you and I and the rest of the Human Family).

When new studies revealed a wealth of rottenness, villany and sin already suspected by the psychologists, although its presence was clearly enough asserted in the New Testament, the world having been brought much closer by rapid communication has also accentuated this problem. The world scarcely seems ripe yet for World Federation. Thousands of years of national governments cannot be swept away at short notice without authority, little if any, short of the Divine. ★

Sir Charles ended his Address with a reference to the coming of the New Dispensation prophesied in the Bible and Man's part in this: "Man is asleep. He must wake up and live in the light of God's countenance. I, myself, am the problem."

I have taken the liberty of telling you about some of my Father's considered judgments because he was a representative citizen of his time – a politician, an industrialist and archaeologist of Biblical sites as his hobby with considerable travel experience as well. He knew about our philosophical studies and would have joined my sister and I if he had been able to – so much of which verified his observation, particularly the necessity to study the science of man. Man is a very complicated machine; he cannot "do" – he must study his machine – it's all in the Bible, and we studied it with Mr. Gurdjieff and Mr. Ouspensky.

The end came in his 80th year when he was still in full 'harness' and mentally vigorous. He was at his Stratford-on-Avon home and had plans to come to London to deliver his Presidential Address for 1946 at the Victoria Institute, and for several other meetings.

On May 21st, he seemed acutely aware that something was about to happen. He went to Communion in the morning, a thing he seldom did on a weekday. He settled all his affairs with his Secretary. He did not want his wife to leave him at any time in the day.

Finally, when she protested that she must go upstairs to change for dinner, he agreed, sat down upon his sofa in his study and began to read a passage from his Bible.

When she returned, in half an hour, the Bible was neatly laid down with the usual pencil for marking passages which specially appealed to him at that moment, and his spirit had left his body.

Looking at the passage he had just underlined, Mary saw they were from Daniel 12, 3 and 4: 'And they that be wise shall shine as the brightness of the firmament; and they that turn many to righteousness as the stars for ever and ever. But thou, O Daniel shut up the words, and seal the book, even to the time of the end'.★★

Here I must insert a note about my Father which particularly affected me.

Sir Charles had never taken any particular interest in the animal

★ Man of Wolverhampton: V. Harten and Marston, pp.212-214.
★★ Man of Wolverhampton: V. Harten and Marston, p.291.

world and had very little contact with any of its members. When I decided to go in for breeding and training dogs, I had no option but to have my own home, where they would be welcome to live with us and not be put into kennels!

However, to the surprise of the family and all members of the household at Stratford, Mary introduced a very small pekinese bitch called "Print" so named because she was prettily marked in black and white with tiny patches of brown here and there. She was delicate, sensitive and dainty, one simply could not put her in a kennel! My Father began to relent. Mary allowed the new arrival to curl up on a blanket at the end of their bed, and when she needed to go out, my Father himself attended to her needs. She would rest with him in the afternoons, and when she grew tired on their daily walks, my Father would carry her in the crook of his arm.

By the time two more Pekes joined the family, Sir Charles was totally won over and a written epitaph to "Dusty" – the third member of the Peke family, gives some idea of the close relationship that existed between my Father and his pets. It was written in 1944 when the horrors of war and rationing were still in force. "Dusty" was a very small Pekinese dog, just a little round ball of chestnut fur. She came to us in June when she was two months old, fully grown, but only four pounds in weight. We expected a certain amount of jealousy over our other two dogs, who were a good deal older and had been with us much longer, but Dusty was quite equal to the occasion. She concealed her nervousness, and immediately began to make advances, which they received with much hesitation, but to which they gradually responded. She was put to bed at 7.30 in the evening in her mistress's dress closet. There she had a window for light and air, and a small radiator for heat in winter, and she slept there, without disturbing anyone, until eight the next morning. The two older dogs stayed up with the grown-ups and went to bed with them. All the dogs had toys with which they played, but Dusty collected them all, and kept them under the dining room table.

Unfortunately, Dusty was not to be long in this world: in spite of the good attentions of a celebrated vet, she caught a germ, which usually only attacks greyhounds. As she was so small and so thin, she had very little chance of survival. It was only when she crossed her little front paws and died that we realized how indispensable Dusty had made herself. The other two dogs felt the same way. They had to begin their lives all over again. Father wrote: "We have felt "Dusty's" presence ever since – only now we realize all that she meant to us. We put a headstone on her grave, which carried on it the inscription: "Dusty, an Angel Unawares."

As you can imagine, I was very touched with my Father's "turnabout with dogs" – he had also apologised to me for his earlier "misunderstandings" of my dogs and through his experiences with the "Pekes", he had begun to understand the 'real' relationship which he could have with them. It had taken him some time to understand – he was now 67 years old, but it was never too late for my father to learn to enjoy them.

CHAPTER 14

I go again to the States 1948

My father, before he died, arranged for me to have investments in the States and Canada so that I would always be able to go to those countries to stay or to visit there. But during the war, our government had insisted that these investments should be called in and that English money was to be given in exchange to help them pay for armaments etc. on lend-lease.

So in 1949 when my stepmother, Mary and I wished to go to the States, we had to find the money for our travel by other means. Margaret, my stepsister, was married and living in Ann Arbor, Michigan, and she asked me to go and stay with her.

My Godchild, Winnie, was away at boarding school and I arranged for a friend to stay in my London flat.

Air travel was still not a regular service, so we went by ship and stayed at Mary's old headquarters, now the Henry Hudson Hotel in New York City. I enjoyed meeting Mary's many friends and her relatives, and numerous parties were given for us. Then I went by train to Ann Arbor. Margaret had a lovely home on a private estate outside Ann Arbor. Her husband, Hickman Price Jnr. had a very good job with Kaiser Fraser as an executive in their automobile industry. Although the actual factory was near – between Ann Arbor and Detroit, his work entailed much travelling and he was rarely at home for long. I arrived at Christmas time 1949 and Margaret was eager to show me a real white Christmas and the festivities that went with it. She already had two small sons, Hickman 111 and Marston and a lively coloured couple to look after the house called Ella and Richard. After my war austerities, this was a wonderful change and Margaret and I were very happy together. I admired her calmness in the face of innumerable crises at home – Hickman would return very tired and sometimes ill, and would go to bed for several days. Ella and Richard were not easy to manage and the children were often difficult to control, but Margaret took all this in her stride and I did my best, as a considerate guest, to help her.

Margaret wished to go away for a time and so I was to act as "mother" in her absence. This meant my taking a test for my American Driving Licence – a written test as well as one in the car. The Prices had two large saloon cars and I had to take my turn with the other parents driving the children back and forth to school. I had no difficulty with the written "Highway Code" but I had the High Sheriff himself to test my aptitude in the car since I was accompanied by a very "high-up" friend, Mr. Eugene Power. However, with true American understatement, at the end of my test, the nice High Sheriff said: "Yes, I think you can drive better than I can! "And so that's O.K.!" I enjoyed looking after the children very much and I had many friends in Ann Arbor to come and see me and the factory managers were "on call" by phone if I needed any advice or help.

When Margaret returned, I went off to Chicago to stay with an old college friend, Jane Rubovits and her husband. In the years that followed, I became very fond of this great city with its high skyscrapers, wonderful shopping arcades, cultural museums and numerous nightclubs. Jane entertained me and brought together my relatives and friends living there. Her mother introduced me to the best musical then running – "Annie Get Your Gun" – and another friend took me out to an evening of visiting night clubs – so cold was it that evening that even with a fur coat on I hated to get out of the car – the wind and snow whistled up each road from the lake.

This was to be the first of innumerable visits I was to pay to this great metropolis in the years to come.

CHAPTER 15

Winnie

By 1948 I was comfortably installed in a ground floor flat in Knightsbridge and once again looking forward to resuming my contacts with my old friends abroad. Evelyn Northcroft had already two young nieces of hers from Germany, and they brought me news of my godchild, Winifred Amelie Melissa. She was living with her family in Marburg, but her Father had been killed at Neustadt in Palatinate in January 1945 and her mother, with five children to support, was having a difficult time. I enquired whether Winnie could come to England to be with me, and I would look after her and send her to school. This was arranged, and one day her English godfather and I were going to Northolt airport to meet her. She was to fly from Frankfurt, but her mother was not allowed to see her off, and when she went with her little suitcase and accordion to the airport lounge, she did not know what to do, and only sat by her luggage and began to cry. Finally, someone came to her assistance and explained that her aeroplane had already left, but it was arranged that she should fly via Brussels to London. She entertained the Captain and co-pilot all the way over with her songs and accordion accompaniment.

So it was that we were unable to meet her that day at Northolt and I had to wait alone for her the following day. I was very touched by her slim little figure and her luggage. She had learnt some English in school, so we were able to communicate. My plan was for her to go to stay with her Godfather in his house in Surrey because his family knew German well and there were wonderful facilities on the farm for Winnie to adjust to English life.

Meanwhile, I was going regularly to "White Walls", my rented house, near the sea at Seaford, Sussex. Nina and Sabina, Winnie's cousins, helped me to prepare it and when Winnie joined us, and later, some of her own family, we spent a very happy summer taking long walks over the downs or riding further afield on bicycles to "Drusilla's" and over the Seven Sisters to Alfriston and Eastbourne. I had also been to a number of well-known boarding schools and chose one nearby where the headmaster and mistress were sympathetic towards German children, and where all their students lived in a nice roomy home with many pet animals for company.

I much enjoyed my new position of standing in loco parentis.

CHAPTER 16

Mr. Ouspensky's Return
1946–1947

It was only in the winter of 1946/47 that Mr. Ouspensky finally and somewhat unexpectedly returned to England. The house in Colet Gardens had been beautifully put in order. An excellent group of some three hundred or more people were assembled to welcome him and hear his first talk, amongst them, many newcomers. It seemed as though after all the waiting, great times had come at last.

Mr. Ouspensky came on the platform accompanied by his new American secretary. We had all remembered the strong and vital man who would come swiftly up on the scene to answer our questions. We saw before us now a sad and ill old man making his way to his seat. We in the audience who had known him, were appalled. There certainly seemed no possibility of a new beginning here. He answered few questions, and repudiated completely the "System" as the theory and presentation of his ideas was commonly called, saying that it had failed and must be discarded! Only work on self-remembering should be continued.

He had several more meetings of this kind, and we went to Lyne, as usual, and my sister hoped she might see and talk to him, but she never did again. People were appalled at his apparent repudiation of his work, but my sister never felt that this was what he meant. Rather, she felt that he was trying to kill off our too certain and superficial approach to it. We had been without him for a long time and had, quite without realising it, come far too much to regard our work as a series of cliches which could be analysed. There must be words, and Mr. Ouspensky was very particular about their exact meaning, but these words could be really understood only in our inner selves. The "Work" is a living, growing thing, always changing, never static or constricted.

Ouspensky's unexpected death in the autumn of 1947 produced no obvious successor to the leadership, although there were many fine men in the group. At last, an appeal went to Madame Ouspensky, still in charge of the arrangements at Franklin Farms in the States, as to what should be done. Her reply came back succinct and clear. People who believed that they could teach should do so. Those who did not want to do further work should leave Lyne, and those who felt they needed further help should go to Mr. Gurdjieff in Paris.

This message caused chaos at the Historico-Psychological Society, as Mr. Ouspensky's groups were officially called. Although the origin of all the ideas taught had their basis in Mr. Gurdjieff's teachings, wonderfully reported by Mr. Ouspensky, Gurdjieff himself was generally considered to be a very dark character. Ouspensky had separated from him, and no member of his group was (apparently) supposed to have anything to do with him, or read the embryo of his book "Beelzebub". My sister knew this because she happened to show her copy to an older member, who had herself worked with Gurdjieff years before. She got into trouble for breaking a promise she had made when she joined Mr. Gurdjieff.

Gurdjieff had disappeared during the war. Now he had suddenly turned up in Paris, surrounded by a large French Resistance group of young people! It all sounds inexplicable now and rather funny. But it was an agonising choice for some people then. My sister, of course, never had any choice at all; she knew at once that Paris was her next step. But we who went to Paris lost many of our old friends; a lady whom my sister and I loved and greatly respected begged us almost on her knees not to go, and never would see us again, and our beloved doctor refused to have anything further to do with us, even medically!

Marjorie would have liked to have gone to Paris with her cousin Daisy Milward, but she was too old and ill now, and did not feel she could manage it. My sister's visits to Paris were always connected, in her mind, with another good friend, a young painter and artist, Kate Adamson, who was at Lyne. She also braved some official ire to go, although I went later and we formed a threesome. Kate and Marjorie had many experiences there together.

My sister went to Paris one day in November, 1948 for lunch at Mr. Gurdjieff's flat in the Rue des Colonels Renards, near the Avenue Carnot and the Etoile. Many people have described this flat, so I will quote Kenneth Walker's description: "The strange mixture of furniture, the incongruous collection of pictures, the haphazard arrangement of the flat's contents gave it the appearance of a junk shop rather than of a home. Everything seemed to have happened there by accident and nothing by design. It was impossible to learn anything of the character of the owner from such a fortuitous collection of odds and ends."* It was already full of people, some of whom my sister knew, who had come for the two hour reading of "Beelzebub" which preceded lunch. A man came forward to greet her at once with his hand outstretched. My sister's first instinct was to draw back with the feeling – I must not meet that man! Fortunately, she came to quickly and shook the welcoming hand with much relief. This was Captain Bennett, one of Ouspensky's special circle of men who used to work with us in groups, but had been "outlawed" for some reason for a time.

After this, the door of the reading room was carefully unlocked, and we all poured in. It was a small and tight fit for us. The lights were on as the blinds were drawn. This was true also of the extremely small dining room we went into a little later. We were told that Mr. Gurdjieff did not care to be overlooked by his neighbours! The reader was Mr. Bennett, who read a considerable amount of "Beelzebub" in English. Mr. Gurdjieff slipped into an empty seat sometime after the reading had started. He had changed little, except that he looked considerably older, and somehow seemed to be more compassionate towards us poor mortals. After a couple of hours' reading, they stopped for a meal.

In the dining room, a long table ran through the middle of it, and Mr. Gurdjieff had his special seat at one side towards the top end of the table. The newest guests were marshalled onto the other side of the table opposite him. As you became less new, you moved down the table to give place to others. Madame de Salzmann, his hostess, sat among the guests. Other members of his groups sat or stood everywhere, with young members of the French group trailing off into the hall.

Before assembling in the dining room, there was an unexpected and mysterious call of "chain" from someone in the kitchen, from which there came some very delicious smells. Everyone available lined up between the kitchen and the dining room opposite, and portions of luncheon (or dinner) were passed from hand to hand: meat and vegetables at the bottom with a plate over and soup on top! It was an excellent idea, for when the company was seated, no one could have got in or out of the room.

* Quoted from "Venture with Ideas" by Dr. Kenneth Walker.

As a new member, I was seated opposite Mr. Gurdjieff. I was, of course, naturally frightened and rather put off by the claustrophobic atmosphere and was frightened of the company. Mr. Gurdjieff sensed this and was trying to make me feel more at home by offering me portions of food which I took with a certain amount of reluctance.

On Mr. Gurdjieff's left was the "Director" for the day with drinks in front of him. There were rules here, too, but they were of quite a different character from those of Mr. Ouspensky! All gentlemen were obliged to drink three (small) glasses of wine or spirits (Armagnac seemed his favourite); all ladies, one. The Director, who was a kind of toastmaster, also distributed drinks to everyone, and the meal commenced, punctuated by the toasts. These were an essential feature of any lunch or dinner, and were called "The Idiots". It was never quite clear what an idiot meant, but one heard that it was some essential type or quality. They varied in number between about four to a rather larger number, each meal depending on the conversation, and were always given in the same order. There were supposed to be sixteen or seventeen toasts in all, but very few people had heard as many as that. Everyone was asked to say which he or she represented in the list soon after their arrival. Curiously enough, everyone did, and even children picked out different idiots for themselves quite seriously. The list started with Ordinary, Super, Arch and Hopeless with a sort of speech to follow No.4, always given by the same person. This was: "To the health of all hopeless idiots, subjectively and objectively. That is to say, to the health of all those who are destined for an honourable death, and to the health of all those who are candidates for perishing like dogs. Addition – By the way, it is necessary to add that only those can die honourably who have worked on themselves in life. Those who do not work on themselves will inevitably, early, lately, perish like dirty dogs." After this came Compassionate and Squirming, and then "We now come to the First Series of Geometric Idiots" to which followed Round and Square and sometimes Zigzag. This was usually as far as the list got! At each toast the Director raised his glass to the people who had chosen it, quite a feat in some cases! No one knew whether the list progressed up or down! Sometimes Mr. Gurdjieff commented on people when their toast came along. My sister remembers something was said to her about square in all things, but something "might get in at the corners"!

Sometimes he commented to people on totally different things – as for instance when a husband and wife – he rather sensitive and small, she much larger and more practical looking – came to sit opposite him. Mr. Gurdjieff leaned forward towards them, saying "She looks as though she could put a knife into you", and illustrating the action on himself. We knew nothing about these two people or their relation to each other, but it was very extraordinary to see how her face changed in the next few days. Another amusing event happened when three Americans came to dinner – one lady appearing as a sort of guide for the married couple, who had never seen Mr. Gurdjieff or his menage before. She kept commenting sotto voce on Mr. Gurdjieff to her friends: "He is not so good tonight" – or "wait until he speaks about so and so." Finally, they all decided they must leave to catch their boat or train. Mr. Gurdjieff behaved as though he had not heard a word of any of it, simply plying them with further delicious things to eat and drink, in spite of their boats or trains, and their voices finally trailed off into silence.

At times, Mr. Gurdjieff would start up a terrific verbal fight with a particular Englishman who responded wonderfully in kind. This went on for some time and then completely stopped and died away! When we came to think of it, Mr. Gurdjieff could be an entirely different character every time he came down for a meal, and say, quite convincingly, things opposite to what he had said at the last meal.

In these extraordinary conversations, you had somehow to be in the right place in yourself if Mr. Gurdjieff spoke to you. It was not always easy! My sister was naturally a rather thirsty person and although quite indifferent to wine and alcoholic drinks, Mr. Gurdjieff noticed one evening that she was drinking a large glass of water and suddenly he railed at her for not drinking wine or something better. He made a sort of laughing stock of her in front of all the company, calling for the feminine of "Jackass" which someone suggested was "Jenny". Somehow she did not feel a bit put out. She simply answered: "I like water, Mr. Gurdjieff" and she never heard about the matter again.

In the late August 1949, I accompanied my sister to Paris and we went together to the flat. Mr. Gurdjieff noticed our close connection although he did not at first know we were sisters. From one of us he got one thing, he commented, and from the other another, but from the two of us together he got something quite different. It was true. We have always been a good working combination together, a thing unusual in sisters, judging by other people's experiences.

But I very quickly ran into difficulties there with the long hours and the heat in the flat. It was a particularly hot summer, and the flat with all its windows shut, blinds drawn and crowds of visitors was difficult to endure. After a long reading, I slipped out without notifying my sister and did not appear for lunch. Mr. Gurdjieff promptly asked for me, which was awkward for my sister, as she had no idea where I had gone. He sent me various messages by my sister and when I turned up for dinner that evening, I was full of apologies. Mr. Gurdjieff brushed these aside and simply repeated – "your loss" several times. I never forgot his words, although I never saw him again and no amount of heat or other difficulties kept me away again from anyone or anything of value.

My sister, too, had the privilege of going on tour with Mr. Gurdjieff and some others – this was an added bonus and one had to be ready and prepared for anything at a moment's notice.

Mr. Gurdjieff was very fond of driving to Vichy where he and his company would take the baths and he was well loved and lionised everywhere. He would go around with his pockets full of sweets, sometimes for one of them, but more often for the children who thronged about him everywhere. On one such trip, Mr. Bennett, who was driving one of the cars, persuaded Mr. Gurdjieff to go to Martignac to view the Lascaux caves – all the party went right through the caves – "As he stood looking at the paintings, he seemed completely to belong there. He explained various symbols, and especially the strange "composite" animal, which he said was like the 'sphinx', the emblem of an esoteric society. I said: 'Symbol', he rejected the correction. 'No. Emblem.' At that time, there were societies with special knowledge, and each society had an emblem by which the members recognised each other. Same way we have enneagram. He said that the deer were the totems of individual people. By the number of points on the antlers, you could know the degree of attainment of the man they represented."*

* Bennett – witness p. 264.

CHAPTER 17

The Movements

When my Godchild, Winnie, went to boarding school in the autumn of 1949, I felt free to continue my meetings in London.

Shortly before Mr. Gurdjieff's death in 1949, his hostess, a great teacher of movements in her own right, Mme de Salzmann, came to London and together with some of her pupils from the French group, we were able to do some concentrated work at Colet Gardens in Hammersmith, South London. We went three times a week and worked on the Movements for about two hours. Both my sister and I were eager to take part in them, having seen some of them performed in New York so many years ago. We had also taken part in some of them in Paris at the Salle Pleyel. My sister knew Thomas de Hartmann and his wife Olga, and we had been to their French home. Thomas de Hartmann, a considerable musician and conductor himself, worked together with Mr. Gurdjieff on the music for these Movements.

When we were with Mr. Ouspensky, we had heard of the "Obligatory" Movements but had never taken part in them. Now they were compulsory for everyone. They were taught by Mrs. Rosemary Nott, a fine pianist herself, who had studied with Thomas de Hartmann.

We were also given the opportunity to learn the last series of Movements created by Gurdjieff and known as the "Thirty-nine". But there were many others, taken from the Dervish Ritual Exercises, including the Great Prayer of the Dervishes of Kashgar, the Cannon of Seven, performed by Christian monks of Essenian origin in Transcaucasia, and also simply "work rhythms" of groups of women knitting or spinning and men sewing shoes, and combing and carding wool.

Gurdjieff had written a ballet of the "Struggle of the Magicians", which also had characteristic rhythms for the Black and White Magicians, but I am not sure that this ballet was ever performed or, indeed, completed. At least we were never given more than bits of it. Most of the Movements were simply known by their numbers, and we heard little of their purpose or meaning, although we were, of course, given careful instructions about the physical steps and postures. They were very varied, and some physically much simpler than others.

One had to keep an inner awareness totally unlike one's ordinary state; it was as though not one of these dances went by itself, or did what one would expect next! One could not just let go and slip into a rhythm like ordinary dancing. One had to be there, physically, mentally and emotionally, every minute, or rather, we had to try to be there. Some of the rhythms, particularly the Dervish ones, were incredibly complicated: the dancer had to follow different rhythms for the body, each hand, the feet, the head and sometimes also to say something, all this at the same time to the rhythm of the music.

Nothing, I found, gave one such a feeling of the utter clumsiness of one's own body as these rhythms did, or the extraordinary energy and power one felt when one was able to perform a movement correctly for a second or two.

Many of these dances were performed by students in seven rows, and very often each row was working on a different movement in a sort of canon.

Work on these Movements brought not exhaustion, as one might have expected, but exhilarating energy, and I was reminded of my days at Lyne Place when hard work there brought the same results.

Some of the best students of the Movements were asked to give a display, and Mrs. Tilley, who was to be in charge of making the dresses, asked me to help her. Mme de Salzmann wanted very special colours for the costumes, and when the material was not available in the colour required,, I was asked to buy some suitable cloth and then dye it. This was a completely new venture for me, but as I was living in Seaford in a house of my own, I had plenty of room and drying space to do it. My Godchild, Winnie, was still in England and came home for her holidays from school and I continued to enjoy entertaining her friends and my many neighbours. Marjorie also joined me at intervals and Luba Gurdjieff came for a recuperative holiday; she was Mr. Gurdjieff's niece. Mr. Bennet also called on his way back and forth to France when he and Elizabeth went for "retreats" at the monastery of St. Wandrille in France.

On one such visit in 1949, Mr. Bennett asked me if I would care to come and stay with them at Coombe Springs and become their housekeeper. Mr. Bennett explained to me that as I had been at Lyne Place, Mr. Ouspensky's house, I could organise the running of his house on similar lines.

Apart from the summer holidays, this meant a lot of train journeys between London and Seaford, but I found the constant train trips an excellent opportunity to read and think about a number of books on our work. There were active groups in Colet Gardens as well as the Movements to go to, and run by members of the French group.

N.B. Description of highlights out of "Finale" of Mr. Gurdjieff's book: "All and Everything".

CHAPTER 18

Our Philosophical Work

Now, I must try to talk more seriously about this "work" that Mr. Gurdjieff and Mr. Ouspensky were trying to show us.

I feel that the cosmological ideas are so important for man's development that I must include some of them in this book, but these ideas are quoted directly from Mr. Ouspensky's book.*

Before the war, I had been able to hear some chapters of Mr. Ouspensky's book entitled "The Psychology of Man's Possible Evolution". These were read out in his groups and discussed by question and answer method. We began to understand by our own verification that before man can evolve, he must try to understand himself. He ascribes to himself certain powers which he does not yet possess: he does not know himself, his limitations or possibilities. He does not know that he is a very complicated machine which must be studied. Man has many "I's" and not one "I", as he thinks, and his machine has many functions. He cannot "do" as he thinks he can, everything happens to him.

We were invited to write down what our aim was in life, why we were here and where we thought we were going? Then there were also the cosmological lectures – entitled "The Cosmology of Man's Possible Evolution", also given to Mr. Ouspensky's groups in 1934-40. Ideas which we found very difficult to understand at first, and only many years later, when reading Mr. Ouspensky's great works and Mr. Gurdjieff's "Legonomism" entitled "All and Everything" Or "Beelzebub's Tales to his Grandson" and developed in the volumes of Mr. Ouspensky's pupil Mr. J.G. Bennett, entitled "Dramatic Universe". I cannot begin to sum up the ideas of the cosmological

* P.D. Ouspensky: The Cosmology of Man's Possible Evolution -The Cosmological Lectures 1934-1940 by P.D. Ouspensky.

lectures – except to say that this universe that we live on is very far away from the sun absolute, and is very dense. Mr. Ouspensky gives mathematical evidence for this i.e. The Ray of Creation. But if man is to study himself he must study the universe in which he lives – Mr. Ouspensky says: Man is an image of the world. He was created by the same laws which created the whole of the world. By knowing and understanding himself, he will know and understand the whole world and all the laws that create and govern the world."*

But before examining these influences, we must study the fundamental law that creates all phenomena in all the diversity or unity of all universes and is the result of the combination or meeting of three different and opposing forces. Contemporary thought realises the existence of two forces – positive and negative magnetism; positive and negative electricity, male and female cells and so on. But no question has yet been raised about the third force. In fact, it is said that people are third force blind. This force is not easily accessible to direct observation and understanding, but by studying himself and the manifestations of his thought, consciousness and activity, his habits and desires etc., he may learn to see in himself – the action of the three forces. His desire, his initiative is the active force. The inertia of all his habitual psychological life which shows opposition to his initiative, will be the passive or negative force. The two forces will either counterbalance one another, or the opposing one will completely conquer the other, and at the same time become too weak for any further action.

This may continue for a lifetime, or this may go on for sometime until a third force makes its appearance, for instance, some new knowledge or method of work which will support the initiative. Then the initiative with the support of a third force, may conquer this inertia and a man may become active in the desired direction. Examples of the action of the three forces may be found in all manifestations of our psychic life, and in the life of human communities and of humanity as a whole, and of all the phenomena of nature around us. But we cannot see the third force; it is a property of the real world, the objective world, which we cannot observe in our subjective state of consciousness.

In the Absolute the three forces are active, but since, by its very nature, everything in the Absolute constitutes one whole, the three forces constitute one whole and possess independent will, full consciousness and full understanding of everything they do. These

* The Cosmological Lectures p.3.

ideas form the basis of many ancient teachings, such as the Trinity, Trimurti, Brahma, Vishnu and Siva etc.

These three forces of the Absolute constituting one whole, separate and unite by their own will and by their own decision and create new worlds, but in these worlds of the second order, where there is no longer a single will, but now there are three wills. The will of the Absolute creates worlds of the second order and governs them, but does not govern their creative work, in which a mechanical element makes its appearance. These three divided forces in the worlds of the second order, create new worlds of the third order, and having been created, manifest three forces of their own and so on, the increasing number of mechanical forces creep in. In the worlds of the fourth order (our sun) is subject to twelve laws and all planets are subject to twenty four laws (3 + 6 + 12 + 3).

If we take world 3, it will be the world representing the total number of starry worlds similar to our Milky Way and world 6 will be one of the worlds created within this world. World 12 is one of the suns that compose this Milky Way, World 24 will be a planetary world and World 48 will be the earth. World 96, the moon.

This chain of worlds, the links of which are the Absolute, all worlds, all suns, the sun, the planets, the earth and the moon, form a 'ray of creation' in which we find ourselves. There are probably infinite numbers of different worlds, each with its own separate ray of creation.

Coming back to our own ray of creation, the fewer laws there are in each given world, the nearer it is to the will of the Absolute. The more laws there are in a given world, the greater the mechanicalness, and the further it is from the will of the Absolute. We live in a world subject to 48 orders of laws, therefore very far from the will of the Absolute and in a very dark and remote corner of the universe. "Organic" life on earth, which is our first world, does not enter into the chain of worlds forming the Ray of Creation. It is a sort of film covering the earth and it serves a definite purpose in the Ray of Creation.

The idea of the Ray of Creation belongs to Ancient Knowledge and there are many copies of it which are either incompetent expositions or distortions of the same idea. Some of the ideas in the Ray of Creation contradict some modern views. The moon, which is one end of the Ray, is, according to this theory, a newly born planet and one that is not fully developed yet. It is becoming warm gradually and, depending upon a favourable development of organic life on earth, will become like the earth and have a satellite of its own, i.e. a new moon. The earth, too, is not getting cooler, it is getting warmer and may in time become like the sun.

We are far removed from the Will of the Absolute on the earth. We are separated from it by forty eight orders of mechanical laws. But the possibility for man to free himself from mechanical laws exists. Can the forty eight laws to which man is subject be defined? They can be studied only by observing them in oneself and by getting free from them, but a great deal of knowledge is needed in order to become free from one law without creating for oneself another in its place.

The Ray of Creation is like a large branch and at the growing end of the branch is the moon. The energy for the development of the moon and the formation of new shoots goes to the moon from the earth, where it takes form through the joint action of the sun and all the other planets of the solar system and of the earth itself. This energy is collected and preserved in a huge accumulator situated on the earth's surface. This accumulator is organic life on earth. Organic life on earth feeds the moon. Everything living on the earth, people, animals, plants, is food for the moon. The moon could not exist without organic life on earth any more than organic life could exist without the moon.*

The influence of the moon and everything else manifests itself in all that happens on the earth. The liberation which comes from the growth of mental powers and facilities is liberation from the moon. The mechanical part of our life depends upon the moon and is subject to it. If we develop in ourselves consciousness and will, and subject our mechanical life and all our mechanical manifestations to them, we shall escape from the power of the moon.

Man is, in the full sense of the word, that is, a "man" whose inherent powers are developed; a miniature universe and in him are all the matters of which the universe consists, the same forces, the same laws that govern the universe operate in him. Therefore, in studying man, we can study the whole world, just as in studying the world we can study man.

We are on the earth and we depend entirely upon the laws that are operating on earth. The earth is a very bad place from the cosmic point of view. It is like the most remote part of Northern Siberia, very far from everywhere; it is cold, life is very hard. Everything must be fought for.

The second fundamental law of the universe is the Law of Three

* Cosmology: p.54.

Forces, or the Law of Freedom, which has already been mentioned. The next fundamental law of the universe is the Law of seven, or Law of Octaves. In order to understand the meaning of this law, it is necessary to regard the universe as consisting of vibrations. These vibrations proceed in all kinds, aspects and densities of the matter which constitute the universe, from the finest to the coarsest. They issue from various sources and proceed in various ways, crossing one another, colliding, strengthening, weakening and arresting one another and so on.

The view of ancient knowledge is opposed to that of contemporary science (which supports the continuity of vibrations) and states the principle of this discontinuity of vibrations. This principle means that the definite and necessary characteristic of all vibrations in nature, whether ascending or descending, do develop not uniformly but with periodic accelerations and retardations.

A study of the seven tone musical scale gives a good foundation for understanding the cosmic Law of Octaves.

Let us take the ascending octave, that is the octave in which the frequency increases. Let us suppose that this octave begins with a thousand vibrations a second. Let us designate these thousand vibrations by the note "do". Vibrations are growing at the point where they reach two thousand vibrations a second. There will be a second "do" – that is, the "do" of the next octave. The period between one "do" and the next, that is, one octave, is divided into several unequal parts because the frequency of vibrations does not increase uniformly. The difference in the notes, or the difference in the pitch of the notes are called 'intervals'.

In relation to the musical (seven-tone) scale, for instance, it is generally considered (theoretically) that there are two semi-tones between each two notes with the exception of the intervals mi-fah and si-do, which have only one semi-tone and in which one semi-tone is regarded as being left out.

This law explains why there are no straight lines in nature and also why we can neither think nor do – why everything with us is thought – why everything with us happens, and happens to us in a way opposite to what we want or expect. All this is the express and direct effect of the intervals or retardations in the development of vibrations. An octave starts in a straight line, and then at the intervals changes direction, and at each interval the octave changes in direction is more marked so that the line of octaves may at last turn completely round in a direction opposite the original one; and some make a complete circle. This change of course can be observed literally in all we do and the same thing happens in all spheres of human activity. A most interesting example of such a change of direction in the line of development of forces can be found in the history of religion, particularly in the study of Christianity. Think how many turns the line of development of forces must have taken to come from the gospel preaching of love to the Inquisition; or to go from the ascetics of early centuries studying esoteric Christianity to the scholastics who calculated how many angels could be placed on the point of a needle.*

This law of octaves and all its manifestations was known to ancient knowledge i.e. even our division of time, that is the days of the week into workdays and Sundays. The Biblical myth of the creation of the world in six days and of the seventh day in which God rested from his labours is also an expression of the law of octaves or an indication of it.

Further indications show that a right and consistent development of octaves, although rare, can be observed in all the occasions of life and in the activity of nature and even in human society. This right development of the octaves is based on accident depending upon the octaves going parallel to the given octave, intersecting it on meeting it, in some way or other fills up its intervals and make it possible for the vibrations of the given octave to develop in freedom and without checks.

In the big cosmic octave, which is the Ray of Creation The Absolute is the "do" of this octave. The worlds which the Absolute create in itself are "si". The interval between "do" and "si" in this case is filled up by the will of the Absolute. The process of creation is developed further by the force of the original impulse and an additional shock. "Si" passes into "la" which for us is our starry world, the Milky Way. "La" passes into "sol" -our sun, the solar system. "Sol" passes into "fa" – the planetary world. And here between the planetary world as a whole and our Earth occurs an interval. This means that the planetary radiations carrying various influences to the earth are not received. The earth reflects them. In order to fill the interval at this point of the ray of creation, a special apparatus is created for receiving and transmitting the influences coming from the planets. This apparatus is organic life on earth".* Organic life transmits to the earth all the influences intended for her to make possible the further development and growth of the earth, "mi" of the cosmic octave and then of the moon, or "re", after which

* Cosmology p.49, 50, 51, 52, 57 of third lecture.

75

follows another "do" – nothing. Between "all" and "nothing" passes the ray of creation.

Shocks may occur accidentally, but accident is, of course, a very uncertain thing and this makes those lines of development of forces that are straightened out by accident and which man can sometimes see or suppose, or expect, create in him the illusion of "straight lines". He thinks that straight lines are the rule and broken and interrupted lines the exception. This in its turn creates in him the illusion that it is possible "to do", possible to attain a projected aim. In reality a man can do nothing and such accidental attainment of aims in small things which can have no consequences create in mechanical man the conviction that he is able to attain any aim, 'is able to conquer nature' as it is called, is able to arrange the whole of his life, and so on.*

In actual fact, man has no control over things outside himself, but he has no control over things within himself. He must first learn that control over things begins with control over things in ourselves. A man who cannot control himself can control nothing. In what way can control be attained? The technical part of this is explained by the law of octaves – there remains for a man the choice either of finding a direction for his activities which corresponds to the mechanical line of events of a given moment – in other words, "of going where the wind blows" or of "swimming with the stream", or he can learn to recognise the moments of the intervals in all lines of his activity and learn to "create" the "additional shocks", in other words, learn to apply to his own activities the method which cosmic forces make use of in "creating additional shocks at the necessary moments."

The man-machine can do nothing. To him and around him everything "happens". In order "to do" it is necessary to know the law of octaves, to know the moments of the intervals and to be able to create necessary additional shocks.**

According to the law of three, twelve triads produce hydrogens of densities ranging from 6 to 12288 "hydrogens" representing categories of matter. Graduations of the universe from the Absolute to the moon. All matters from Hydrogen 6 to Hydrogen 3072 are to be found and play a part in the human organism. Hydrogen 768 can be defined as "food". Hydrogen 384 will be defined as "water". Hydrogen 192 is the air of our atmosphere which we breathe. Hydrogen 96 is represented by rarified gases which man cannot breathe, but which play an important part in his life, and further this

* Cosmology p.54.
** Cosmology p.57.

76

the matter of animal magnetism, of emanations from the human body, of rays, hormones, vitamins and so on and are almost imperceptible to our chemistry, or perceptible only by their traces or results.

Hydrogens 48, 24, 12 and 6 are matters unknown to physics and chemistry, matters of our psychic and spiritual life on different levels.

We want to "do" but in everything we do we are tied and limited by the amount of energy produced by our organism. Every function, every state, every action, every thought, every emotion requires a certain definite energy, a certain definite substance.

We come to the conclusion that we must try to remember ourselves – but we can do this only if we have in us the energy for self-remembering and the same holds good for understanding, feeling or studying.

This is a dilemma for man until he begins to understand that he has quite enough energy to begin to work on himself. It is only necessary to learn how to save the greater part of the energy we possess for useful work instead of wasting it unproductively.

Energy is spent chiefly on unnecessary and unpleasant emotions, on the expectation of unpleasant things, possible and impossible, on bad moods, on unnecessary haste, nervousness, irritability, imagination, day dreaming and so on. Energy is wasted on the wrong work of centres, of unnecessary tension of the muscles, out of all proportion to the work involved, on perpetual chatter, which absorbs an enormous amount of energy; on the "interest" continually taken in things happening around us or to other people, on the constant waste of the force of "attention" and so on and so on.★

In beginning to struggle with all these habitual sides of his life, a man saves an enormous amount of energy, and with the help of this energy he can begin the work of self-study and self perfection.

Then further on the problem becomes more difficult – having to a certain extent balanced his machine, and ascertained to himself that it produces much more energy than he expected, he nevertheless comes to the conclusion that this energy is not enough, and that, if he wishes to continue his work he must increase the amount of energy produced.

The study of the working of the human organism shows this to be quite possible.

Actually all the substances necessary for the maintenance of the life of the organism, the psychic work, for the higher functions of

★ Cosmology p.83.

consciousness, are produced by the food which enters it from outside. The human organism receives three kinds of food:

1. The ordinary food we eat
2. The air we breathe
3. Our impressions *

For its normal existence the organism must receive all three kinds of food, that is physical food, air and impressions. We can exist without food for some time. Without air for only a few minutes and without impressions we cannot live a single moment. The flow of impressions coming to us from outside is like a driving belt whose principal motor for us is nature, the surrounding world, and if that inflow of energy is arrested, our machine will immediately stop working.

The process of transforming the substances which enter the organism into finer ones is governed by the law of octaves. If the human organism is represented in the form of a three storied factory, the upper floor consists of a man's head; the middle floor, of the chest; and the lower of the stomach, the back and lower parts of the body.

Physical food is Hydrogen 768, or la, sol, fa of the third cosmic octave of radiations. This hydrogen enters the lower storey of the organism as "oxygen" do 768. "Oxygen" 768 meets with "Carbon" 192 which is present in the organism and from their union is obtained Nitrogen 384, which is the next note "re".

Re 394, which becomes "oxygen" in the next triad, meets with "carbon" '96' in the organism and together with it produces a new 'nitrogen' 192 which is the note mi 192. Here an additional shock is necessary and there enters the second food – air – in the form of do 192 – that is mi, re, do of the second cosmic octave of radiations. This note 'do' possesses all the energy necessary for transition to the next note and gives part of its energy to 'mi' 192 and force enough to pass, while uniting with 'carbon' 48 already in the organism, with 'nitrogen' 96 which will be the note fa.

Fa 96, by uniting with 'Carbon' 24 a product of nitrogen and present in the organism passes into 'nitrogen' 48, the note sol.

The note 'sol' 48 by uniting with carbon 12 present in the organism, passes into 'nitrogen' 24 – la 24.

'La' 24 unites with 'Carbon' 6 already in the organism and is transformed into 'nitrogen' 12, or 'si' 12. Si 12 is the highest

* Cosmology p.87.

78

substance produced in the organism from physical food with the help of the additional shock obtained from the air. But the third octave begins with do 48, this is la, sol, fa of the second cosmic octave – sun – earth. Do 48 has sufficient energy to pass into the following note but at that place in the organism where 'do' enters the 'carbon' 12 necessary for this is not present. At the same time, do 48 does not come into contact with mi 48 so it stops here unless we can remember ourselves at this point, which is the additional shock required and very often the additional sensation connected with "self-remembering" brings with it an element of emotion, that is, the work of the machine attracts a certain amount of 'carbon' 12 to the place in question. Efforts to 'remember oneself', observations of oneself at the moment of receiving an impression, and simultaneously defining the impression received, all this taken together doubles the intensity of impressions and carries do 48 to re 24 and gives this note the necessary energy for transmission of mi into fa. The shock given to do 48 extends to 'mi' 48 and enables seven octaves to develop.

Mi passes to 'fa' 24, 'fa' 24 passes to 'sol' 12, sol 12 passes to 'la' 6 which is the highest matter produced by the organism from air. Mr. Ouspensky explains here that we all breathe the same air, but the air exhaled may be different. He explains – Let us suppose that the air we breathe is composed of twenty different elements unknown to our science. A certain number of elements are absorbed by every man when he breathes. Let us suppose that five of these elements are always absorbed. Consequently, the air exhaled by every man is composed of 15 elements, five of them have gone to feed the organism. But some people exhale not fifteen but only ten elements, that is to say they absorb five elements more. If the organism is able to extract and retain them, they remain in the organism. In order to extract more, it is necessary to have in our organism a certain quantity of corresponding fine substances, then the fine substances contained in the organism 'act like a magnet' on the fine substances contained in the inhaled air. We come again to the old alchemical law: "In order to make gold, it is first of all necessary to have a certain quantity of real gold." If no gold whatever is possessed, there is no means whatever of making it!

The whole of alchemy is nothing but an allegorical description of the human factory and its work of transforming base metals into precious ones.*

* Cosmology pp. 98-99. Development of Air and Impressions Octaves.

We have followed the development of two octaves. The third octave, the octave of impressions, begins through a conscious effort. 'Do' 48 passes to 're' 24, 're' 24 to 'mi' 12. At this point, the development of the octave comes to a stop.

For the two octaves to develop further, a new conscious effort is necessary which will enable the two octaves to continue their development. This effort is connected with our emotional life.

The practice of not expressing unpleasant emotions, of not identifying, of not considering inwardly, is the preparation for the second effort, which is connected with the transformation and transmutation of these emotions and man can only change when this transformation is attained.* Work on this is only possible after long practice of self remembering and of observing the impressions received. When the work of the food octave is really understood and with it the work of the different hydrogens, it can further begin to understand the work of the centres. The thinking or intellectual centre is the slowest of all our three centres and it works with hydrogen 48 and the intellectual centre is never able to follow the work of the moving centre. The moving or instinctive centre works with hydrogen 24. (Hydrogen 24 is many times quicker and more mobile than hydrogen 48) and the intellectual centre is never able to follow the work of the moving centre. We are unable to follow either our own movements or other people's movements unless they are artificially slowed down. Still less are we able to follow the work of the inner, the instinctive functions of our organism, the work of the instinctive mind which constitute, as it were, one side of the moving centre. The emotional centre can work with hydrogen 12, but it seldom works with this fine hydrogen, and in the majority of cases, its work differs little in intensity and speed from the work of the moving and instinctive centre.

In order to understand the work of the human machine properly, we must know that we have two more centres fully developed and functioning properly, but not connected with our usual life nor with the three centres in which we are aware of ourselves. These two "higher" centres are recognised in all mystical and occult systems, although in many cases they admit their existence and capacities only in the form of possibilities and speak of the necessity for 'developing' the hidden forces in man. This teaching differs from many others by the fact that it affirms the higher centres exist in man and are fully developed. It is the lower centres that are undeveloped.*

* Cosmology pp. 101, 106.

In order to obtain a correct and permanent connection between the lower and the higher centres, it is necessary to regulate and quicken the work of the lower centres.

Moreover, as has already been said, lower centres work in a wrong way, for very often, instead of their own proper function, one or another of them takes upon itself the work of other centres. This considerably reduces the speed of the general work of the machine and makes acceleration of the work of centres very difficult. Thus, in order to regulate and accelerate the work of the lower centres, we must first free each centre from work foreign to it and bring it back to its own work, that it can do better than any other centre. Also, a great deal of energy is spent on work which is completely unnecessary, and harmful in every respect, such as the activity of unpleasant emotions, the expression of unpleasant emotions, the expression of unpleasant sensations, or worry, or restlessness, or haste and on a whole series of automatic actions which are completely useless. Examples – constantly moving flow of thought in our minds, which we can neither stop nor control and which takes up an enormous amount of our energy. Then there is the quite unnecessary constant tension of the muscles of our organism. Muscles are tense even when they do nothing. As soon as we start to do even a small and insignificant piece of work, a whole system of muscles necessary for the hardest and most strenuous work is immediately set in motion. We spend muscular energy continually and at all times even when we are doing nothing.

Still further, we can point to the habit of continually talking to everybody or if there is no one else, with ourselves, to the habit of indulging in fantasies, in day dreaming: the continual change of mood, feelings and emotions and an enormous amount of quite useless things which a man considers himself obliged to feel, think, do or say.

It must be noted that the organism usually produces in the course of one day all the substances necessary for the following day, but every so often these substances can be consumed upon some unnecessary or unpleasant emotion. All psychic processes are material and there is not a single process that does not require the expenditure of a certain substance corresponding to it. *

* Cosmology: p.111.

CHAPTER 19

Coombe Springs

In 1955 when my sister moved to her flat in Kensington, I went to stay at Mr. and Mrs. Bennett's house at Coombe Springs, Kingston. This was in accordance with a promise I had made when I saw Mr. Bennett and Elizabeth at Seaford, and also because I had had a very clear vision of what I was and what I wished to become at Seaford. I remember it clearly. I was walking down a street in Seaford town when I had an intuitive feeling that everything within me was part of my ego and there was nothing there which really belonged to me as a person, only my ego or false personality, but I also felt that it was possible to discover something more real if one worked hard with others who were trying to experience the same sort of difficulties. So I gave up my house in Seaford and my flat in London, put most of my furniture in store, my cats went to a holiday home and I presented myself at Coombe Springs, a Victorian house in five acres of ground, with a celebrated ancient well which was in use in the days of Cardinal Wolseley. Mr. Bennett and his wife lived there with a community of people; about thirty regular residents, some families, single men and women, and when I went there in 1955 – two older ladies, Mrs. Bennett and her sister, who had to be cared for round the clock. On weekends, many more came to talks, meetings and seminars.

I had a bedroom and sitting room at Coombe Springs. There were about thirty five or so residents, some families together in bungalows, a dormitory called the "Fishbowl" for single people, and another building with single rooms and a sauna had been newly built in their five acres of garden. Mr. Bennett himself, half English and half American, a scientist in his own right and a soldier, was a considerable linguist of Greek and Turkish languages. He had met his present wife, Polly, in Greece.

I was no stranger to Coombe Springs as my sister and I had been to groups there for some years, and Mr. Bennett had been interested in and was taking an active part in our Glastonbury work. But now I was to partake more regularly in the work there and help to organize the regular daily activities at Coombe Springs. Since 1951, my sister and I had been attending groups in London with one of the French teachers, but our work with Mr. Bennett was especially valuable, as he organized his groups with a leader and assistant leader and we were obliged to try and answer others.

Mr. Bennett had the brilliant idea of asking Mme de Salzmann if she would come and "sit in" on the student groups. Obviously she could not come to each one of them, but a special Saturday was arranged when all the groups were asked together with their leaders. Mme de Salzmann attended each group for some moments in turn and presumably commented afterwards on their composition to Mr. Bennett. Both the leader of a group and their assistants were appointed by Mr. Bennett and both positions were interesting and, perhaps equally important, then Mr. B. himself took the leaders group and tried to answer any questions still outstanding or any problems which needed to be sorted out. The whole work seemed like a pyramid: it formed a complete whole with the leader, sub-leaders and students of various experiences down to beginners. This did not necessarily mean that the most important people were always at the top, sometimes very interesting things started from beginners, or at any other level in the pyramid.

Mr. Bennett also had "seminars" with more intensive work, either in the summer vacation for approximately a week or so, or for long weekends such as at Easter or Whitsun. I well remember a very original one, when the sexes were divided – the men came to work at Easter and the women at Whitsun. The men were not to smoke, and we were not to talk – particularly at meals! I rather think we came out better. When asked about the result, Mr. B. thoughtfully commented that the ladies were more practical, dedicated and down to earth. He found that the men tended to philosophise and were all chasing different hares!

In all our groups with Mr. B he himself would give us a theme which he would discuss very fully, and it was up to the groups to take it from there with the question and answer regime.

In the autumn of 1957, Mr. Bennett gave my sister and myself another project of a very interesting kind – these were the small "Super Groups". Each group consisted of about seven or eight people, with a leader and others drawn from the groups of less experience down to beginners.

Mr. Bennett's point was that people should try to meet more informally and be able to ask and answer questions if they wished. The Chairman was responsible for sending in a short report and the groups went on for a year or more and proved successful, animated and in general all members took part.

Another task undertaken at Coombe Springs was the building of the "Movements" Hall or Dyamichinatra (Dyami for short) as it was to be named – Coombe Springs did not have a very suitable hall for meetings.

In the autumn of 1953 Mr. Bennett had gone to the Near East and the idea had come to him of building such a hall, and he had intentionally studied the dimensions of many sacred meeting places there. Upon his return to England, he talked to the community of his travels and his idea of building a hall. A team of some fifteen to twenty architects, engineers and craftsmen began to work on the building, and whenever a specialist was needed he or she appeared from somewhere. As Mr. Bennett himself explained: "The Building seemed to have a plan and a purpose of its own, and all we could do was to wait until one part after another of the plan was revealed." There were "mock-ups" or models put up for the benefit of everyone during the summer of 1955 and work on the foundations and framework was started.*

It was hoped to have the building ready by June 1957. It was to be a nine-sided building on a site a short distance from the house. Teams worked all summer to put up the Portal frame and I can well remember the moment of triumph when our architect-in-chief Robert Whiffen climbed the scaffolding and attached the ends to a small circle in the centre. The Dyami had come alive and was in being.

Of the many parties held at Coombe Springs, the most enterprising was the production of Mr. Ouspensky's only novel entitled "Ivan Isokin". This book had been adapted by Mr. Bennett into a play which was produced by him and Mrs. Pat Terry Thomas. An excellent young actor played the title role and there was a cast of amateurs living at Coombe Springs to support him. It was performed in the dining room on a makeshift stage and refreshments were later served in Mr. B's study. I can also remember the redoubtable Mr. Terry Thomas himself in a maroon coloured dinner jacket looking debonair and friendly.

Although much was always going on at Coombe Springs in the

* Bennett – Witness p. 319 American addition.

way of seminars, groups and visitors, I felt that there seemed to be a kind of "Spiritual pause" – the pause that comes before something is about to happen! Actually, preparation for a work of quite a new order began. The emphasis was now to be on the actual "Force" brought – a force which could be inwardly passed on from person to person rather than taught by a Master in meetings. As the Leader put it, "Subud is a direct action that is beyond mind and heart and cannot be transmitted by any kind of teaching."*

Gurdjieff, before he died, seemed to have given some hint that someone or something was to follow him – he spoke of the necessity to have a Dutch group and to keep in contact with their India. Actually, there were two Dutch Gurdjieff groups, one in the Hague and the other at Eindhoven, who looked to Mr. Bennett for help and guidance, and my sister used to go at intervals to visit them.

It was, as I remember, in May 1957 that the new development suddenly burst upon us. Mr. Bennett spoke to us about it in our leader's group. In 1956, an Ouspensky member, living in Cyprus, had spoken of a new "prophet" who was in Indonesia, a country very little known since the War and the expulsion of the Dutch. A pupil of this member, Husein Rofe, brought the news to Cyprus and eventually came to England to meet several of the leading Ouspensky Gurdjieff pupils.

The Indonesian himself was Mohammed Subud, and he claimed that he had been given a "Force" which could be passed on to others at a spiritual exercise called "The Latihan". Unbelieving, a small group of ex- pupils – all men – worked on this with Rofe and found it to be true. As the rule was that men and women had separate groups and only men "opened" men, and for women there were no separate groups at first. Only the wives of the new male group were allowed to be "opened" by their husbands as a special concession.

Now a quite different element had entered our work – what would happen? The instinct of the English leaders was to give only their more experienced pupils the opportunity for this if they so wished to have it. But Mohammed Subud, when he came to England (which he and his party did shortly afterwards), claimed that he had no right to refuse it to anyone if they wished to receive it.

Was this the leader whom Gurdjieff had implied would come? Some of the first people to hear about the new development were the Dutch groups It chanced that my sister had an appointment to go

* Bapak at 2nd International Congress, Coombe Springs

85

there in early June, and as Mr. Bennett felt the matter to be so very important, he went with her himself to explain the new undertaking.

My sister said: "in looking over these talks now, I feel that almost too much was expected from this new work in the beginning. On the other hand, I felt then, as I do now, that "Bapak" (Father in Indonesian) as he was called, did have some extraordinary power to bring to mankind, for those who could accept it."*

In England on May 22nd in response to a telegram sent by the six members of the group who had been working on the "Latihan", the new movement spread like wildfire over here. Unknown and unheralded when it arrived, by December Subud was known throughout the country and its adherents numbered eight hundred or more.

Living at Coombe Springs I remember vividly the arrival of Mohammed Subud and his party. They were holding a kind of reception in the garden under the big oak tree. I was working in the kitchen and went out to the garden to see them. They were standing in the garden altogether and when I looked at Bapak he seemed to be almost translucent, when everyone else appeared normal, round, fat or thin.

Subud brought us to the image of God. I was purified – both inwardly – and, I hope, outwardly as well.

On May 29th, Bapak and his party came to stay at Coombe Springs, where many foreign visitors came for the summer seminar, and became converts to the Subud work, inviting Bapak to visit their countries when he was able to do so. Many others also came to Subud work who had no previous connection with Gurdjieff.

In November 1957, further newspaper publicity – a thing which had never happened before in the Ouspensky-Gurdjieff movement on the same scale – broke with the healing of the well-known actress Eva Bartok and the birth of her baby, and some very extraordinary scenes occurred at Coombe Springs. People's reaction to the Latihan were totally different: some were quiet and seemed full of a wonderful new force, others were noisy or violent, and some felt nothing at all. Others could not bear it and left precipitously. The Latihan externally was always carefully controlled. "Helpers", the new name for the men and women in charge, gave the signal to "Begin" and also in a half hour the word "Finish". What happened in between was entirely up to each individual.

My sister and I went on working for Subud as "helpers" until 1962. There was an excellent and varied group of Women Helpers in

* HARTEN – "A Way of Living" – page 64

86

Kensington who did manage, my sister felt, to put their various capabilities together constructively. But it was difficult to see that the results were always beneficial as a whole. People came and left very rapidly so that there was always a core of enthusiastic supporters. Certainly, to those who were moved by it, were very stirred up (sometimes very negatively) that was evident. But whether this made people more sensitive or understanding of themselves and others when it came to the test? Rather, in the domineering type – they became more domineering, and more certain of the rightness of their interpretation.

The first visit Bapak and his "entourage" paid abroad was to Holland for meetings in the Hague and Eindhoven. My sister and I also went with them. Bapak gave a talk to the Dutch members about the Subud Latihan in Indonesian, which was translated into Dutch, which he spoke also. Not one word of either language did my sister or I understand, yet somehow, through the timbre of Bapak's voice something came through to us. It was always so with Bapak. He spoke of fine matters, and had his own interpretation of the Forces of Life which he spoke of to us – always in Indonesian with translation afterwards – but the actual words were conventional and were simply repeated over and over again in each talk.

The whole force in the Latihan seemed to work towards the purification of the individual and some of the worst and most unpleasant individual manifestations certainly expressed this. It undoubtedly developed health and vitality in one, at least that was our experience. Quite soon after "Helpers" were appointed by Bapak, a certain number of us were told we could exercise with the sick people, usually two helpers at a time. We were also instructed to do a short Latihan with each other afterwards to take away any bad effects. My sister had a very interesting experience of this kind in her Kensington group. She remembered a friend in Subud who asked her to substitute for another helper at the last moment for a visit to an unknown lady living in Park Lane who was very ill with cancer. She arrived at her destination to find her friend already there, and they both went into the patient's room. An emaciated lady, with almost nothing left in her face – she could remember it vividly.She heard afterwards that the patient died the following day. Another occasion was quite different. She worked with a drug addict, and although the lady appeared well and quite charming, she never had a worse experience. Being a healthy person, she seldom felt ill. This time, she had a headache and terrible internal pains so that she wondered if she could finish the exercise. All this passed off when doing the Latihan with a fellow worker afterwards. It seemed to be something she had picked up!

Shortly after this work began, an increasing need arose from people who were suffering from serious diseases and who could not come to Coombe Springs, that there should be a "Subud Hospital". Bapak told us that such a development was necessary and I volunteered to try and find a suitable place, as I was especially interested in medical and spiritual healing (owing to my own Mother's strange illness – multiple sclerosis). From a group of possible houses, near where I was then living in 1957, Bapak selected Brookhurst Grange at Ewhurst in Surrey. It was a house of a suitable size with a large market garden in good condition, and the whole place could be easily equipped with a trained staff of nurses and visiting doctors were available – all members of Subud. I felt that we pioneered an attempt which led to many such ventures in the future.

With the coming of Bapak, I decided to resume my independent life again. I bought a house on Pitch Hill, Ewhurst, near Cranleigh, Surrey, but I was still in close contact with Coombe Springs and attended their second World Congress in August, 1959. Thirty five countries were represented with more than 450 delegates. Subud had really arrived! The Conference was divided into seven sections: International Organization, National Organization, External Relations Communications, Human Welfare, Growth of Subud and Finance, all with Chairmen from different nationalities. Bapak gave a talk each morning on one of the separate sections and answered people's questions arising about it.

I drove over each day from my new home to Coombe Springs during this Congress and back late each evening, and one evening after my return home, I found myself for some hours able to see the unity behind everything – the place of myself, this community and its members and what would be said and done the following day. Time did not exist as it usually does for me. Perhaps I had earned this insight into another realm for a short time.

*Bapak and his retinue came several times to my home on Pitch Hill, Ewhurst and was, of course, interested in the new hospital – the staff who were assembling there hoped that he would take up residence there for a time, and give us some direction on the whole subject, as we all felt ourselves to be "blind leaders of the blind". But like so many other times when we hoped for some direction, Bapak

* Subud. Brookhurst Grange – Report on first sixteen months of the Subud Nursing Home.

seemed too busy with the many demands the various countries made upon him to stay.

Consequently, Brookhurst Grange was given up after two years and the house sold, not due so much to lack of money, but to the collapse of the staff, who felt they were unable to go on working there without direction.

But this was by no means the complete story of the experiment. I quote from a report from an inmate in June, 1959 about results: "In writing of our results one is reminded of the story at the beginning of Chapter IX of St. Matthew's Gospel, and the rebuke of Jesus to those who always demanded outward manifestations. Nevertheless, Brookhurst must, of course, produce results to justify its continued existence and the efforts, financial and otherwise, of Subud members, to keep it going, that our results are not impressive." Here follows a discussion of the various groups of patients and the fact that they have, of course, benefited from the peace and good food in beautiful surroundings." But there have been few patients who have not had much more than this; we have felt that they had a much greater benefit on the spiritual side, and in some cases a foundation has been laid or an obstacle overcome as a result of which developments can continue in a way which did not seem possible before. We are sure beyond doubt that Brookhurst must continue."

CHAPTER 20

Glastonbury

The trustees of my Father's will drew our attention to a gift that my Father had made to the local Church of England in Glastonbury, Somerset. My Father had been for many years especially interested in Glastonbury Abbey and the Chalice Well. He had been stirred by the ancient tradition surrounding the Abbey and had included us both on some of his visits there. My Father was keenly interested in giving money for the excavation of the Abbey and he had American friends, Mr. and Mrs. Van Dusen from Palm Beach and Sir Herbert and Lady Grotrian in England who believed that the Abbey had not yet yielded up all its treasures. Following my Mother's illness, my father had been in touch with the Society for Psychical Research and was interested in the attempts of Mr. Frederick Bligh Bond, an excellent architect and member of the Society for Psychical Research, but he had been dismissed from his post as Director of Excavations there. The Abbey Trustees were suspicious of Mr.Bond's unorthodox methods, i.e. "automatic writing" to reach certain archaeological conclusions about the size of the Edgar Chapel in the Abbey by excavation, research – and automatic writing, and in his two books entitled "The Gate of Remembrance" published in 1918 and the "Company of Avalon" in 1924. He showed how he had arrived at certain archaeological conclusions about the size of the Edgar Chapel by these methods which included – automatic writing!

My Father and his friends had applied many times to the Trustees of the Abbey for permission to finance excavations there, but the final refusal came again to him just before he died.

So Marjorie and I went again to Glastonbury to try and sort out a misunderstanding about a Church hall belonging to St. John's Church in the High Street. My Father had given money to the

Church so that they could purchase this building and to save it from becoming another car parking area. Now both the Vicar, Rev. Lionel Lewis, and his Churchwarden wanted to own it and we were asked to go to Glastonbury and mediate between them. For the first time, we came up against the very special controversial forces present there.

Before my Father died in 1946, he had met Colonel Garton who lived near Glastonbury at a little village called Pylle. Both men shared a common interest – they were both deeply religious and both interested in Glastonbury Abbey. The old Trustees at the Abbey were about to retire, and we were deeply interested in the vision of the new and younger men who were to take their place. Col. Garton was to be one of them and Edmund Page, living at Ivythorn Manor, Glastonbury, was another. We were also greatly encouraged by other old friends of my Father, Mr. and Mrs. St. George Grey. Mr. Grey, together with Arthur Bullein, had carried out excavations in the Lake Village at Meare beginning in 1908, and following up their earlier work in the Glastonbury Lake Village. Mr. Grey worked under the auspices of the Somerset Archaeological Society and was, in 1951, the Society's Secretary. From 1901-1949, he was Curator of the County Museum, Taunton Castle. Both he and his wife were thoroughly conversant with the excavations in Glastonbury Abbey and it was through his kind offices as Secretary of the Somerset Archaeological Society that a new excavator, Dr. Raylegh Radford, a medieval specialist, was found who would continue with the Abbey excavations from 1951 onwards. The money for these excavations came chiefly from Mrs. Blanche Van Dusen. There were certain places in the Abbey grounds where it was thought treasure might be found and she wished that these places should be excavated. There was a fine group of young men and women there to aid in these excavations. One of them, Kate Woodward, was a personal friend of ours, and Mr. Bennett. Dr. Radford, from the beginning, was not ready to excavate as deeply as would be necessary, to uncover possible hidden treasure. He told us that the ground there was virgin soil and that if he tried to excavate he would disturb the whole surface of the soil and run into difficulties with water drainage. He was, after all, a medieval specialist and was more interested in finding traces of the old Benedictine Abbey which he did with great effect. The excavations which only took place in the summer months were not continuous, as Dr. Radford had other commitments and no work was done in 1953, 1958, 1960 or 1961, although the Glastonbury Abbey Excavation Committee of which my sister was a member, met regularly.

Meanwhile, my sister and I were busy studying the ancient prehistoric zodiac signs round Glastonbury. We had read Mrs. Maltwood's book "A Guide to Glastonbury's Temple of the Stars" re-published in 1934, and we had also the ordnance survey maps around Glastonbury to help us. Clearly this ancient Zodiac Circle is visible on it and the signs are outlined there by earthworks, rivers and ancient tracks. They were said to have been made by the Celts. This Zodiac is ten miles in diameter and thirty miles in circumference with its centre not at Glastonbury but at Burleigh, but it was not, however, until aerial photography became perfected commercially in the thirties of the 20th Century that the layout of this vast solar calendar with its giant earth effigies became plainly revealed for all to see.

We, during our visits to Glastonbury, were able to drive around these earth-effigies and see for ourselves their outlines – especially Leo the lion and the Gemini Twins in their boat and the horn of Capricorn with its earthwork known locally as "Ponters Ball". This massive earthwork, five eighths of a mile long, and rising to twenty one feet above the ground, may have been used as well as a landing stage for ships unloading cargoes at Glastonbury, when the seamoors were navigable for a considerable distance into the interior of the Somerset countryside. It is said that as long ago as the Druids this Zodiac was venerated by them and later the Celts held the Circle in equal veneration until the time when the whole area came under the direct jurisdiction of the Ecclesiastical authorities. Even the monks at the Abbey knew the purpose of this Zodiac and had a tradition of preserving these ancient signs.

My sister and I did put together this Zodiac and proved that the star constellations do indeed fall on the back of these giant effigies. Our Zodiac map now is housed at Glastonbury at the home of Mr. and Mrs. Jevons of the Ramala Community.

Of course, the Fishes of Pisces are centered on Weary-all hill, and their outline can be seen clearly from the Street-Glastonbury motor road. Centred above the Abbey's Chalice Well is the Phoenix or Aquarius sign with its crested head turned towards its tail as it drinks at the Blood Well (Chalice Well) with its wings spread out above the town.

Our teacher, Mr. Bennett, had relatives living in North Cadbury and nearby Pilton, and he and his wife Polly came often with us and explored the neighbourhood. We introduced him to Colonel Garton and there was one memorable visit to South Cadbury when Mrs. Bennett, rather ill with chest trouble, insisted on walking to the top of Cadbury Hill to see the view up a very steep and muddy hill. On our way down, we encountered live pigs wallowing in the mud, and when I asked facetiously some enthusiastic tourists to whom they thought the pigs belonged, they said, without hesitation, "To Arthur!". Later in the 1960s, Cadbury Hill was excavated by a group of enthusiastic young people under Dr. Leslie Alcott of Bristol University, and there was evidence that Arthur had, indeed, lived there.

To return to the excavations at the Abbey: They did afford a great deal of interest, and many people came to see the work that Dr. Rayleigh Radford did there. Before I read out his report of his excavations, I would like to make a point of telling you the history of the re-burial of Arthur and Guinevere, his wife. In 1191, monks at Glastonbury Abbey claimed to have found his remains just south of the Lady Chapel, and King Edward and Queen Matilda witnessed their re-burial in front of the Abbey High Altar in 1278. Dr. Radford found, when excavating the ruins of Glastonbury Abbey that the oldest monastic settlement lay west of the crossing of the great church of the later middle ages. It was bounded on the East by a great bank and ditch which were located in the crossing of the great church and in the Chapterhouse to the South. This ditch was twenty five feet across and about ten feet deep. The bank which lay on the West side had been largely levelled by subsequent building , and the base, originally about thirty feet wide, remained in position. It had been pared down to a height of barely eighteen inches at a period when the bank was much spread, glass furnaces dating from the ninth century were dug into the inward slope.

The oldest remains within this enclosing bank were those found in the ancient cemetery. Post-holes were found belonging to at least four oratories of the wattled type. In every case, the area was so disturbed by later structures that no full plan could be recovered. There were also two mausolea within the ancient cemetery. These tomb-shrines were rectangular structures, large enough to take one or two bodies. They were quite low and probably marked by a standing cross. They were designed to hold the bodies of saints or revered founders of the community.

A trench was dug south from the bay of the Lady Chapel lying east of the doorway. Forty feet south of the chapel, a hole three to four feet across was found. The damaged edges showed that a large object, probably a monolith, had been carelessly dragged from the hole. The shaft of a great cross could have left such an impression if it had been violently pulled down. In the filling of the hole was a scrap of pottery dated c.1500. Fifteen feet further south was the mausoleum already discussed. It measured overall eight feet by seven, and must have been marked on the surface by a cross, of which no trace was found. These two pyramids, or crosses, form an essential link in the Arthurian connection with Glastonbury. Both the contemporary writer, Gerald of Wales and the earliest account in the Glastonbury tradition agree that the bodies of Arthur and Guinevere were found in 1190 between the two pyramids in the ancient cemetery. In this position the excavation disclosed a large irregular hole, which had been dug and filled in, after standing open for a very short time. At the bottom of this hole had been destroyed two, or perhaps three, of the slab-lined graves belonging to the earliest stratum. One of these destroyed graves was set against the wall of the mausoleum, a position likely to have been granted only to a person of importance.

At a date before the twelfth century, mausoleum and graves were covered by a bank of clay which still remains to a depth of three feet six inches. On the outer, south side, this bank was de-limited by a stone wall of which the foundation trench was found. On the other side, it sloped down toward the Lady Chapel, which stood on the same level as the mausoleum and graves. It is recorded of St. Dunstan that, while he was Abbot, in the middle of the tenth century, he enclosed the cemetery of the monks on the South side of the church with a wall of masonry. The area within was raised to form a pleasant meadow, removed from the noise of the passers by, so that it might be truly said of the bodies of the saints lying within that they repose in peace.*

During the 1960-70 period, limited excavations were in progress at the Chalice Well and on top of the Tor and at Cadbury Castle 1966-70.

Perhaps the most interesting find was discovered during the Chalice Well excavations which were carried out under the direction of Professor Philip Rahtz in 1961. At a depth of eleven feet nine inches, the excavators found the stump of a yew tree which had the remains of roots and was apparently in situ where it had formally grown. Professor Rahtz believed that it may have been an ancestor of the yew trees which grow by the Well at the present time. Professor Rahtz, in concluding his report on the Chalice Well excavations, said that if further excavations were contemplated in the future, they should only be done if expert advice could be obtained as to the best way of excavating deeply over a large area below the water table,

* Report by Dr. C.A. Ralegh Radford on the excavations at Glastonbury Abbey in "Quest for Arthur's Britain" by Geoffrey Ash.

either mechanically or by hand. He further suggested that there were two areas which could be explored:

1. The area around the well and 2. the large area in the lower part of the orchard between the Well and the long cutting, too, of 1961. He believed that this would establish conclusively whether there was any settlement just above the spring of Christian or pre-Christian date.*

In 1964, Archaeologist Professor Rahtz and his helpers started excavations on the Tor – St. Michael's tower, situated on the summit is all that remains of the medieval church built to replace an earlier one destroyed by a landslide or earthquake in 1275. Professor Rahtz established that the Tor itself is a natural structure and not man-made, but there was evidence of instability in the lower stratas which makes archaeological interpretation very difficult. There are numerous terraces on the slopes which may be the result of agriculture or, more importantly, the remains of an early three dimensional maze.

These excavations on the Tor extended over nearly all the summit and part of the shoulder. The middle of the summit was probably levelled for the medieval church. Two graves were found on the north side of the summit, both of young people, with heads to the south, generally a non-Christian arrangement.

A dark age settlement was found on the west side where a series of wooden platforms had been built, though very little remained of them. There were a quantity of bones of animals: cattle, sheep and pigs and also charcoal, burnt stones and fossils. On the east side was a fence or protective barrier and many objects were found, such as a Roman tile, a bone needle and other objects.

The most curious feature in this area was a cairn, some ten feet by four, found on a structure of large boulders, some burnt, lying among the dark age layer – it looked like a grave, but it contained nothing at all.

The most important area was on the south platform. There were the remains of a level shelf four to five feet below the level of the chapel area, some of it had been cut off but it was undoubtedly a major timber building. There were two hearths, they may have been for domestic use or used for metal working. The other finds were Roman tiles and imported Mediterranean ware, and a remarkable head of bronze.

* Report of excavations of the Chalice Well, Glastonbury reprinted from the proceedings of the Somersetshire Archaeological and Natural History Society, Volume 108 1964, pages 145 to 163.

Professor Rahtz thought that this indicated a permanent residence of a local chieftain's estate and that there would have been other buildings, long since disappeared on the lower ground.

This chapter would not be complete without mentioning my sister's friend, Mrs. Janette Jackson and the wonderful work she inaugurated.

Some of the original meetings between Janette Jackson, Elizabeth Leader and Professor Mary Williams were held at my sister's flat in Kensington when that inspirational trio founded R.I.L.K.O. (Research into Lost Knowledge) and they were soon joined by Keith Critchlow and John Michel and their Chairman, Commander George J. Mathys. It should be remembered that the original concept of R.I.L.K.O. was not so much to form a group which would seek to 'inform' but rather one which would ask pertinent questions and seek to maintain awareness of the existence of those questions.

It was, however, Mrs. Jackson who applied most of the padding-out of living flesh upon those concepts. Her work-loads were prodigious, despite her advanced age, her increasing infirmity, bad sight and failing health. It is true that her co-founders and the Members of Council made the collective decisions and mapped out the directions of progress. It fell very largely, however, to Janette herself to implement them, usually with brilliant injections of her own quality and by the distinguished and capable personalities she drew into them.

Based upon an outright donation by Professor Mary Williams and an original gift of £100 from John Michel, Janette obtained financial aid from my sister for their first publication of 'Glastonbury – A Study in Patterns'. Ultimately she persuaded 'Gothic Image' to undertake a 50-50 participation in its latest edition. She was also responsible for getting a translation done on "The Mysteries of Chartres Cathedral", and, due to one of the many inspirations of Elizabeth Leader, further delicate negotiations with many very distinguished representatives of Westminster Abbey which led to the translation and publication of 'Cosmati Roundel'.

But it was to Glastonbury that she turned then. From an original idea of the Geoffrey Russell's and an initial grant from the Royal Society of Arts, Janette then obtained the main monies from the Van Dusen Trust enabling the Photogrammetric Survey of Glastonbury Tor to be carried out, so showing the Labyrinth there.

Janette was responsible for nearly a score of main publications of which some had several reprints: the arrangement of illustrated lectures – over 60 Council Meetings – AGM Socials since 1969 –

Newsletters, membership and normal correspondence – Janette was the faithful focus about whom they revolved.

Janette was especially interested in above all others which she would wish to be recognised and stated firmly, loudly and unequivocally. She was the redoubtable and successful Champion of Frederick Bligh-Bond. Based on her collation of evidence from the time of his appointment as Director of Excavations at Glastonbury in 1908 and right up to letters exchanged within months of her own death, Janette sought to clear his name and professional reputation. In so doing, Janette was more successful than perhaps she realised. Today, Frederick Bligh-Bond is known, respected and admired by a great number of our contemporaries who have much more open minds than those few of blinkered mental vision so much earlier in this century.

Had he not been misjudged seventy years ago, we might not have become so aware of his work today. Janette kept those treasures alive for our notice and appreciation. 'The Gate of Remembrance' by Bligh-Bond is probably the most important work Janette helped to see into re-publication.

Incredibly, within the last six months, and entirely unknown to Janette, I have heard discussed the serious suggestion that Glastonbury be restored to its former glorious whole as a living, working, source of prayer and spiritual power.

Perhaps in its restored Edgar Chapel there might be a simple plaque to the memory of, and in thankfulness, to God for Frederick Bligh-Bond and the ever loyal Janette Jackson.

Janette died in the 1970s, but R.I.L.K.O. has gone from strength to strength. Many specialised themes have been taken up and considered by authors, such as Professor Alexander Thom, Emeritus Professor of Engineering, Oxford University, who indicates possible use of Glastonbury Area as a Stone Age Lunar Observatory. Professor Mary Williams, University of Wales and Mrs. Jackson herself provide an introduction to the remarkable spiritual and archaeological work of Frederick Bligh-Bond, F.R.I.B.A. at Glastonbury and Professor Keith Critchlow's interpretation of the secret geometrical structure of the Abbey, while Mr. John Michel shows the continuation of the prehistoric magic tradition in the geographical location of the Abbey as it relates to Stonehenge.

References throughout this chapter from Geoffrey Ashe, F.R.S.L.

References re: life of Janette Jackson, M.B.E. A.R.C.M. from R.I.L.K.O. Newsletter No.25 Autumn/Winter Newsletter 1984 by Commander J. Mathys.

CHAPTER 21

Slow Opening up of Travel after the War

Our first trip to Switzerland after the 1939–45 war
1946 June–July

I had been many times to Switzerland on holidays. We have always enjoyed the lovely scenery there, the mountains and the meadows and the pure air, this country being a relatively stable one. I remember I went first with my Father and Ruth in the 1920s and we stayed at the Maloja Palace Hotel near St. Moritz, a wonderful Victorian building built round a large glass domed hall. This visit was memorable for an earthquake we all felt one night. I was asleep and suddenly I awoke to find the glass in my room shaking, and I heard a familiar voice outside my own door, saying: "What is that?" It was my Father coming to fetch me to go down to the hall where most of the guests were assembled in a variety of sleeping attires. I remember sitting down and wondering what else Fate had in store for me. Fortunately, no further quakes came, and we finally went back to bed.

Another year, when I was a little older, my sister and I had stopped off in Switzerland to be near some American friends. We all stayed in Grindelwald and took many trips in the mountains nearby on the little mountain railway as far as the Jungfraujoch where we had lovely views of the Jungfrau Mountain. When we found it was possible to climb to the top if we took guides, we decided to try and go. In the end, only three of us set out - my sister, myself and one other American girl, with two guides. We were suitably attired to face the cold, and in boots with clampons. Our diet consisted of strong tea with sugar. I cannot remember how far it was, but we all made it, and felt very brave. Coming back, as an anti-climax, we were attached by ropes to our guides, and gently tobogganned down the hills to the Joch.

So when we could once more set out for our holiday in Europe, we made certain it would be to Switzerland that we should go, to give us the maximum rest, comfort and pleasant conditions.

Marjorie and I flew to Switzerland for our first holiday abroad after the War in June, 1946. I remember landing in Zurich to stay at the famous Baur-au-Lac Hotel. We were met at the airport by the Hotel car and whisked off to Zurich. It was market day, and the streets were full of barrows of fresh fruit, bananas, oranges, pears, grapes etc. We eyed them with great enthusiasm. We were only just beginning to come off rations in England and had been so used to it that we could not get over the amount of fruit shown here in Zurich. The plane which brought us to Zurich was a little late on arrival and we were fearful lest the hotel dining room would be shut when we reached our hotel, and we asked the Head Waiter perhaps, could we have a sandwich. He replied at once - "A nice salmon mayonnaise with salad, perhaps, and followed by strawberries and cream." We simply could not believe our luck. We enjoyed every mouthful.

Our night's stay in the famous hotel was equally captivating and comfortable, and the trains that took us to Locarno and on to Wengen and Murren were equally satisfying. There was a giant lift that took us to Murren at the top of the mountain, and we spent most of our holiday high up in a comfortable wooden beamed Swiss Chalet Hotel with breathtaking scenic views of the Swiss Alps, the wild flowers in the fields and the sounds of bells on the cattle and goats.

In March/April 1949 we took our first trip by air across the ocean via Canada to the Caribbean. When we got to the air terminal, we were told that the weather was so bad on the Atlantic that it was doubtful whether we would be able to start, and we were delayed by the authorities, who wished to decide whether we should go by the Azores, a much longer route, or to Goose Bay in Labrador, a shorter and more northerly one.

Finally, the latter was decided on, and at Heathrow we were shooed through Customs and Immigration, literally no interest taken in any of our belongings, and on to the waiting plane. It was a large, four engined one of rather a different style from the Pan American one I had taken to New York in 1947. On the whole, I preferred the American one. The Canadian one had Rolls Royce engines and was very safe and good, but there were too many people on board, with not quite enough room for the individual passenger physically and psychologically. When one has to sit up all night and be confined in such a small space for so long, one needs a certain amount of privacy and freedom. Also, the service, although adequate, was not over-good. As the plane started late, we had no meal until 11 o'clock at Shannon, Eire, although we had had no warning. Indeed, we had been told we should have been fed on the plane if necessary. We took off and landed at Shannon airport without incident and left there again about midnight, a fairish dinner, including an excellent piece of steak.

The crossing to Goose Bay took about ten hours, and we consumed about two thousand gallons of petrol, I was told. However, we were so continually altering our watches that I soon lost count of time entirely. It only seemed to be about two nights rolled into one and we were waiting indefinitely for the sun to rise, which it did finally with great beauty over the snowy wastes of Labrador.

My sister relaxed in her chair by the aisle and went to sleep. I stayed awake all the time. I was cold and shivery and worried. I was looking out of the window, and there was a mixture of storms, flashing lights from our plane and general desolation of a rather frightening sense of void and loneliness. My sister finally woke up and saw me shivering, and so she suggested that I should take her place on the aisle and she should stay by the window.

The weather temperature was somewhere about zero when we landed at Goose Bay. Snow was covering the ground and the air was magnificent. Our fellow passengers fled ignominiously to the overheated waiting room, but we went exploring around the airport, slipping around on the ice, sniffing the wonderful air, much to the amusement of the bored but pleasant officials. It was too cold to stay out too long at a time, but we went to the waiting room for rests and coffee and then emerged again for another voyage of exploration. This time was about 7 o'clock by Labrador time. We left in an hour and had a most beautiful four hour trip to Montreal, cruising over Quebec and ice floes on the St. Lawrence river. The day was glorious, blue sky and bright sun.

Finally, we came down at Montreal. There was a considerable delay and fuss over Customs and Immigration, which seemed curious as we were only in transit, but one trouble seemed to be that they had me down as a Canadian citizen for some reason we never fathomed. George Bonney and his wife, Frannie, were waiting for us at the airport, which we thought heroic as we had arrived about three hours early. It was, I believe, somewhere about 11 am but the clock appeared to have been doing things again and on account of not having gone by Gander, the ordinary route, we had failed to put in a call at Nova Scotia, "Goose, not Gander", as the children plus Frannie and George cabled Mary.

Montreal, March 2nd. We checked our tickets and went to stay at the Laurentian Hotel the excellent new hotel here. Two very nice single rooms and a bath apiece, and all our meals paid for apparently, with as much as we could eat. George and Frannie motored us from the airport in their car and we all had lunch. After that, we had a sleep and a bath and finally dinner in their sweet little house. Lovely cold weather, bright and dry, slippery roads and frozen ice everywhere, but no-one seemed to mind. If we could only have decent winters like this in England!

The next day, we went shopping attired in our woollies as we battled against the icy wind. I remarked that in all probability, we should be bathing the next day, a remark to which my sister did not feel at all responsive. Actually, we bought nothing, possessing few dollars, but it was fun to look at the things in the windows and dart into a shop every now and then when we felt cold. Frannie and her sister took us to lunch, and then we motored round to see the sights of Montreal. Marjorie did not recall the city at all, and when she last visited she was escorted by South African students and collapsed with exhaustion whilst her troupe was being escorted around McGill University by their students. Later, we had an early dinner with George and Frannie, who then motored us to the airport to catch our Jamaica plane. There was a full quota of passengers. We tucked ourselves, without incident, into the Jamaica plane, which was very comfortable, as far as Toronto, but far too full after that. We stopped at Nassau also, as the main part of the passengers left us there. It was a pity they crowded these planes so badly, seats too near together, and there are too many of them in the two compartments. The result is that the passengers are rather restless and unhappy, especially, the larger men. The trip was a steady one, but we felt rather tired and sick from the incessant vibration and the fact that there was so little room to move. All this for a long time after a rather cramped night.

The sun rose suddenly and most beautifully as we were approaching the Bahamas. Kipling's line came into my mind: "An' the dawn comes up like thunder outer China 'crost the 'Bay!"* Not that we were near China then, but it seemed about the same thing. Then we came down at Nassau and were all turned out for breakfast and I was suddenly conscious that it was hot and that the birds were all singing! Coats, woollies, stockings all seemed irksome and out of place although we had hugged every woolly close in Canada.

The American accents changed to British, and the very solid plate

* Kipling Rudyard: "On the Road to Mandalay".

of eggs and bacon appeared for breakfast on an open porch with roses all round us. We simply could not believe it all, and felt that we were getting a new series of scenic effects. "From the snowy wastes of Labrador to the land of palms amd sunshine." I remember the half of this caption as we entered Florida. Up we went again, and after skimming over Cuba and some beautiful blue sea in which we could see the fish swimming about, descended on Jamaica, an exquisite place, even from the air. We went round in circles, having considerable difficulty getting our large plane down to so small a runway, as it appeared to be, going straight into the shiny, clear water, but actually we just slipped across it and landed on the airport runway on the beach.

The Jamaican airport I shall never forget. It looked like a picture of the World's Fair, and some sort of wine and fruit shop. Huge signs everywhere advertising Jamaica's products. We were at once presented by a soft voiced lady of rather mixed antecedents - with large flower decorated glasses of "Rum Punch". After the official formalities, we were siezed upon by a reporter and interviewed. I could think of nothing to say except that some members of our family had been here before and so liked the island that we had decided to visit it. This went down well, and duly appeared in the "Daily Gleaner" the next day, a copy of which appeared at our bedroom door at some dark morning hour. But we had to fill in this form, sign that piece of paper, give these details and then retain bits of the forms for when we left. I remembered about Dad, who had finally lost his last form just as his boat was sailing from here, and handed the official his coat check folded in two, or something of the sort, hoping it would not be discovered until the boat got away. Finally, we all piled into a car and drove along to our hotel, the Myrtle Bank. I had not yet discovered the origin of the name, as no-one here appeared to have heard of the name of the tree. The driver pointed out the usual Queen Victoria monument (we found it all over the East) and Nelson's headquarters, but knew nothing about the interesting side of the Island's layout.

The Myrtle Bank is all green and white and greatly resembles in its layout the Bar-au Lac Hotel in Zurich. It is far more open everywhere. Porches all open, dining room also. In fact, everything. The Hotel goes three sides round a lawn with palms, flowers and several little arbours. It all faces on the sea with swimming pool at sea end. No beach bathing of course because of sharks, etc. The climate appears to be a marvellous one. No rain, cool wind, sun, no sunburn and very little glare.

Monday March 7th. it seems to be rather warmer, but the cool wind is still with us, and I see by the local paper there is snow in England. We somehow missed this in mid Atlantic. It is incredible we only started out last Tuesday from home. England and all of our friends there have simply dropped out of our lives. I can't help wondering if Time is not the same as Space. If one is at a certain moment of time, all the other moments seem to have entirely disappeared, although in reality they are still all there just as you and England are still all there. The amazing development of the aeroplane makes me feel I understand all this a lot better, but I cannot stress enough the extraordinary quality of this trip through the annihiliation of space by this means of transport. Also how quickly one adapts oneself to it all. At first I felt everything here was a new "scene drop", and changed gingerly into thin clothes. Now I seem to have been in these conditions for weeks, and cannot imagine anything else!

The hotel does not seem to be very full although it seems to be the centre for all sorts of people. Quite a few English-looking and awkward in their unusual summer weight suits and summer dresses, Americans and Canadians more at home and better dressed. One particularly large lady we have nicknamed "You have been Warned", and my sister points her out when the food gets too good and we are eating too much.

The U.S. Navy have just been here in full force and left, we hope, for good. They do make a bad impression in bulk in their creased bell trousers, propping up the bar or making noises either in the swimming pool or somewhere else. A few of our lot appeared in freshly ironed shorts and looking smart, alert and cool.

Kingston does not seem to be a very interesting little town, although it is the centre for some lovely residential districts, beautiful open air houses, mainly bungalows, and gardens with hosts of lovely flowers. There is charming scenery all around, especially the part leading to the Blue Mountains in this island. The coloured people all speak English as their native tongue, and seem a fine, hard working and independent lot, far less self-conscious than the U.S. darkie, they seem very proud of their island and to feel very much part of the Empire, a point of view I have not come across in my travels before. There seems to be much more a spirit of co-operation and less of revolution, although I understand there is quite a strong force for separation. There is a tremendous interest in Mr. Churchill's advent, next month, I believe. People living in islands seem in general more happy and much less strained than those in big cities or big land masses.

The wealth of the island is, like Java, prodigious. Everything seems to grow all the time, and a continuous supply of everything necessary is obtained by simply growing the same crop at different times in different places. Bananas grow all over the place: so do oranges, lemons, coffee, cocoa, castor oil, pineapples etc. And there are dozens of new vegetables, which we sample daily at meals, and at least three kinds of potatoes - yams, yammies and something else I have forgotten. Why can't we have some of these in England instead of the everlasting spud? Fruits are the best I have tasted anywhere, and have soft lovely flavours which the exported variety seems to lose at once. The limeades with which we constantly refresh ourselves are a real dream! Lastly, flowers are wonderful too, all the various varieties of bougainvillaea are full out now - reds of all kinds, white, yellow, purple, etc. The mass of bright red bougainvillaea at the Botanical Gardens is one of the loveliest things. Poinsettia too, and hibiscus, and a wonderful orange thing on the tops of the trees known as "Flame of the Forest".

One correction: the varieties of potato are yams, yammies and chochos, and I believe there are even more! There is something called "Ackie", a vegetable eaten with salt fish, most delicious, also a wonderful fruit called "Sour Sop" which makes the best flavoured ice cream and tastes like a combination of fruits all rolled into one, and the coffee from the Blue Mountains is out of this world!

To continue our adventures! We left Kingston on Tuesday, March 8th for the north side of the island to a place called Ochio Rios. There seemed to be three possible hotels, a rather humble sort called Windsor, run by two English ladies, which somehow did not appeal to us, the Shaw Park at which I suspect Dad had stayed when he was here, the last word in luxury, and Tower Isle which has only been open for two months or so. We somehow found ourselves booked at the last of these and I felt vaguely annoyed, as I thought it would be simply wasteful extravagance. So we insisted upon visiting Shaw Park first. They had no room for us there, but I was glad to see the place, as the whole surroundings were too lovely for words, built high up on the hills overlooking exquisite sea views. The place had been erected by an English family who, English-like, had worked on the garden terraced down the hill until they had almost every possible flower growing there. It was simply a paradise, and beggars description of the whole island. I have never, in all my travels, seen such a supremely beautiful bit of the world, really almost too beautiful. The Shaw Park could not put us up in the house, but they offered us a lovely little villa with two bedrooms, bathroom, kitchen and sitting room, in their grounds. Of course, it was the sort of place one would have stayed in for months, but they wanted eventually to sell it and I had difficulty in restraining my sister from giving them an offer for it there and then. It seemed miles away from anywhere, though. I had the impression of all Jamaican country places that they have heavenly views, and one feels cut off completely from everyone except the immediate household.

Well, to continue our tale of hotels. We left the Shaw Park rather regretfully, and came about seven miles along the beach to Tower Isle. As I said, everything seemed far away and isolated, quite a feature of this country. A simply mammoth place, in excellent modern architecture - right on the beach and backed by palm covered hills. Our first reaction - we were fairly tired - was that it was rather too much for us humble souls, and a kind of whirlwind struck us. The charming young manager - a Southerner from Florida- welcomed us in ringing tones by our names. Two porters siezed our bags and we were whirled upstairs to a couple of the most colossally magnificent rooms I have ever seen. Enormous in size, twin beds, bathrooms, special alcove for bags and hanging things, large balconies with chairs and tables, etc. Every kind of new gadget. I spent about two days getting used to them. We dizzily ensconced ourselves and walked downstairs, which we were quite sure was wrong - to beg for tea. However, we were promptly presented with more "Planters Punch" with a note of welcome on it, and Mr. Issa introduced himself to us. He is a very nice old gentleman, rather resembling that Swiss charm at Stratford who brought chocs to Dad. He is the local millionaire - I presume - and runs the Myrtle Bank Hotel in Kingston and the local big department store there.

This new hotel is his special baby, and he seems to have thought it out and planned it all. He was specially interested in us, as we were English - most of the guests appear to be U.S. or Canadian - and also more so when he heard about Dad. Said he was born in Bethlehem - he is an Arab I believe - and told us about his difficulties in getting out of Palestine when it was still under Turkish rule, and the mere chance which brought him to Jamaica. Of course, he was very inter- ested in both Dad's business concerns and his excavations. He is going to give us a letter of introduction to the manager of his store in Kingston so that we can order what we like from there. (As far as I can remember, nothing materialised in this direction. Ed.)

This place is the last word in modern "beach play" luxury, but on a tasteful and efficient style, and the people seem really very simple and nice. It seems a far cry from that awful Palm Beach "Breakers" where Dad took me as a girl. It is really an experience to be here a few days - I doubt whether we shall get anything better in the whole of our trip. It will certainly become famous when it is better known. (As far as I know Tower Isle did not improve, although many similar places were started up. Ed.)

We have a gorgeous sandy beach with a reef around it - to protect us from sea monsters, I presume - also a swimming pool in part of the verandah of the hotel. If there is too much wind or the sea gets rough, every kind of beach appliance and chairs and hordes of servants at our elbows every minute. Perfect place for Hickman Price, and he would really have to relax here! Perfect for Neysa Perks, too, I should think. And Sir Malcolm could pose as a "sugar baron"!

We learnt much of the local history of the island from the Manager. This beautiful island has produced the most extraordinary wickedness, and is known as the "White Man's Grave". Both Spanish and British adventurers made fabulous riches, and had, of course, no sort of control from their mother countries. They pirated, looted and lived in splendour out here in the most fantastic ways. One man in particular - an English adventurer called Henry Morgan, at the time of Charles 11 or thereabouts, was the leading buccaneer and raided and looted all the countries around, and appears to have been a most magnetic character, and completely talked the London officials around by saying that he alone knew all the pirates and local buccanners and would clear them up, if officially appointed by the English. Accordingly, he was knighted and sent back here as Governor! His adventures would make a marvellous film, with possibly Lawrence Olivier! Port Royal, the Pirates' capital before Kingston was built, was considered "The richest and wickedest city on earth" and was completely destroyed by an earthquake in about half an hour. This interested me very much, because there is something very sinister about all this beauty.

We had an interesting visit to a friend of mine, a Mrs. Todd, who, with her invalid husband, had been loaned an old manor house at Monesque near here. It is in colonial style, lies far from the road in beautiful scenery – house stands high, very primitive, no electric light, telephone, nor running water,, with old "slave pens" still under the house! Just as glad I didn't live in those days.

We spent exactly a week at the exotic Tower Isle, and felt we had had full value for money in every way. This out of door life and sunshine is truly wonderful. I suppose we are practically out of doors 23 hours out of the 24! The half hour being allowed for bath and natural retirements per day. Everything is open everywhere - it is impossible in England to conceive of such a thing - one seems to need a roof in case of excessive sunshine and heavy showers in the rainy season, otherwise, dining rooms and living rooms have either no walls, cut away walls, or enormous windows wide open - usually a combination of all three. Same with bedrooms, these usually have large porches at one end with only shutters and very often huge ventilators through the ceiling. These natives appear to be very honest, as literally anyone could get in anywhere as far as I can see. The sun shines continuously and the temperature does not increase greatly during the day. We are told that "sunburn" is more likely between one and three, but there is no sunstroke, and one only occasionally needs dark glasses, and never hats! There is generally a breeze, quite different from Far Eastern heat. What a Paradise of Nature!

The island is very mountainous, and they have occasional bad earthquakes, but no volcanos. Main crop is sugar cane, which is just being cut now. This is all over the place, but especially along the fairly level north coast, in lovely waving fields of light green mile after mile. The interior of the island grows bananas by the million - very prolific - as soon as one tree dies, another comes up. The fruit comes in huge bunches, sometimes about four dozen or even more, with a lovely purpley-red flower at the end of the stem. It is hard to see the bunches at first, but if one looks first for the flower, one soon spots them.

The coffee tree, or rather bush, grows mainly in the high mountains, but one sees it in other parts too. The fruit of this - the bean - looks larger and a different colour until it is fully dry, when it becomes the bean we are used to. Strange vegetables and fruits abound of which the most popular for the native is the breadfruit, which tastes rather similar to a good slice of bread! The natives are the most pleasant coloured group I have ever seen. They are all descendants of African slaves - from four main places in Africa, I was told, brought here by Spanish and English settlers, the original Indians living here, i.e. the Arawaks and Carribs, having been wiped out by the Spanish. But there appears to be little colour bar and no segregation, although we are told that certain groups who have settled here keep very much to themselves racially and won't inter-marry with the blacks although they live native. There are, of course, classes and different varieties of colour, but even the poorest people seem to be clean, intelligent and well-groomed. Their English is not always the variety that we can understand! The principal difficulty seems to be that everyone gets so brown from the sun that it is quite impossible often to tell where people belong racially. The negro through the South American to the white gets shaded into a rather general brown variety. The groups of small children - especially when massed in their open air schools - are too sweet for words. They are gay, and grin widely at you, their shining black faces and little woolly heads of hair carefully cut, slates in hand. Once a child put out his hand for a lift, not realising, I think, that we were white tourists in the back. I told the chauffeur to stop and pick him up in the front, and a couple of the cutest little fellows got in front. One looked around and spied us, his jaw dropped and he was quite deprived of speech. But he left the car with a most polite little bow of thanks! It seems to me that the coloured faces have far better natural manners than the white, more dignity, and they feel what to do even if bereft of speech. The white man en masse seems a very poor individual.

We had a pleasant little three days' trip of the rest of the island back to Kingston, our starting point, beginning with a ride along the north coast westwards to Montego Bay, the smart centre of the Island. The popularity of this place is one of those unaccountable things which happens, I suppose, owing to the push of one or two people and much imitation from others. It is a large and fine bay, not particularly Jamaican in character, with a small quantity of very white sandy beaches. As far as we could see, the best place is occupied by an enormous old cemetery, or rather, three cemeteries, we were told, and the main hotels are huddled together around a minute and expensive bit of beach with coloured umbrellas -the celebrated "White Beach", Sunset Lodge, the most exclusive hotel of all, we are told. Only company directors are admitted - has a wee bit more beach of its own, and charges $50 per person per day for food and board. It all appears to be rather a racket and not to be compared in value to our "palace" at the other end of the island.

The rest of Montego Bay lies mainly on the hills around and there are polo fields and country clubs and other hotels of a pleasant, if very ordinary, cosmopolitan variety. On the way, we passed miles and miles of sugar plantations, all with large signs up telling who they belonged to. The most notorious is "Rose Hall" with a fine old 'Great House' which can be seen from the road, although it is now ruinous. The novel sold all over the island, "The White Witch of Rose Hall" is a villainous tale of Jamaica, and native magic in the old days. We also passed on the way Discovery Bay, where Columbus is supposed to have first landed. There is a charming little new hotel being put up in the hills behind with its own beach below. We also made a slight detour of the coast to 'Good Hope' Ranch, one of the nicest spots in the island. Originally an old plantation house, situated in the hills with a high commanding position overlooking the whole estate, this "Great House" appears to have been well modernised although little altered in its original construction, to catch the maximum amount of wind, and its large and very charming outside dining room on the other side of the house. This is now a hotel, but of the "ranch" type. It has horses, and one can ride at will. If I ever return to Jamaica, this is certainly one of the places I should like to stay at. Either the traditional home or the very modern seem the best out here - it is the intermediate smart business that seems so appallingly dull!

We also passed a pleasant little road house on the sea where one catches and eats oysters; they just stick around on rocks looking dirty and very closed.

March-April 1949

On our departure from Jamaica and a nice little British South American Airways plane, we picked two very nice Englishmen, who came from Birmingham and Kidderminster. They were spending a week at Nassau and Bermuda before returning to New York to sail back to England in the Mauretania. They proved excellent companions to sightsee with in both Nassau and Bermuda.

We were fortunate, too, to have an excellent coal black driver to take us sightseeing. Nassau seemed a charming and rather old-fashioned island and not at all the ultra-smart affair we had expected. We visited the enormous Sugar Palace Hotel, the Fort Montague Beach, an enormous Butlins affair, and enjoyed a buffet lunch while an organ player rolled out the Hallelujah Chorus from The Messiah. My sister thought that everyone processing around and collecting choice morsels of food as though it was their solemn rite. She thought it suitable Sunday music, as each one's plate became heavy with food, a darkie waiter rushed forward with a tray so that the guests were free to choose their coffee, tea, cheese, cake etc., and then each guest was escorted back to their table by a remarkably good looking head waiter.

We made several trips, all quite different, and enjoyed the bathing facilities on the protected beaches. The nicest trip we took by ourselves was in a seaplane to another small island called "Eleuthera", where Rosita Forbes, the novelist, has built herself a home. We took off from the seaplane base in Nassau, shot across the water for a bit, then up into the air, landing about half an hour later at our first port of call - in the water again, and when the plane comes down one hears a sort of crunch as it hits the water. Then a small launch comes out to take the passengers. We got out at the last port of call, and as we were about the last passengers left on the plane, our pilot obligingly flew low and pointed out the sights of the island to us, and when we landed, to our great surprise, we came down on the ground. We had no idea our plane was an amphibious one. We suddenly shot out a nice, tidy bit of landing gear and came down neatly on a sandy track. Eleuthera is the ideal tropical island of one's dreams, being undeveloped so far and has comfortable little swimming pools with restaurants here and there. We did make enquiries about buying land there, I doubt whether these dreams reach fruition, but what a place for a writer or an artist to live in peace. There are two farms on the island, which send their produce to Nassau, as well as fresh water springs, so the island is really quite self-supporting.

After a delightful excursion from Nassau to the "Sea Gardens" where one rides in glass bottomed boats out to sea, observing all the flora and fauna of the ocean bed, we left Nassau for Bermuda, where we had some difficulty in finding accommodation. The only hotel that could take us was again a Butlins run one, another vast affair, newly decorated in pink and white. Our escorts were still with us, as they, too, were staying in Bermuda and had booked their rooms well ahead. We had lovely views from our hotel of the Bay of Hamilton, but our escorts were housed in a rather poor affair on the other side of the island. Although all the people on this island are friendly and well clothed, we did not feel that it compares with our beloved "Tower Isle" in Jamaica.

Bermuda is a charming place in construction and type, but rather too crowded for us. Very much a holiday place with clear sun, fine air, charming views, and beautiful flowers, but it seems rather out of place in the present world as it is. We flew home direct from the West Indies some ten days later.

In the early 1950s, my sister and I went by my car to Europe. We thoroughly explored the Chateau district, visited the Lascaux caves and drove south to Lourdes and on to St. Jean de Luz to visit some English friends living there. We also went to Rome and studied the Etruscan towns on the hill tops and drove north to Florence, but the car trip which interested us both, we took in 1951 to Germany, when my sister and I were the guests in Hamburg of Brigadier Dunlop in his beautiful house on the Ulster. He was the Commandant in Hamburg and I knew his sister quite well in England. There we were able to feel like royal guests. We had a flat each in his house and were looked after by his hostess, a titled German lady.

We were entertained to the opera one evening, had seats in the front row and at intervals, the singers would bow directly to us all. The Brigadier was very popular in Hamburg as he could speak excellent German and was genuinely fond of the people there. Another evening, we were taken to see the Austrian Lippitzaner Horses performing in a barracks in the town, two great events which I shall never forget.

Each day, our German hostess would acquaint us with the social events, and she made sure we were ready and on time to take part. We were truly sorry to leave this lovely place and to drive off in our little car to Neumunster to be with my sister's mother-in- law and her family. There we had one very small bedroom each - I find it wonderful and interesting how one can adjust one's life style to suit the occasion! After a brief visit to Marburg where my friend and mother of my Godchild, Winnie, entertained us and showed us that beautiful medieval town where she lived and worked we drove to a little town on the border of East and West Germany near Bayreuth, where we could easily take the motor road. Bayreuth was just re-opening after the long trauma of the war with Wieland Wagner, Richard Wagner's grandson, in charge. Our mother had been here years ago with her mother, and now we were following in her footsteps.

There is a very solemn atmosphere in Bayreuth for the Wagner Festival and especially this one - the first after the war. We had tickets to see the whole of "The Ring", Parsifal and the Meister Singers with Herbert von Karajan conducting. Each day for a week, we drove in our car to Bayreuth, processed along the main street where crowds turned out to see us and wave us on, then having driven to the theatre and parked our car, we walked through the gardens of the theatre until a tune was heard from the opera on a small porch outside the theatre and we all filed in. We had been joined by our escorts who had tickets close by. There was some subdued talking while people took their seats, but when the orchestra started to play the prelude there was wrapt attention, and when the curtain went up on the undulating waters of the Rhine for "The Rhinegold", one could hear a pin drop. That's the way it was from beginning to end, and thereafter for all the other performances.

"The music of Wagner captured the moods and emotions of its

characters and helps one to listen, and as in all the "Ring" operas the dramatic events are coloured by it. At first, the orchestra plays and the Rhine Maidens sing their theme song Weia! Waga! while the Rhine Maidens swim about guarding the gold which lies at the bottom of the river. Then the ugly dwarf Alberich comes up from the darkness below. He is the chief of the Nibelungs, a race of dwarfs who live in the bowels of the earth. He watches the maidens, desire is awakened and he starts trying to make love to them. Thus, through the character of Alberich, repulsive, crafty and sinister, the element of lust and greed is introduced into the innocence of primitive nature, and this is reflected in the music. Finally, after being goaded for sometime by the behaviour of the Rhine Maidens, he loses patience altogether and he curses them with clenched fist, his arm raised in imprecation and with this gesture, enter the evil forces of nature whose aim is destruction. With this gesture, Alberich begins the disturbance of the virgin peace of the world. Suddenly the sun from above breaks through the surface of the water, and the depths of the water shine with a golden glow - it is the Rhinegold, lit by the soft rays of the morning sun and reflected brightly in the waters. The music here follows the text, bursting into the fanfare - like Rhinegold motif, one of the chief motives of the 'The Ring'." ★

★ "The Rheingold" by Berta Geissman: pp. 6 & 7.

CHAPTER 22

Greek Cruise

In the summer of 1954, my sister and I went on the first of the Greek Cruises ever to be made. It proved to be the Mother and Father of the later cruises.

Our American Aunt Rosalie Edge wrote us about it and said she was going and would like to have our company. It was a dollar earning cruise and so we had to part with some of our small store of dollars to join it.

The cruise was to start in Italy and was to include Greece, The Aegean Islands, Egypt, the Middle East, Sicily and the Dalmatian coast. Our cruise ship owned by a Greek Company, the "S.S. Aegean", was to sail from Genoa, July 16th and was due to return to Venice on August 15th.

The S.S. Aegean was the former "Princess Alice" owned by the Canadian Pacific Steamships, now under Greek registry and owned by the Aegean Shipping Line. Our brochure stated that this ship should be of sufficient size and comfort to undertake a cruise of this scope and yet small enough to enter many of the small harbours which will be visited. Actually, as it turned out, it was a little bigger than our cross channel ferries with cabins to match. We only found one bathroom on board and the door had no lock!! However, after our initial disappointment we quickly adjusted to it and it turned out to be the most comprehensive and fascinating tour one could ever hope to make.

When we boarded the ship in Genoa it was only partly sold out and so after some days at sea, we were left in Taormina, Sicily, while the ship sailed off to pick up further passengers.

Meanwhile, we sailed serenely along the Mediterranean, passing the volcano of Stromboli looking mild and pleasant with only a few lava streams visible. The sun was gorgeous and Marjorie and I took out our store of books and began to read "Bull of Minos" which gives a short account of Cretan civilization and remains a reason for worship of Bull – the sign of Zodiac in force at the time. What was the meaning of Athlete's leap over Bull? As we passed through the Straits of Messina, the sun grew hotter and there were some wonderful sunsets with the evening star shining out above them.

The clock was being put on during the nights and Rosalie often got up too early. The ship was lazing along toward the south coast of Greece as we sat reading and watched the islands of Greece slip by.

We were to land at Crete, and woke up early to watch the sun rise and our entrance into the little harbour. It was cool until the sun rose suddenly, lighting up the little grey houses and bare hills behind them. There were a few people on the long quayside to which we were tied up.

We went ashore about eight and boarded the buses with their guides and bumped along about five kilometers to Knossos. What a place! Beautifully situated amidst pleasant hillsides covered with trees and grapevines – the ruins are many acres in extent and about four or five stories high. It reminded my sister of the Alhambra in Spain, every window seemed to open onto a beautiful view. It had all modern plumbing devices including a modern W.C.

Later, we were taken to the little museum – what life in everything Minoan. They must have seen everything as living things, birds, animals and especially Bulls, wonderfully portrayed on vases and jewellery. What we have lost nowadays!

We both wished to return again to see more of these cities. Perhaps we could stay at the Villa Ariadne – home of the British School of Archaeology. There were very few hotels nearby in those days.

But we were driven back to our ship and after a very warm time aboard we landed at Alexandria, where we were due to take the air conditioned train for Cairo (about four hours). What a relief, for it was very hot. We had an excellent room at the Semiramis Hotel overlooking the Nile with Giza Pyramids on the distant bank. However, we were rather disturbed by work being carried out all night on the foundations of the new Shepherd's Hotel next door. We had decided to stay close to our American Professor of Archaeology, Dr. Robinson, who was on our cruise with his wife, as we knew he was going out to see the new excavations at the Giza and Sakhara Pyramids – as the Cairo Museum was shut in the afternoon – but we had great good fortune, as our Professor arranged his expedition for that afternoon. We started in a car with the Professor and his wife, an unknown American and ourselves, plus a dragoman and driver. We went first to Giza Pyramids and the Mena House Hotel, then drove to Professor Fakhery's house (the Egyptian archaeologist in charge of excavations at the pyramids) but found him not at home and no message for our professor. Fortunately, however, the Arab in charge of the excavations was finally persuaded to show us outside where two boats were hidden at the base of the Giza pyramid (the peephole now sealed up temporarily).

Many years later when I returned to Egypt, I asked about a modern building put up beside the Pyramid, and I was told that it housed one of these boats hidden originally at the base of the Giza Pyramid and the many difficulties the archaeologists and curators had to try and preserve it in a modern air conditioned museum.

We continued on to Sakhara and with much bribing and many difficulties, we were able to see through a grill the coffin of Ka, and an ancient cutting of shaft down – well worth seeing. Then in another tomb, we saw beautiful sculpture.

Then we drove home, glad to be back to have a bath at our hotel and dinner on the roof garden. Next morning, we were able to visit the museum before departing for our trip back to Alexandria.

On the following day, we docked at Beirut, a large modern port with new buildings and herds of American automobiles. We drove uphill to the American University, a fine set of buildings in a lovely garden – then to a museum – another fine building, but not much in it but an interesting map of the ancient world. Then we set off over the Lebanon Mountains – up 5,000 feet, where it was nice and cool, over a fertile plain, finally reaching Damascus in the evening. We stayed at The Orient Palace Hotel in a nice quiet room on the back, but were up again at 7.30 am. We then saw the Omayade Mosque the street called Strait, the house where St. Paul was let down in a basket, now turned into a church – house of Ananius and Caiphas now in a Christian quarter – and the only Arab Palace. Our cousin Rosalie Edge and her friend Blanche Evans had lunch with us at about 11.30 and then we drove to Baalbec, another lovely drive over the mountains, a large place which is growing rapidly. We noticed that the people, both at Damascus and Baalbec, looked vital and happy. We returned to Beirut and boarded our ship in the evening.

We had another quiet day at sea before landing early at Rhodes, a beautiful water front with the Castle of the Knights and other buildings making an impressive line with the coastline of Asia in the background. The Professor bundled us into a car for Lindos, but we never reached it and went instead over high hills to the Valley of Butterflies – where a particular orange butterfly with closed black and beige wings lives in millions. There was a sort of cloud over everything. We walked a little, then returned to our car and continued, but the car's brakes boiled, so we decided to return to Rhodes, where we visited Museum and Castle and returned to the ship.

Our next call was at Cos – "Poor Man's Rhodes" – where we drove in buses to Asclepius – a beautiful terraced place, where in the old days people were brought for cures – air, religion and water (very effective – works in ten minutes) herbs, beautiful surroundings, with a small, attractive museum, and finally back to the boat.

Next day, we found ourselves in a deep crater of water surrounded by high hills. This was Santorini. There was a town on top of one hill with many white houses (Thera). In order to reach it we were all put on mule back and then ascended a long series of zigzag slopes to reach the top, where there was a wonderful view of the other islands. We saw two churches, one Greek Orthodox and a Catholic one and a small hotel. This island is now famous because of the excavations which have been done by well-known Greek archaeologists. It is thought that the tidal wave caused when its volcano erupted may have been responsible for the sudden disappearance of the Greek Minoan Culture centred in Crete and even may have extended toward the Egyptian coast across the Mediterranean Sea when the Children of Israel under Moses crossed the Jordan and started toward their "Promised" land.

When we rejoined our ship, we took another trip through the Corinth Canal and back to Sicily where we sightsaw in Syracuse. We left our ship and went to Taomina to stay at the "Miramare" Hotel, a small hotel with a lovely view, where we had dinner on top of the hill overlooking the sea. The next day we went on a spectacular trip to Volcano "Etna" where we went right up the side of the crater. The lava had flowed down in huge black lines from the various craters which have overflowed in different years – large clusters of bloom alternated with the black (stone) flows of the lava – a very awesome sight – also very fertile soil, with grapes, olives, oranges, lemons, corn, vegetables and sometimes bananas growing there.

We finally once again returned to our ship at Messina, where we found other passengers in our old cabins, so once more we had to be firm until we negotiated fresh cabins – my new home was right on the deck and so when it became hot again and some people chose to sleep on the deck rather than in their cabins (they did not have air conditioning), I had to learn to step over their recumbent forms, but I was always cool in my new cabin!!

Tuesday August 3rd. We sailed up to the port of Katakolun for our trip to Olympia and then took some very ancient buses for about an hour, a wonderful town containing everything. Temples of Hera and Zeus, sort of fraternities known as Treasuries, which belonged to different sports groups, a stadium (not much excavated then), a hippodrome, heaps of statues, principally of athletes, a theatre, etc. A huge area for sacred activities. There must have been a large number of people co-operating peacefully and effectively. Here, also, in the temple of Zeus stood the wonderful ivory and gold statue of Zeus, the seventh wonder of the World which has now completely disappeared. All these were in beautiful surroundings of grapes and cedars amidst gentle green groves.

There was also a very handsome museum containing parts of the two great frescos for the Zeus temple, one active, one passive. The head of Apollo, a beautiful victory, Apraxitiles, Hermes, with Dionysius, bronze weapons and headbands found recently by German archaeologists who were still excavating there.

We returned finally to our ship and found it was stuck in the mud until about 1 am. There was an awful noise – quite impossible to sleep. We believe the engine that winched the anchor went wrong. However, we finally got away and sailed to Nauplia, but we were late in arriving there and so we had only the choice of going to Mycenea or Epidaurus. Mycenea is wonderfully situated on top of a hill with gorgeous views of the country round about. There are beehive tombs well made, also the Treasury of Atreus. There was a new row of royal tombs discovered recently, one the day before, of a lady skeleton with a gold diadem and another wonderfully constructed with nothing in it. We met the Greek American excavator and Professor Wace, later at our hotel, "La Belle Helene".
We called at Tyrans on the way back, with its "Cylopean Walls".
 Next day we landed at Delos, a fascinating place surrounded by blue sea all whipped up by waves. There were ruins of an ancient town like Pompeii in Italy. Little streets, houses, shops and temples, also a theatre, and some beautiful mosaics. The inhabitants were evidently wealthy and able to trade extensively.

Our next port of call was at Lesbos, or Mitylini, home of Sappho. We sailed right into the dock to land and walked about the town. We found an exhibition in the local school of a "Lesbos House", rooms full of Greek products with ladies in costume. There was a statue of Sappho, which I saw as we were leaving the dock. After some delay in loading supplies, our ship steamed along up to the Gallipoli Peninsula (with the British and Australian war memorials) and started up the Dardanelles.

After a short time we reached Canakkale, where we docked in Turkey for the first time and the whole local population were there to meet us. We got into some of the shakiest buses I have ever seen and rattled to the site of Troy in about an hour. Nothing very impressive left there, only old walls of various "Troys", but we had a great thrill in seeing the wonderful sight of the Plain of Troy and its command of the Hellespont. A whole lot of my childhood memories about stories from Troy slid into place in one piece. We wished our Father could have got out there too. The Walls of Troy, the Scaen Gate and Achilles chasing Hector around that wall. We bumped back to Canakkale, and went on board again, with the local crowd still staring at us.

On August 7th at some early hour, we were awakened by the loud speakers aboard. We finally made out that they were giving us a description of the skyline of Istanbul, which we were passing, i.e. Santa Sophia, the Blue Mosque, Golden Horn, Sultan's Palace etc. all very fine in the early morning light. We went out to join the sight-seers and then to breakfast. The professor thought we would dock about 10.30am. The first day on land was to be free, so everyone could shop and go to the bazaars. We joined the professor's party and went to the Park Hotel where we checked into the last free rooms and stayed overnight, then we went with a few people to Santa Sophia – where the pillars had been taken from the temple of Diana at Ephesus and constructed in a great square with circles everywhere. We thought it a wonderful city, much more modern than we had remembered it from our first visit, but as ever, very much at the crossroads of the world. We sailed the following day, having seen the Blue Mosque and museum before we left.

Our next port of call was to a very important island of Samothrace. There was some doubt whether we could land there, as any roughness of the sea would make it impossible.

However, we were able to make it in a local boat with difficulty, and then there was a long, hot walk with the excavators, who had come to meet us, to the ruins in a sort of cleft from which there was a beautiful view to the sea. The famous winged Victory originally stood on top of all this, facing the sea – the prow of her ship standing in some water and her hand upraised (part of her hand recently found here) – a wonderful setting again. Part of the temples found here belonged to the Mysteries. My sister asked the excavators what they thought the Mysteries were, and they said: "Oh, something like theosophy."

I have omitted to mention our lovely sail around Mount Athos. This occurred after we left the island of Samothrace and before we landed in Salonika. We could not, of course, land there, but we sailed straight toward the beautiful mountain headland and then skirted right round it, getting a very excellent view of the single houses and clusters of dwellings on its slopes. Our ship's siren boomed out – most disrespectfully, I thought, but the monks waved banners back at us, and although we did not see many of them, they did not appear to be upset by our presence.

After paying a brief visit to Olynthus from Salonika, where our Professor had excavated and was, therefore, his special interest, we proceeded to Piraeus, where we disembarked and went by buses to Athens. The professor was in his element here and took us to too many places, dragging us hither and thither by foot and finally in the heat of the day, to the Acropolis, where we were expected to view every detail in turn. We were finally allowed to board our bus and were left at the Grand Bretagne Hotel in the centre of Athens where we were grateful for air conditioning and stayed there until the evening when we again saw the Acropolis by moonlight and returned to our ship. We were able to see both Istanbul and Athens on much more auspicious occasions in the future.

Next day, we landed at Itea and we had a lovely drive round Mt. Parnassus to Delphi – much finer than we had remembered it before. We visited the ruins, the great stadium and theatre and admired the gorgeous views to the sea. In the afternoon we cruised through the Corinth Canal for the third time and out into the Adriatic, north through the Straits of Ortranto and cruised into and along Kotor Bay Fjord, beautiful, – like the Norwegian fjords, but light much softer. There were many people in boats and they all waved to us, but there seemed to be few inhabitants in the various houses and settlements along the coastline.

We arrived at Dubrovnik in the evening and went ashore in a launch. Dubrovnik is a white walled city, particularly fascinating at night, when the lights overhead and the white houses look like a stage set, with small streets dimly lighted climbing up the hill leading off it. Crowds of people, but no wheeled traffic. We went to a cabaret – the Labyrinth – a rather poor European Show, but a beautiful place – all out of doors with a walk leading around that part of the city wall – with views all around. We all tried drinks there and they all turned out unexpectedly. Marjorie, for instance, asked for a "rhum Punch" and it turned up boiling hot!!

Next day we went ashore again, officially for sightseeing. We saw two Catholic Churches and convents and some baroque houses of the merchant princes, who really made the place rich and famous, then back to our ship sailing for Venice.

We arrived next morning in the pouring rain, but we managed to get ourselves and our baggage to a comfortable hotel. Aunt Rosalie and her friends could be seen in the distance, but they did not see us. Meanwhile, the rain cleared up and so we went to St. Mark's Square where we found Maxime and Katherine.

We all climbed the clock tower to see the "Strikers" in action, but were too late to go inside the Basilica. We had a farewell dinner with our friends and said goodbye to Rosalie and Co who went off for a gondola ride.

The next day, we flew back to London via Milan. Oh dear, how cold it was there when we arrived after our 90° to 100° temperatures for the past month.

CHAPTER 23

Ancient Sources

After our travels to Europe, Greece,the Carribbean and the United States, my sister felt that we should try to go to the South American States. No one in our immediate family had been there before, and although we had many friends in England who were acknowledged travellers, they could not give us news of South America, but when we went to the States to spend Christmas with our stepsister in Ann Arbor, Michigan, we found that her husband, Hickman Price, had his business connections and agents in South America. He was an executive with Willy's Jeep who were busy opening up there and had many agents who could help us on our way. There were others, too, from Canada, who went there in the winter to avoid the freezing snow. So we came back to England again feeling that this travel plan might indeed be possible.

Mr. Bennett, as always, was encouraging and wrote to us the following letter dated 28th November, 1955 from Coombe Springs:

"If I were, myself, fortunate enough to be making the trip that is ahead of you and Melissa, my chief object would be to acquire an organic sensation of the pre-Columbian civilisations. Whenever I have visited ancient sites, I have found it possible to sense the quality of the existence of the people who live there, and in this way to understand their history as it is said with all three centres.

My next aim would be to assimilate the chronology and connect it with the general conclusion that I have reached about the existence of time cycles in the spiritual life of mankind. The periods that are of special interest to me are 9,000 to 10,000 B.C. which corresponds to the final retreat of the glaciers and to the cataclysm known as the Lost Atlantis.

Next, I am interested in the period of about 7,000 or 8,000 B.C. when agriculture began in many parts of the earth. Then again, about 5,000 B.C. when great buildings of megalithic and also brick construction began to appear. This was also the time, I believe, when astrologers established the calendar and kept records in which climatic cycles were predicted.

From 3,300 to 2,800 B.C. was the transition from priests' rule to kingship and the arousing of the dynasties in Egypt, Mesopotamia, China and India. The next great crisis came between 600 and 500 B.C. with the appearance of the great teachers and the beginning of what I call the megathropic epoch. The drama of Christ appears to be a unique event without parallel anywhere else in that period of history. At the end of the millenium of revelation, there was Mohammed in the West and Hui Neng in the East with similar missions. Once again, in the 11th century, there was the flourishing of Art all over the world and the appearance of Great Mystics like St. Francis and Jalalul-Din Rumi.

It would be of the utmost interest for the purpose of my studies if you could ascertain whether there were any synchronous patterns corresponding to this in America. The dating of the pre-Columbian civilisations is still so uncertain that perhaps not much can be discovered, but I would like you to take with you a most valuable and scholarly book – Frederick Zoyner's 'Dating the Past' . The third edition may now be available.

The third feature which I would try to understand are the migrations of races and the present status of the theory that the Americans came from Asia through Alaska. You may not have heard that Gurdjieff once said that when the civilisations of Maralpleicie dispersed as a result of the drying up of the central Asian plateau, some of the remains went northwards and their descendants are the Eskimos and the Red Indians. When we were together at Lascaux, I mentioned the fact that the Magdelanian people painted corpses with red ochre, and he said that they were the same as the Maralpleicie people and that they had red skins. You probably also know that he made more than one special journey out to the West of America to see the Pueblo Indians and regarded them as the inheritors of a very ancient and important tradition. References in the chapter on Hypnotism to the knowledge possessed by the people of Maralpleicie is somehow connected with what he said about the Indians.

This leads me to the fourth, and by no means the least interesting of the points that I would like to study, and that is the nature of the spiritual powers possessed or claimed by the priests and astrologers

Melissa Marston Macleod
(nee Marston)

Melissa and her sister,
Marjorie in South Africa

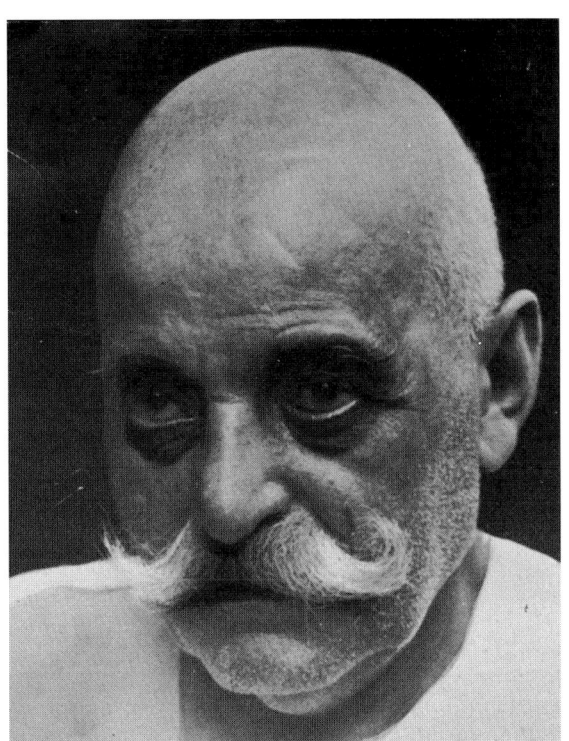

Mr. G. Gurdjieff –
philosopher and writer

Mr. P.D. Ouspensky –
Russian philosopher and
writer

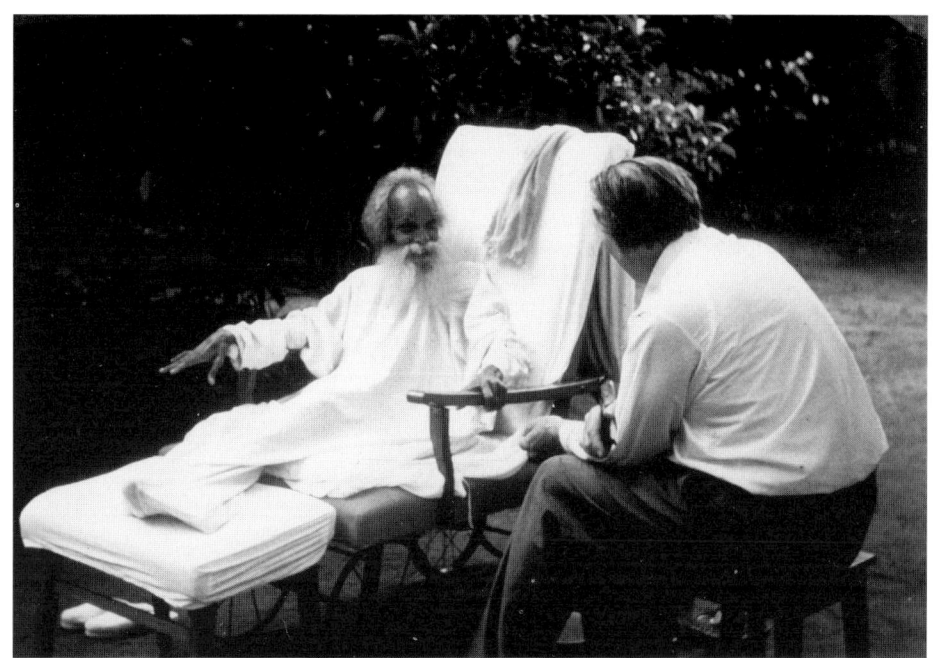

Shivapuri Baba with Mr. Bennett

John Bennett – soldier,
scientist, philosopher and
writer

Mohammed Subud and his wife Ebu at Coombe Springs

Bapak and family in front of their house in Indonesia

Paramahansa Yogananda

Mother Meera

Sathya Sai Baba – Avatar of the Age

Archaeologist Professor Raleigh Radford and interested parties connected with the Glastonbury dig at the Abbey

of the various pre-Columbian civilisations. What is known of their magic, their astrology, their healing powers? what interpretations are given by scholars of the rituals, and especially of human sacrifice? Undoubtedly these people understood and made use of special drugs, and much of what is written in Beelzebub about the polomedekhtic products is especially significant for the pre-Columbian civilisations of South America. Indeed, much strange knowledge has been preserved, even to the present day.

Fifthly, and again, by no means last, there are the art forms and the connection between American art and contemporary expressions in Asia and Africa.

I hope that you will collect as many pictures, drawings, brochures and other written material as possible. Such things are not easily found in books, and if you do not wish to preserve them yourself, I would like to keep them in our archives in Coombe Springs.

Signed: J.G. Bennett

Then two other coincidences occurred while attending some lectures in London given by Mr. Bennett. We met an old friend, Rodney Collin-Smith. He had been a member of Mr. Ouspensky's group in the '30s and later had gone to Mexico to forge his own connections there. He told us that he knew the country well and that things were just "coming up and starting again." It might be ripe for further work and he was firmly of the opinion that we should come. As he had many archaeologist friends both here and in Peru, we should be sure to see interesting places.

About the same time, a banker from Valparaiso, Chile, Snr. Biggs-Delano, called on Mr. Bennett. He represented a group of three Chileans who were eager to hear about the work of George Gurdjieff. They knew nothing of him except Louis Pauwel's book entitled "Gurdjieff". In this book, the author had been so abusive that they felt strongly that Gurdjieff must have been a very great character! How Gurdjieff would have appreciated this!

On account of these two coincidences, we saw that a visit from us might be useful in at least two places in Central and South America. Later, we were able to meet the three Chileans, and a small group was started in Santiago under the leadership of Mr. Figini, with whom my sister corresponded for a long time.

So we made a firm decision to visit Central and South America in 1955-56. We were greatly helped by our American brother in law, Hickman Price and his friendly agents who turned up to meet us nearly everywhere, offering us cars or any other help we might need.

This was invaluable, but many of them would have found us very odd. What on earth were two middle aged women trying to do coming a long distance to visit some old temple or archaeological site?

We had a rough passage by ship across the Atlantic, but we arrived in Ann Arbor, Michigan in time for a sumptuous family Christmas with our American sister and her family. We spent New Year with some cousins in Chicago and finally launched ourselves south, with endless visas, permits and introductions into the unknown.

Actually, we had arranged far too elaborate and complicated a trip: Mexico, Guatemala, Honduras, Panama, Peru, Chile and then all the other countries the "Panagra" plane went to on the way round South America – Buenos Aires, Montevideo and Rio de Janeiro. By the time we reached the last stop, where our brother in law was waiting for us, we could not look at anything and longed only to lie on a beach where everyone could speak English.

Mexico City, with its sunny dry climate high up on a plateau, descends in all directions to the most fascinating places we had ever seen. In 1948 Collin-Smith and his friends had bought a beautiful site at about 9,000 feet, midway between sea level and the top of the two sacred snow-capped mountains – Popocatepetl (Man) and Ixlaccihuatl (Woman) – with a glorious view of the Valley of Mexico. The name of the site was Tetecala: "The Stone House of the God". Here they planned, in 1951, to build their own homes as well as a large building to be known as the "Planetarium", of which only the understorey was ever to be completed.

It was conceived as a large circular building with a diameter of 43 feet. In earlier travels, we had often found sacred buildings of this diameter, for example the Chapter House at Wells Cathedral. The same dimensions are also found in the Indian Kivas. This was to be used for Work, Movements and plays with a smaller circular part as a Christian (R.C.) Chapel. Combined with this, in a separate building, was a Clinic which functioned at weekends with doctors and helpers in attendance for the village people who were very poor and had practically no medical help.

The signs of the Zodiac stood out on the specially designed plaques set along the approach to the main building, which was built of the black lava stone of the district. As one reached the top of the slope, one could see that the base was actually two circles, a larger one and a smaller one. The two were linked by a still smaller circle between them. Under these formations a crypt had been designed and was already constructed. It represented the mineral world, the geographical realm, the petrified traces of the life of men and of the earth in the past. Around the edge of each circle there were paths with niches and one could take a journey back in time: each niche representing in mosaics an epoch twice as ancient as the one before.

1. 200 years ago Colonial Times (Tree of Jessie)
2. 400 years. Pre-Columbian (Aztec Fire Ceremony)
3. 800 years Virgin from Chartres (Mayan Priest)
4. 1,600 years Greco Roman
5. 3,200 years Egyptian
6. 6,400 years Sphinx and Pyramids
7. 12,800 years Magdelanian
8. 25,600 years Aurignacian

Under the larger circle, a Movements Hall had already been made, with the circle and lines of the enneagram outlined in tiles on the stone floor and with a huge figure of Deity on the ceiling, with arms outstretched in blessing. Large carved doors separated this chamber from the one beyond which was a private chapel dedicated to the Virgin and Child with a central stone font above which the sun poured down. Each chamber might be used separately or the whole could be thrown open to make one.

The understanding used in the conception of this building was put into one of Collin Smith's books entitled "The Theory of Eternal Life", which concluded with a diagram of four states of matter as four worlds or spheres, united at a single point, where individuals may pass from one world to another – Death, Judgment and Rebirth.★

We had many interesting talks with Collin-Smith about the future. In his book "The Theory of Celestial Influences", he had outlined his expectations for the coming age, calling it the "Age of the Conquest of Time". Time was suddenly introduced as a dimension into phenomena where there had been no room for it before – as, for example, the microphone and television, etc. In other words, that mechanical motion and electromagnetic motion were interchangeable.

In consequence:- "that which separates and divides belongs to the past – that which reconciles and unites belongs to the future. And the way towards unity lies in escape from time"

In speaking of the astrological influences of the past and present decades, he mentioned the Piscean Age just passing with the Virgin

★The "Planetarium"

as the opposite sign of the Zodiac, The enormous influence of the Mother can be easily seen through the past centuries as, for instance, at Chartres. He pointed out to me that in the coming Aquarian Age, the main influence will come from the opposite sign Leo, the King. Then he said: "Wait until Leo sounds!"

While in Mexico, we came into contact with the processions visiting the Shrine of Our Lady of Guadeloupe, a sort of Mexican Lourdes,*

On the occasion of the New Year, the Collin Smiths took us to the Church, filled with Pilgrims from the local villages. Its fine and powerful atmosphere, the picture of this mass of simple people kneeling in front of the altar with flowers in their hands, will remain long in our memories. On one day, the people of Toluca (about 64 kilometres away) came, some with babies strapped on their backs or carried in shawls, walked there and back in bare feet!

We also saw the Acolman Convent nearby with a Monastery and farm attached, and were told that many of these churches were founded in the district by the monks, who came after the Spanish Conquest and really ran the country until a Civil Service was established.

We left Collin Smith (never, unhappily, to see him again), but we had acquired permanent friends there in the persons of a young Peruvian couple, the Costas who were his students and who later in Lima introduced us to the members of their group, the first of the ones in Central and South America who had had direct contact with a pupil of Mr. Ouspensky.

Modern Mexican cities are pleasant enough, but to the person interested in archaeology, all directions are alive with mysterious ancient places. Even those comparatively well-known and fairly well excavated seem to hold many more mysteries. Always their excavators claim how much more there is to do and find out, and there are supposed to be some 2,500 ancient sites not yet even explored.

* In 1531, ten years after the conquest of the country by the Spaniards, a poor Indian Peasant Boy, Juan Diego, claimed that a beautiful lady had appeared to him telling him that she was the Virgin Mary.

Diego took this message to his bishop, Fray Juan de Zumarraga, several times, and finally on his last visit, showed the bishop his "Tilma", or cloak, on which according to tradition was revealed the beautiful image of the Virgin Mary.

The cloak with the image still hangs in the Basilica, unfaded and perfectly preserved. It is now covered with glass but, for the first hundred years of its existence, it was not. No painter has been able to explain just how it was painted, or why it can remain in 'this combination of harmony and majestic beauty'.

America's Treasure, The Virgin Mary of Guadeloupe by Helen Behrens.

Little seems to be known abroad about these sites – at least in England. There is a vague feeling about the part played by the Aztecs of Tenochtitlan conquered by Cortes on his triumphant trip to Mexico, where all the temples ran with blood sacrifices to their Gods, or possibly something about the remarkable calendar discovered by the Mayans.

What is not understood is that long before the Aztecs (a rather unpleasant people) came on the scene, there had been vast earlier civilizations in the late B.C. and early A.D. centuries, originating in their sacred cities races of men who were astronomers, engineers, stone cutters, potters and who had a written language.

Their works were everywhere, now sometimes lost in the jungle, as the great Mayan City of Tikal – with its enormous pyramids, some as high as a modern 20 storey building – was, or the great pyramid city of Teotihuacan, whose builders are still unknown. These pyramids are as large or larger than the Egyptian ones and the city of Teotihuacan, according to some authorities represents the body of a man – an idea found constantly in Peru, also. The moon pyramid represents his head, the sun pyramid his heart, the processional way his spinal chord, and the temple of Quetzalcoatl, his feet (The great plaza for the people).

We spent several hours in this wonderful place. The name means 'Where the Gods are made', or 'Place of the Gods'.

A prehistoric civilisation probably starting about 500 BC, it must have extended over a long period, as the Aztecs knew it as a ruin only. The earliest building is the Pyramid of the Sun – height 210 feet, base measurement 735 feet on each side and which covers an area of 540,000 square feet. Its volume is well over 1,500,000 cubic yards of lava stone and adobe rock with an outer covering of plaster which was originally painted. The magnificent flights of stone steps ran up from the base, divided and came together, and then divided and came together in six tiers with the seventh tier buried below the ground. The stone steps were so deep that each time one climbed gave one a feeling of almost total height above ground. From each platform it was difficult to see the steps at all. Marjorie was able to climb to the top, but I was not sure whether I could get down again, and so I climbed three flights and then waited for the others. I am gradually getting accustomed to these climbs!! At the foot of this pyramid runs "the Avenue of the Dead" – named thus by the Aztecs who thought that the unexcavated mounds on either side were tombs.

At the other end of this avenue and in line with the Sun pyramid stood the Moon Pyramid, which has now been excavated, as indeed are so many of the mounds which fill the surrounding areas. At the other end of the avenue and in line with the Sun Pyramid stands the Citadel and Pyramid of "Quetzalcoatl" or "The Feathered Serpent".

The Citadel, a big rectangle with high walls crowned with platforms, this citadel was probably the scene of many large and spectacular ceremonies.

There are many other buildings in this area, and a Rain God temple, only a few of them have been excavated. We saw some charming open houses, which must have belonged to the priests, and wonderful pieces of frescoes in red, white, blue and green paint. Also, vivid images of Tlaloc – the rain God – whose eyes followed one everywhere.

After Teotihuacan we saw many other pyramids and we began to be interested in the actual pyramid form. Very little was then known about it. The Great Pyramid of Cheops was thought to have represented a sort of 'map of the affairs of man'. Now, much more study is given to the actual effect of the pyramid shape, and the effect it may have on anyone or thing inside it. Experiments have shown that there is a relation between the shape of the space inside the figure and the physical, chemical and biological processes going on inside that space. For example, bodies can be preserved in a mummified condition, and a razor can be sharpened.* The rudimentary pyramid of Cuicuilco is probably about the earliest one and is situated on the lava bed just south of Mexico City.

Some days later, we went to Tula, a newly excavated site some 50 to 60 miles north west of Mexico City, founded by the Toltecs, a very ancient race, and supposed to be the home of Quetzalcoatl, The Feathered Serpent, who was presumed to be a real historical character who taught man science and showed him the calendar. He lived as a King in Tula (originally named Ancient Tollam) and was 'exceptional in moral virtues like King Arthur among the English'.** The Aztec State was founded on his spiritual inheritance, which it betrayed and transformed into a weapon of worldly power.

Two smallish pyramids, the remains of some palaces, and a large 'ball court' have been excavated at Tula, but many other buildings are still untouched. No one knows the meaning of the ball game, it may have originated with the Toltecs from earlier times. We found an even older court later at Monte Alban. There were some extraor-

---

* Lyall Watson – "Supernature" pp.97-100.
** SAHAGIN, quoted by Laurete Sejourne in "Burning Water".

dinary sculptured figures (described as "Atlanteans"). They were square, severe and vivid things, like a living being boxed in. Of course, they are not Christian but the same direct and vital connection is felt. Only they had quite a different life to our own, something we could not understand. Some of the bas-reliefs – an animal eating human hearts – made us shudder. Collin-Smith thought we should find something similar in Peru.

Later, we went to Toluca, about 64 kilometres from Mexico City, to the village of Calixtlahuaca, where there is an unusual round pyramid, dedicated to the Wind God. Of moderate height, it has the usual upright stairway on one side and also a path winding around it to the top. I understood that Indians in feathered headdresses made their formal marches here, giving the impression of a 'feathered serpent'. The most interesting thing is that from the top of this pyramid one can see the roof on a smaller building with an 'Egyptian Cross' or the sign of Everlasting Life', cut into the roof. When we looked at the walls of the smaller building, there were a series of sculptured skulls on its walls. This must surely mean that death comes before real life.

That same evening we were invited to have supper with Mrs. Dickins and her family in their lovely Mexican home. Mrs. Dickins introduced us to several cosmopolitan couples who together with the Collin-Smiths, the de Costas and the Grepes made a nice gathering, Spanish music was played and a Spanish buffet supper was served.

Before leaving by plane for Oaxaca we were able to see another pyramid set in the midst of a lovely Spanish town, Tenayuca. This was a pyramid known as "The Edifice of the Serpent" because it is surrounded on three sides by a wall of serpents. Two coiled serpents lie at the base of the pyramid. Like so many of the religious places in Mexico, the pyramid has been rebuilt five times. That means five different epochs have built over the original one, superimposed structures. It was possible to see this because tunnels had been made into the pyramid itself and the different epochs were clearly distinguishable. This style of superimposed structures was due to the belief prevalent amongst these people that life was renewed after definite periods of time; for instance, the Aztecs after fifty two years and the Zapatecs two hundred and fifty years.

The thing that strikes one architecturally in Mexico is that the whole country, particularly the Southern part, is a mass of ruins with only a small area which has been excavated. Interest in excavation only started in about 1900, and though it is now speeding up there is still much to be done. Group after group of people have lived on each site and no-one seems to know their dates for certain or just how they were related.

We had a pleasant flight to Oaxaca in the early morning, seeing the sun rise over the sacred mountains, Popocatapetal and Ixlaccihuatl. With the red desert mountain land beneath us, this early morning was most beautiful.

Our destination was an informal, gay little airport in a warm valley with masses of flowers and orange, lemon and grapefruit trees everywhere. It was good to have a country atmosphere again, and the perfumes and crickets at our little motel were most reassuring at night.

The first day, we drove round the little town of Oaxaca, a colourful Zapotec and Spanish one centred on another 'Zocalo' or square like Mexico City. Cortes, the Spanish conqueror, styled himself 'Marquis de Valle' and chose his marquisate from this part of the country. But there is no statue to him, nor remembrance of any kind in Mexico. And no wonder! What did he do, or any other Spaniard accomplish, but destruction and debasement of everything they found there.

On the following days we were introduced by our excellent guide, nicknamed "Pepe", to two wonderful examples of Indian architecture – at Monte Alban and Mitla. Monte Alban (the Spanish name as the Indian one is lost) was a great ceremonial centre on a mountain, the top of which was levelled off to build the great Plaza on which the main buildings are grouped. There are about 25 miles of ruins as well, which have never been touched yet: it would take a very long time to excavate, says Dr. Alfonso Caso, the excavator.*

No-one seems to know where the founders came from. They were great experts in astronomy and building – all the main temples were exactly placed, also there is a special astronomical observatory with aspects of its own. It is said that all the city was plastered, delicately

* Acosta, the museum's archaeologist, gave me the following dating for Monte Alban:

Period I. The Dancers, i.e. the odd bas reliefs on stones of figures dancing – 1000 B.C. to 200 A.D. (this by carbon dating).

Period II. 200 to 400/500 A.D. Probably early Mayan.

Period III. 400 to 800 A.D. Zapotec – Golden Age – Great building.

Mitla was probably started during Period III and carried on until destroyed by the Spaniards.

Period IV – 700-800 A.D. to 1300 – when place abandoned probably with the Mitkes who conquered it for a time.

carved, and all the surfaces were painted red. Fortunately, the Spanish, when they came, never found it, owing to the mass of blossoming trees which hide it.

The exhaltation one feels on arrival at the great plaza is quite indescribable: (something like our own Glastonbury). We came a second time to Mexico and Oaxaca five years later, and again ascended the mountain to the great plaza and it was as though we had never been away and might have been paying a second visit the following day.

Monte Alban was the first of the sacred cities such as Uaxactum, Palenque, La Venta, Cholula, Xochicalco and El Tajin started about 600 BC, and there were probably many more of these sites.

The plan of Monte Alban is the Great Plaza with buildings. Exactly north is the huge Jaguar Temple, south is a pyramid, east The King's Palace, and two unidentified pyramid temples and west, The Priest's House. In the middle of the Plaza, a pyramid facing east is the Sun Temple, and an Astronomical building orientated south west and north east. Here, too, one comes across the first sacred ball game court. this looks like a large capital "I" and a rectangular alley with slanting walls and alcoves for the heavy rubber ball at both ends. Later, these alcoves were changed into large stone rings placed at the centre of the court on either side. Five or more players (possibly less) took part in the game and the object was to put the ball through one of the alcoves or rings. Play was extremely difficult, since each player could use only his shoulders, hips or knees to move the ball and it was never thrown or kicked. According to some reports, only the aristocratic youths were allowed to play, and the game was in honour of the Gods, with some cosmic meaning concerning the movement of the sun, moon and planets. The ball game had very deep symbolical significance and we find it mentioned repeatedly in the Popul Vuh. The various characters there are always playing against their superiors, whether angelic or diabolical, and the result may mean survival, or not, as the case may be. It seems to have been a dangerous game, in every way. Sometimes, the losing players, or at least their captain, was sacrificed.

Another day, we were taken to see Mitla, which was really a shrine, a holy of holies rather than a ceremonial centre, and it was probably still in use when the Spanish came. Originally, there were four groups of low, flat-roofed palaces within plazas but there were no pyramids. Only the two central palaces are now still left standing. Two were taken over by the Spanish, who built there a church and parish house in their place. When archaeologists first came, they found the court of the palace was the Spanish priest's stable, and a whole section of murals had been destroyed to build a pig sty. Besides the murals, there were stone mosaics adorning the walls of the remaining plazas. There was also a temple with six huge columns reminiscent of Karnak, and said to be unique in Central America. Large subterranean passages and tombs were found under some of the buildings with entrances from the main patios. These were said to be entrances to the Underworld, and it was believed that Mitla stood on the site of the approach to the spirit world.

The most wonderful and, to us, original, part of the temples were the facades which have sunken panels or entablatures. The Zapotecs cut and polished blocks of trachyte (light coloured volcanic rocks) about the size and shape of Tapestry bricks. On one end, hardly more than one-inch-and-a-half in width, they carved part of the total design. Then, thousands of these blocks were fitted precisely together without mortar, and set in a facing of hard stucco painted red. Since the designs are an integral part of solid stone, they have worn evenly and well and have supported the walls against earthquakes and time.

The designs are taken from the sacred symbol of the Staircase Sign found in the very early levels of the Tiahuanaca ruins and which appear everywhere in Mexico. This staircase design rises two or three steps, the last often ending in a spiral to signify Heaven and Earth, or the stepped spiral that represents the head of the Sky Serpent. But what do these designs signify? Surely, again, that Man can rise above himself. Collin Smith referred to them as representing different levels of energy. He also said that he understood that these designs appeared to those who had taken mescalin, which undoubtedly the priests used. I had the impression, as I watched them in the strong sunshine, that they were moving rapidly. Perhaps there is a link here with the old observatory on Monte Alban, and were the mathematical relations between the heavenly bodies, which the astronomers worked out so precisely, developed into an astrological mysticism which linked them with people and the divination of human fate. Can they be taken as symbols of celestial mechanics? Or do they represent different elements, for example, thunder and lightning? One feels there is a host of meaning here we do not understand.

Before leaving Mexico City for Yucatan we were able to watch some members of Mr. Collin-Smith's group doing "movements". They had learnt several of the Obligatories and some Dervish numbers. They were practising for a small demonstration. Previously when this group, who had been studying astronomy, had given a demonstration of the movements of the planets, the sun and moon and their relationship to each other and this had proved most effective. Now they were trying to find movements which would express their group.

The next day was our last in Mexico City, and before we left, we called on the archaeologists who had been in charge of excavations, Mr. Acosta about Tula, Monte Alban and the Mayan pyramid of Chichen Itza, and then a nice chat to Mr. Noguira who gave us some helpful hints about Peruvian museums.

After a farewell lunch with the Collin-Smiths, we left by air for Yucatan, landing at Merida, and had our first introduction to the Mayan cities of Uxmal and Kabah. Their most important God was the "Rain" God – since rain, in this area, was scarce and hard to come by. The Mayans also fashioned circular cisterns on concrete catchments for their water, which would run down and be collected in a circular well. The whole system was so marvellously fashioned that it is still in use today.

Chichen-Itza, which we visited next day, has been widely excavated, as it was owned at one time by Mr. Thompson, the American Consul General, brother of the writer. He dragged the lake there, and many of the treasures found were sent to the Peabody museum at Harvard, and therefore American funds were further used to excavate there. The Mayan art found here was further strengthened by the Toltecs who came up from Tula and conquered Chichen-Itza and they helped to build the great observatory, the dominating pyramid with its nine terraces and 91 steps and other pyramids and a magnificent ballcourt (already mentioned.)Certainly, the Toltecs started new and warlike influences among the Mayans. They introduced the queer, statuesque Atlantean figures to Chichen-Itza as well as the plumed serpent and that queer reclining form, whose purpose was not known, the "Chac-mool" half God, half man - possibly a representation of life or "sleeping man".

With hurricanes, pestilences and internal wars, the end of the great Mayan Empire came and the Spanish Conquistandores put the finishing touches.

The following day, we flew on to Guatemala City to see another Mayan stronghold buried deep in the jungle called "Copan".

Central America – Guatemala, Honduras and Panama - proved to be rather more difficult to travel in. Most of the inhabitants are so busy making money, or existing on practically nothing,that they care very little for their heritage or the ruins that lie practically at their doorsteps. Neither have they any particular desire to show them to visitors.

Mr. Nicols, the Willys representative, met us at the airport with his entire family and two large bouquets, and with these extra items we had to go through the customs, and when we were rather wearily installed in his car, we found a whole family of newly purchased birds (in cages) already in the car! Although Mr. Nicols had been told of our archaeological interests, he had made no arrangements for them and we had to spend the rest of that day battling with travel agents and airlines where we found that in order to view Copan, we needed to fly on to Tirgucigalpa, capital of Honduras, and take a plane there for Copan.

We were taken to Antigua to dinner that evening, a rather precarious journey, as the car was misfiring, and while it was being repaired, we had an excellent dinner and listened to eight men performing on a kind of double xylophone, a national instrument, so I understood, here very melodious and charming, while romantic young officers sauntered in and out of the restaurant, part of the retinue, I was told, that were part of the conference of Central American Military Staff. We were later shown the conference halls and offices in the University building, part of the "ruins" that Mr. Nicol thought we should see in Antigua!

We were met the next day at Tegusi airport by Willy's Representative, Mr. Jim Walters, and we were delighted to find that there was plenty of room for us and our bags. Mr. Walters quickly informed us that the airtickets obtained in Guatemala City for Copan were no good and many manoevres had to be made to permit us to take an "air taxi" to and from Copan the following day. In fact, this almost failed us also as the pilot, who was due to take us, had another "rush" job to perform first, fetching and carrying to hospital a man who had been shot. However, with a certain amount of persistence and patience, Copan was finally in sight, after a rather precarious air trip above the rainforests and over high hills and deep valleys - we landed on a rough runway by the ruins. We were delighted to be practically alone with Copan amidst mounds of fallen masonry, extraordinary stone stelae, grotesque stone heads and glyphs over which the jungle had grown, large trees were growing up amidst pyramids and flights of steps. There was only a Spanish guide book available, but a little English Guide book was fetched for us and Marjorie and I did our best to find our way amongst the ruins climbing up and down, photographing some of the stone heads, the ball court and hieroglyphic stairway and the stone altars, on which were recorded the important happenings of the time.

After having our picnic lunch on the steps of a large pyramid, we made our way back to the little airstrip where we took a ride in a truck to the local museum and a drink of coca cola and then waited by the airstrip until our little air taxi appeared with an American pilot to take us away. Jim Edwards told us his whole life story while we soared up over the forests and mountain peaks to the airport at Honduras.

Next day, the Walters invited us to view a modern agricultural school at Zamorano, run by the Standard Fruit Company. The valley where the school was situated did not have very good soil, since it was thought that the students from the city should work in conditions nearly appropriating their own. They were busy crossing breeds of pigs and we saw cattle, poultry and turkeys there. There were also gardens with English vegetables with a green garden in the centre where the staff had their homes. The school was self supporting and had its own laundry, class rooms and mess.

The Walters family lived on one of the sides of the hills which surround the city. Mr. Walters Senior came from Manchester, England many years ago and never went back. He married an American lady from Connecticut. They had a son and daughter.

The following day, when we were due to depart, we discovered to our dismay that all sorts of exit permits were necessary before we would be allowed to leave the country, and as the airlines refused to take any active part in obtaining these permits we threw ourselves upon the mercy of the local "high class" grocer from whom my sister was buying cigarettes, and who proved to us that chivalry was still alive in some hearts when he gallantly accompanied us from exit permit authorities to Police and back. Then Papa and Mama Walters drove us to the airport in their luxurious Chrysler car, their son having escaped on a hunting trip over the weekend.

Panama was to be our next destination, and we boarded our plane, and with two hops, we swiftly descended to it, but were held up at immigration for sometime after landing, only one officer on duty for the whole plane load of passengers. Then we were whisked away by our Willy's Representative, Mr. Robbins, eighteen miles to our hotel in the American zone, the "luxurious" El Panama. It was hot and sticky here and we were glad to have cool quarters, although a corner house opposite our window screamed and hissed jazz until 5 am that morning. We were able to catch up with our diaries, do some shopping and catch up on our sleep before boarding our next plane, importantly named "El Interamericano" of the Panagara Airlines - at 4.30 am for Lima, Peru.

At 7 am a cheery stewardess offered to serve us breakfast and we had our first view of Peru. Canyons and craters of sand everywhere, with the high Andes mountains on one side and the blue sea on the other side. This time when we flew into Lima Airport, we were quickly and efficiently pushed through the customs and were greeted by our Willy's Representative and a "group" member, Mr. Schuster. When we reached our hotel, the Bolivar, we quickly unpacked and tucked ourselves up in bed for a few hours' sleep. Then we drove out and saw some of Lima's residential suburbs situated on wide streets lined with shady trees, flowering bushes, canna lilies, geraniums and gladioli, and then out along the seafront to Miraflores and the Country and Yacht Clubs. This was their summer season and there was little rain, so the population depended upon irrigation ditches and water from the Andes and hose pipes. Next day, we drove along the Pan American Highway, where the sandy deserts touched the road in some places and the mists from the sea came down and obscured our view of Pachacarmac, which was older than Lima, a most important Peruvian centre, a ceremonial city, with a kind of Inca fort overlooking the sea and a much earlier temple "To the Creator God".

A further temple to the moon has been reconstructed near the Highway, with plastered walls and niches with a central ceremonial altar and pool with ingeniously thought out plumbing system: a kind of siphoning from one level to another. This monument was different from the Mexican ceremonial centres and shrines and we thought that there had been even less modern excavations here than in Mexico. Practically nothing is labelled properly or protected and very little has been written down.

We visited the town Museum where there are on display intricate woven Indian blankets and tapestries, pots with endless decoration, bas reliefs, etc. of a very varied culture. The exhibits came from the south, from Paracas and Nazca, from the necropolisis i.e. graveyards. The grounds are so dry that the grave clothes are all preserved. But who the people were, and even where they lived, was quite unknown.

For the next few days our visit to Lima was gay with carnival festivities, bands and decorated floats processed outside our hotel in the square. The custom of throwing water and cheap scent was successfully evaded by our kind friends who frequently took us out in their cars.

After a day when our Willy's Jeep guide took us out of Lima to wine and dine on chickens cooked deliciously on spit irons over a charcoal fire and drinking "Vicious Virgin" cocktails in cocoanut shells, we returned to Lima and from the relative safety of the Hotel porch watched the procession of "floats", the grand climax of the carnival and our friend, the travel agent, Mrs. Cook, from the air office, told us that her daughter was one of the beauty queens whose float won a first prize.

The next day, our friend Carlos Matchelajaoic, called to take us out in his car, and he told us about some of the customs of the Indians. He told us that he had heard that on Good Friday night, the Indians become quite wild and they invade the burial grounds, dig up the graves and rob them, scattering and trampling on the bones far and wide. He himself had not believed that this was true, until he and a friend had been out on an expedition and had seen for themselves with their own eyes people doing it. They apparently believe that God is dead and that there is no power that can harm them. Carlos took us to see some of these old burial grounds near by where bits of cotton cloth were lying in disorderly array everywhere and already this old cemetery was being used for new burials since there were fresh graves with stones and crude little crosses on them.

There were many "haciendas" nearby and we were told that the Indians working for these haciendas were badly paid, sometimes they got nothing at all and a state of almost "slavery" existed there. There were few churches there and no schools. The Indians care very little about money and live on practically nothing at all, but one cannot help but feel that this state of a few very rich Peruvians, apparently caring very little for their fellow men, will be levelled up someday. We talked also to our Peruvian "work" friend, Mr. Costa, and he thinks it is possible that some of the early traditions from the very early civilizations have been kept alive and that when the time is ripe they will show themselves. There is certainly evidence to show that in the jungle regions in Brazil and near the Amazon river, there may live groups of people unknown to the white man who may have been able to preserve something. Certainly, they are waiting for the end of the epoch of the "white man" and they believe that now to be near.

After an abortive attempt to get to Cusco, our next calling place, when the weather conditions were too bad and the flight was postponed, we rang our nice Mrs. Cook in Lima and she booked us into the hotel for another night as well as booking us an air trip for the following day.

Another early rising at 5.30 am turned out to be a little more successful, although the plane was late in starting. Our cargo consisted of a mass of small children with their parents, who we thought must have been on a brief vacation in Lima. However, we finally reached Cusco and our plane descended between the mountains to a tiny airport and amidst a jumble of guides, visitors, lookers-on and others we were ushered out to waiting automobiles and quickly driven to the Tourist Hotel, where we settled down for a little rest.

The whole town is built on the beautiful "Inca" stone foundation - large rounded stones, beautifully fitted together without mortar, but interlocked so that they have withstood constant earthquakes and the ravages of time. There are narrow paved streets running up the sides of the hill and groups of Indians in their wide and brightly coloured skirts and wraps with their high crowned panama hats sit or walk about. The Indian men wear heavy blankets or ponchos over their shoulders and trousers, sometimes knee-length. These clothes, of course, dated from Spanish times and were not their original clothes. These Indians own their own herds of sheep, goats or llamas and they cut, comb and spin the wool of these animals and dye them in lovely bright colours and then weave them for their clothes.

Cusco is known to have been a sacred city from the very earliest time and may date back to pre-Inca days. According to some, the word "Cusco" meant in Quechu "Indian Navel" and this may have meant that it formed the central position of the sacred cities with Tiahuanaca at the feet, Pachacarmac the heart and another sacred city in Quito (Equador) the head. The old glories were badly damaged by the Spanish and one can only imagine how glorious it's Cooricanchi (Temple of the Sun) looked since only a foundation of Inca Stone is left standing. It had occupied over 17,520 square feet and contained a refulgent gold disc representing the sun which was placed at the eastern end of the line in such a way and the rays of the sun falling upon it at dawn illuminated the whole sanctuary. There were further sanctuaries dedicated to the moon, Venus, Thunder and Lightening and Rainbow. Now only some of the foundation stones are left, but even these stones show the extraordinary technique known to these early builders which made for greater solidity of the whole structure and accounts for their standing today when the younger buildings convents, churches, etc. have all fallen in recent earthquakes.

Other ancient sites near Cusco which we visited were the fort at Sacsayhuamar, above the city and the ruins of Ollantaytambo, some distance away in the sacred valley of Viracocha.

From hot Panama, we sped to Lima, Peru, over the coast and in full view of the snow-capped Andes. There is nothing quite like this: the Andes lined up on the left, then the great coastal desert, with occasional patches of green where the rivers run, and the sparkling sea on the right.

Lima and the Bolivar Hotel seemed almost European and stable beside Mexico, although the poverty amongst the poorer people and especially the Indian groups, was soon evident. We were met by a charming couple, the Schusters, members of the Collin Smith group there, and later they introduced us to other members, notably Carlos Matchelavjovic, of Baltic stock, like my sister's husband, who became our chief friend and guide in Lima.

In many respects the stories of South and Central America are similar. They both go back long before the coming of the Spaniards and, in Peru, like Mexico, it is always difficult to tell the boundary between Inca and pre-Inca, so few of the older ruins have been explored.

The Incas, whom the Spaniards under Pizarro destroyed as Cortes had the Mexicans, were a much more admirable people than the Aztecs. Their rulers were complete autocrats but, like the Romans they at least had some system of government which looked after all their peoples. The ruins around Lima, notably Pachacarmac, are different from the Mexican ceremonial centres and shrines. There is a large ruined temple to the Creator God, built by no-one knows whom, and an Inca sun temple, set on a high place and built up in more of a fort plan than a pyramid. There is also a temple to the moon. Our main impression was that there had been much less excavation here even than in Mexico; that nothing is labelled properly or protected and very little has been written down. But wonderful things turn up to astound one: for instance, in the large town museum there are wonderful woven Indian Blankets and tapestries, pots with endless decoration, bas reliefs etc, a very varied culture, or cultures. Where did they all come from? What type of man produced these varied embroideries, for instance? Nobody knows. The exhibits came from the south, from Paracas and Nazca, from the necropolises, i.e. graveyards. The grounds are so dry that the grave clothes were all preserved. But who the people were, and even where they lived, was quite unknown.

It is an extraordinary thing to drive up some pleasant valley near Lima, as we did, climb a hill and find curious 'etchings' or broken shards depicting odd faces, sun signs, snakes and long flat lines. Nothing appeared known about our finds except that they came from a temple called Amuk, which had fallen long ago.

It was all overwhelming, but we decided to fly to Cusco, the head of the Inca Empire, to see what we could there. The journey was trying. The smaller planes were not pressurised and oxygen had to be taken from a tube by one's seat, in a long cold and unpleasant draft through the mouth. I found myself nervous too: was I stifling, did I really need oxygen? And so forth.

Cusco is at one end of the Sacred Valley of the Virachocha – fertile land which is watered by the Urubamba, which runs into the Amazon. Originally it held palaces of the Incas and other ruling families, and is certainly one of the most beautiful places in the world. Vivid colours, snowy mountains, beautiful flowers and grasses, wonderful terracing reminiscent of the hanging gardens of Babylon, all made doubly beautiful by the vivid light and clear outlines. Not much habitation there, only a few 'haciendas' and simple Indian huts with straw-thatched roofs. But I am anticipating – actually, we did not see the beautiful valley until a day or two later when we were driving from Pisak to Ollantaytambo, and it stayed in my memory, as one of the loveliest places I have ever seen. A few Indians in colourful costume stroll along the roads, or squat looking after their flocks, sheep, oxen, goats, donkeys and mules, which tend to cross the road at the most dangerous moments!

Our first day was spent in Cusco and its environs and our first real excitement came when a herd of Llamas (pronounced Yamas) suddenly rushed down upon us from a nearby hill: brown and white beasts, with a queer dignity and character of their own. They are far more attractive than camels. I am told they will only carry a certain load; if it is too much, they lie down and refuse to move! There are three varieties of llamas: llamas proper, alpacas and vicunas – the latter have the softest and most valuable wool. The baby llama is the sweetest little beast.

Cusco is a very ancient city, certainly the holy city of the Incas, and probably dating to a race far further back. It must once have been wonderful, with its great temple to the sun, moon and stars, lesser temples to the gods, and charming palaces and residences, all built of slabs of stone so perfectly fitted that no earthquake ever toppled them. Around the city centre, we were told, stretched a chain of pure gold, which somehow mysteriously disappeared when the Spaniards came, and has been hunted for ever since. There was a golden disc representing the sun, and a silver one the moon, with jewelled circles for the planets. There were priests, vestal virgins (sacred women of the sun) and all manner of beautiful ceremonies – until the Spaniards destroyed everything.

One interesting comment is that in the 1950s an earthquake destroyed the churches but the "ruins" still stand. The church of Santo Domingo (over the sun temple) is in ruins still.

Mexico City celebrated human sacrifice, but Cusco and the Incas were an orderly and cultured people of quite a different order.

What would have happened if we, the British, in India, had destroyed the great Hindu temples of the south, the Mohametan buildings of Agra and Delhi, the caves of Elephanta, Ellora and Ajunta? Yet this is the equivalent of what the Spaniards did here. There is nothing left of the great sun temple (the Cooricanchi) today, except its perfectly fitted stone base, and indeed this is true of all Cusco: it literally lives on its Inca foundations. One sees them everywhere: under churches, government buildings, houses and roads; and one marvels at their perfection. What other things did these people know?

In the hills around Cusco are Inca forts and palaces; one known as Kquenco, being a sort of amphitheatre of stone seats with a large monolith, now ruined, in the centre, which appears to have been some sort of initiation centre. But the most extraordinary is the building at Sacsayhuaman, whose purpose is unknown, with its immense fitted stones, some cut concavely and some convexly depending upon the slope of the walls. It reminded me somehow of Stonehenge, although far more extensive and impressive. Much of this is not excavated at all, and its tower at the top, which is a circular enclosure, may have been a form of zodiac.

On February 19th we took the lovely trip by car to Pisak over the colourful hills to the Sunday market in the village square. Here the different villages send their people to exchange goods for what they need. It is almost barter, although I understand money is in fact used. The bare-footed women all wear long colourful skirts or dresses and wide gay hats. They weave the materials themselves (often we saw them spinning whilst walking along the road) and are expert with dyes. But these are the clothes the Spaniards taught them to wear, and not their original designs. Often they have a baby, or a bundle, or both strapped on their back beneath a large shawl. The women seem to carry most, the men lounging along, hands in pockets.

Small children start work early; it is very common to see a small boy or girl carrying a smaller infant on their backs. As a rule they do not mind being photographed, although, we were told, they believe something of the person goes into a photograph and the one taking it should pay something. We were quite often asked for tips: small children would murmur 'money' at us, as their Eastern compatriots cried 'Baksheesh' in older days. Sometimes they refuse to be photographed; I remember one lady in a beautiful orange hat, who took it off, and lay down on the ground under it. But mainly the

Indian silently observes the visitor with as much interest as he himself is observed. There is little he misses about the "gringo's" behaviour and dress, which he comments on in his own way.

Dirty and living in the most primitive conditions the Indians here, nonetheless, looked happy and healthy. Their main trouble seems to be the premature ageing of the women owing, I suppose, to over-work.

If the women do not wear the wide upturned brim hat, they wear a man's high white panama, usually with a coloured band. Such was the fashion in Cusco; in La Paz they all wore a sort of brown bowler.

The market was the usual square plaza where the Indian women sat on the ground in long lines, with their wares in front of them. Beautiful corn (double the size of the U.S. variety) seemed to be their main food, but there were many other vegetables, including varieties of the bean family, especially the broad bean, carrots, onions, marrows etc. Also plentiful were eggs, and there were chickens and some meat. Some women sold herbs and had many different coloured piles in front of them. We were told they were considered to be witches also, and often gave charms for various needs. We particularly noticed the quiet of the market, no-one was shouting, gesticulating, or playing radios as the Spanish and semi-Spanish do. But they all seemed quietly occupied and taking everything in. We both felt much more in tune with the Indians than with the rest of the population, and I was interested in a Peruvian comment on this, which I will relate later.

After leaving Pisak we had the beautiful 40 mile drive up the valley of the Urubamba River to Ollantaytambo. Only some fertile valley in Tibet can be anything like it – with its radiant atmosphere and feeling of happiness, youth and all possibilities – release from the strain of our civilisation and its complications. If one stayed there one would somehow become quite different. It was the beginning of the sensation we had later at Macchu Picchu.

Ollantaytambo came at the end of the valley as a fort to guard the entrance to it. It was sacked and destroyed by the Spaniards when they took Cusco, but this did not appear to be the beginning of its history, although what it started as, is difficult to say. It is beautifully placed on the side of a hill, and has some fine ceremonial stones of an immense size, at the top. Fortifications, dwellings, water cisterns and terraces for food, all made in careful stone jig-saw still stand today. You can climb to the top, which we did, and be rewarded by the magnificent view on both sides. But the climb is a great physical effort at the altitude.

The wonderful heights and sights of Cusco prepared us well for our next venture, the trip to Macchu Picchu, the city discovered only recently by Hiram Bingham.

We had decided to spend the night there as we arrived at Cusco station about 7 am to catch the famous 'Autocarril'. It was a nice little English-type tram, painted green, and made at Ware, Herts. This is for tourists only, and gets to Macchu Picchu in three to four hours; the regular train takes eight hours. Our little car was hauled from one level to another in a series of zig-zags to the top of the mountain behind Cusco. Then we started at a brisk pace along a fairly level patch, finally following the course of the little river Warakitta (phonetic). After some time and more zig-zags, we reached the gorge of the Urubamba, and ran along that mighty torrent until we again saw Ollantaytambo in the distance. After that the route, and the river, became wilder and wilder: huge rapids, dense jungle on either side of us, beautiful flowers including many wild orchids. I felt that we were really in the South American jungle at last. Finally we stopped at a quite ordinary little station which said 'Macchu Picchu', and transferred to two ancient Ford buses for the corkscrew ascent to the top of the mountain.

The peak of Macchu Picchu is an enormously high island with the Urubamba River running all around it. Everywhere one looks down sheer precipices to the river, and out at equally sheer drops on the adjacent snow-capped mountains. I never saw such a place. It is so vast and awesome that one forgets to be afraid of the immense depths.

Later we climbed high above the city to the cemetery from which Hiram Bingham is first supposed to have seen it (he climbed the mountain on the opposite side of the road and railway). The city is practically complete, undestroyed by the Spaniards who never found it, or could never reach it.

Archaeologists disagree about its origin. The popular verdict seems to make it a purely Inca conception, but some consider it was merely used by the Incas. Others suggest that neither Incas nor Spaniards ever found it. One authority suggests it was founded by Manco Capac and his wife (the first Inca, who appeared miraculously from the islands of the sun and moon in Lake Titicaca to found the Inca Empire). I would like to believe that, because for a school or initiation centre to be here, safe from everything, might have produced some wonderful results. The generally accepted dates seem to be that it was founded about 800 A.D. as a refuge for the descendants of the 'old regime', who fled from invaders. It later became the capital of the new empire, until it was abandoned for Cusco, about 1300. It was again used as a refuge, when the Spaniards came.

Since Bingham's discovery many smaller ruins have been discovered nearby, whilst five or six other cities on other peaks have come to light. At present there are no roads to them, but it is hoped to build these shortly. Huge populations must have lived here once a complete enigma to the outside world. How many more cities will be found in unexplored Peru, Bolivia and Brazil.

Many people claim that Macchu Picchu is only interesting because the Spaniards never discovered it. We found this quite erroneous; its size and completeness, its position and atmosphere make it unique. Also (as we found in the Alhambra in Granada) one is still in touch, in a curious way, with its old inhabitants. They might have only just left.

The city is entered from the top of the mountain, in the cemetery area, by a gate which still stands. Inca roads ran all over the mountain and were guard houses and nearby a wild puma tethered as an extra deterrent. Its post is still there, as indeed are several others, notably one near the Inca's palace, and another near the Holy of Holies. The beasts were used like guard dogs.

One walks down the beautifully proportioned steps, through the little streets of 'high class' houses to the palace of the Inca and royal family; the royal bath and the Inca's seat commanding one of the most beautiful views. Below this were the royal tombs, the sacred enclosure and priests' houses leading up to the sacred sundial on a specially constructed hill.

The temple proper has three large windows, three altars, and seven niches in the wall above – a play of three and seven everywhere.* The sundial, reached by steps, is supposed to be for astronomical purposes (it has complicated lines and planes) but there is also a sacrificial stone. Sitting quietly here, surveying the immense grandeur and with the river thundering in the distance, gives one strange impressions. From here you can see the highest peak of Macchu Picchu with its beautifully cut terraces, and a little temple at the summit. How anyone ever walked up there, let alone cut the steps and planted things is quite beyond our comprehension. The Indian of those days must have been far more aware and in control of his physical presence than we now are.

* According to Gurdjieff, the Law of Three (Triamazikamno) and the Law of Seven (Heptaparaparshinokh) are the two great laws of the Universe from which everything is developed.

The slopes everywhere are terraced for crops. Water was brought in an aqueduct from the mountain through the city and down the main Street in a series of fountains. They are still there, and we walked down this steep street tracing out the water ducts as they ran from one level to the other.

The street of fountains leads to several squares and plazas, where the markets and fiestas were held, and to the houses and shops of the ordinary people. Staircases everywhere, and one can explore indefinitely, unless one is afraid of 'Mr. Viper'. Still lower than the town houses are rock tombs. We spent three half-days exploring and we could have stayed much longer.

Our host, Mr. Soto, who knew Hiram Bingham, was a real character with a fine library. How lucky we were ever to have got there. My sister expressed her appreciation to our host with tears in her eyes, and he remarked quietly: "Yes, you have been looking all the time. Some tourists do not see anything."

The Incas certainly used and modernised the old cities. Their sacred cities were Cusco, the 'navel' as it was called: Pachacarmac and a city in the north near Quito, Ecuador, all linked by ancient roads. Lima is a comparatively modern town founded by the Spaniards.

Frederico Costa had some interesting theories. He believed that there was a similar layout here to the old Mexican cities (i.e. the moon temple of Teotihuacan is the head; the sun, the heart and the processional way the spinal cord). He told us the Indians still travel en masse, at certain seasons, from north to south, and back again. No-one knows much about these movements, except that they take place. He also believed that many of the archaic treasures, and much of the ancient knowledge has survived, and was never found by the Spaniards. Indian mythology speaks of five ages, of which the fourth is the present one starting with white domination. The tradition is that this will shortly pass, and the fifth age will come when the Indian will come into his own again.

Our last researches led us to Lake Titicaca and Tiahuanaco, that most ancient of cities.

We left, by plane, for La Paz, Bolivia, the highest airport in the world. The pilot pointed out to us the extraordinary lines of the Nazca plateau, of which we were to see much more on our next trip to Peru.

At La Paz we had no members of our group to help us, but my brother-in-law's 'distributor' and his wife came to meet and look after us and could not have been kinder.

We went for a boat ride on Lake Titicaca which we had already flown over the previous day. One's main impression is of an unearthly and heavenly blue, very still water surrounded by snow-capped mountain peaks. Collin Smith had described it to my sister as "a region left untouched from some immeasurably ancient time". We encountered a group of fishermen in their ancient balsa boats. We had hoped to visit the sacred islands of the sun and moon but, alas, they were too far away.

The next day our friends took us to Tiahuanaco. It was most uncertain whether we should ever get there, as the road was the worst we have ever travelled. But at last there was Tiahuanaco and its famous Gate of the Sun, ready for our inspection. The city must have been enormous and densely populated. Also climatic conditions must have been quite different from today, as both Bellamy and Posnansky maintain.* Either the place was surrounded by water, or it must have been on Lake Titicaca. Beyond that we got a feeling of familiarity and home: Avebury came to mind when we saw the large standing stones of the Kalasasaya Temple and, indeed, Posnansky's book mentions this likeness. He considers the Kalasasaya temple was a true solar observatory located on the astronomic meridian, and the Gate of the Sun a magnificent stone calendar.

The Gate of the Sun, and the great stone statues with their extra-ordinary detailed markings must surely stand from some intricate calculations or possibly, some form of language. But we drank our American cocktails on the ancient stones, and I hope the gods forgave us! I think they must, because by incredible chance we managed to meet Mme. Posnansky on our short visit and to obtain her husband's book, as well as help from her.

Tiahuanaco is one of the most mysterious cities in the world. Its roots go far back in time. But why was it built at this inaccessible height? Or was it built at coast level, as some think, and thrown up to this height by the earth in her movements? Experts scoff at such an idea, but cannot solve its mysteries themselves. The late Arthur Posnansky lived in La Paz and made most of the excavations and studies of the district. He believed that a very early race of people, the Khollas, originally developed the city, like so much of Mexico and Peru and that they were great builders and astronomers.

Before closing this chapter, I want to put in some notes about the great country of Brazil, which is as large as the U.S.A. with an extra Texas!

* H.S. Bellamy, Built before the Flood; Arthur Posnansky, Tiahuanaco.

Most travellers there know the beautiful bay on which Rio de Janeiro lies, Sugar Loaf Mountain and the spectacular beach of Copacabana. But if one goes further into this lovely land, what strikes a traveller first, is the enormous variety of races. There seems no limit to variously coloured people everywhere and everybody appears to be happy with everyone else. There is, apparently, no race problem. There was no monopoly or friction but more racial groups than I have seen before.

How is it that such possibilities have developed in our time, something so different from the other side of the continent, in Peru, and other western states conquered by the Spanish? It speaks very highly for the Portuguese. They seem to have traded and fraternised with the native peoples, instead of conquering them and destroying their cultures. The Christian churches alone in Bahia and Ouro Preto, the old towns, are far more beautiful than the heavy Spanish architecture in Peru, and they seem to have given birth to a regular school of architecture and sculpture, notably of Aleijadinho, a native sculptor of genius. He had a dreadful form of leprosy and lost most of his limbs, but in spite of this, his strong fine sculpture shows no negativity. His most famous works are the statues of 12 prophets outside the Sanctuary Senor Bom Jesus at Congohas do Campo, near Belo Horizonte.

Our next stop was a complete contrast to the old, namely the new capital, Brasilia. It is an astonishing place formed in the shape of an aeroplane (or a bird, some say a bow and arrow), and is modern from end to end. One wonders how well it will last. The hotel, the Brasilian Palace, the first building to be put up, was already shabby. The President's Palace and his helicopter base are very forward-looking and impressive and so, too, are the Congress buildings. We were very thrilled with the building on first arrival; the next morning we were not quite so sure! When we went everything was unfinished with thousands of workmen everywhere, all of whom seemed to originate from a shanty town called "the Free City". But this was all 20 years ago. Possibly now the bird-aeroplane-bow city is much more mature and inundated by modern technology.

In early 1961 we were visiting the old capital of Brazil, Bahia (Salvatore). We were fortunate to be there for one of the New Year Candomble (Voodoo) ceremonies. This represents there a fully-fledged religion: Christian in principle but mixed with ancient African rites. Our only other companions were an Israeli couple who spoke good English and were very helpful, as they were studying the subject of voodoo.

We drove some distance to a country area outside the city where the ceremony was already in progress. The company of negroes welcomed us most pleasantly and carefully placed a bench for us. Girls in white were singing and dancing, some softly and some wildly. Two women appeared to be in charge, dressed oddly in leather costumes adorned with peacocks' feathers. It suddenly struck us as rather similar to a Subud Latihan, with the same idea, apparently, of "casting out devils" or purification. There also seemed to be simple attempts at healing, some successful, others not. The worst feature, which certainly had nothing to do with Subud, was the sacrifice of a chicken which made us feel very peculiar.

After a couple of hours we decided to leave, and the two "priestesses" came over to say goodbye with a "Brazilian embrace" – similar to the Russian one. My sister braced herself for this, but it was not unpleasant, simply a primitive earthy force. The high priestess suddenly looked straight at her and spoke. What she was sure she heard was "You Know". As few people in Bahia spoke English, (Portuguese being the 'European' language), I think she must have got it by telepathy. A very strange experience, and one wishes one could understand more clearly these unknown forces.

Part 2

In our 1956 trip to Peru we had covered a great deal of historical ground, Inca and pre-Inca, with Cusco and the mysterious city of Macchu Picu, but we had done little with the country north and south of Lima. These parts were equally interesting both from geological and historical points of view, so as soon as we arrived in Lima for our second visit there, in 1961, we arranged an elaborate trip to Trujillo, the northern capital, and Callejon de Huaylas (the Switzerland of Peru) the home of Chavin, one of the most ancient centres. I have seen castes of the very individual and extraordinarily carved stones from the latter site in the Lima Museum, but their originals were still in Chavin itself, a most difficult site to reach, as it was necessary to cross the high Cordillera Blanca on a more than dubious road.

So we engaged a car (a rather aged Dodge) and an English speaking Peruvian, who answered to the name of Ralph.* We nicknamed him 'Saint Rafael' as he turned out to be a real hero. We were first to proceed to the Callejon de Huaylas, a long high valley lying between two ranges of the Andes (the Cordillera Negra, with

*Raphael Aparicio

no snow, and the higher, the Cordillera Blanca, with snow) to its capital Huaraz. According to schedule, we were supposed to go from Lima to Huaraz, about 216 miles, in one day, and then stay for four nights.

Partly owing to the bad road we did not realise the time the trip would take. After leaving Pativilca on the main Pan American Highway from Lima, we took a ghastly metal road similar to the horrors one finds in New Zealand. Added to road troubles, our car was difficult: boiling at intervals and stopping. We went on all day, and finally, as dusk was approaching, discovered we had a great distance to cover. We felt rather alarmed, as the car had proved unreliable, and there seemed a possibility that we might be left out all night. However, after telephoning at a nearby town, to check that our accommodation was secured, we finally arrived, weary and cold and 10,000 feet high. It was very cold, especially after Lima.

When we arrived at the hotel triumphantly, the front of our car fell into a hole and had to be extricated before reaching the hotel.

Next day our car was overhauled, and we took a short trip around the picturesque villages full of brightly dressed Indians.

The following day we started at 8 am for Chavin, our great excursion from here. We retraced our steps to Recuay along the gorge of the River Santa, intending to take the only road to Chavin open, from Catac several miles further on. As we left Catac, Ralph asked the tailor, working in the last shop in the village, whether the Chavin road was open. The tailor thought a bit, and then said he supposed so, as two trucks had come through two days previously! Heavy rain could wreck these mountain roads at any time; and we were at the beginning of the rainy season!

Never have I seen such a road! It was rough all the way with enormous precipices and horse-shoe bends. First we climbed to the top of the Pass of Cahuish, (13,600 feet) then down in endless long swoops. In the bright sunshine the scenery was glorious beyond words.

Chavin is a hidden shrine, about 6,600 feet high in beautiful country. Hardly ever have I seen such views. It has been devastated by everyone, but still holds a flavour of its beautiful peace and devotion, which is strengthened when one looks at the little relics in the Huaraz Museum afterwards.A landslide came down on the Palace here, obliterating most of the top storeys. Much that is left consists of curious underground chambers carefully planned and built, for what purpose no-one knows. I have heard it referred to as an underground city. In one of these chambers is a most original sculptured stone idol, or monument, actually hanging from the ceiling. The beautiful carving on this strange triangular-shaped monolith is of some feline deity known as the Lanzon (spear). There is a replica of the piece in the Lima Museum, but this gives no idea of the reality. Even seen under the difficulties we encountered (rough footing, pitch dark except for a candle, noisy children constantly getting in the way) it was most remarkable and had great atmosphere. We were told the Great Spear monolith must be viewed in both directions, ascending and descending. Its many parts have also many meanings, and it really represents 'The Stone which Came Down from Heaven'. This marks the end of the Great Work according to the symbolism of the builders. (One is reminded of Moses and the Ten Commandments.) From Chavin, also, was taken the Raimundi stone which is now in the Lima Museum; it stood in front of the main building. Also there are some curious carved heads on the wall, which again do not resemble at all their replicas in the museum.*

The legend runs that first came the gigantic Huaris who settled in the fertile valleys on the far side of the white Cordillera. These Herculeans were followed by their descendants who returned to the Callejon, and spread out through the vast land. Behind the complex mythological and symbolic language, there is a source of metaphysical concepts, a way of looking at Nature and at Man which is father to a great primordial tradition that goes back to humanity's beginnings; to the Valley of the Euphrates and the Nile, and from the Mediterranean to the Far East.** 1.

The creative force of these first inhabitants who were able to live in peace and develop such high culture, inspired by the deep desire for the sublime and transcendental, which is so passionately and

* The Stela Raimundi is described as an extremely formal carving of the feline deity, with a huge headdress consisting of cat-like faces and snakes' heads. It is considered to be a forerunner of certain Nazca designs. This isolated valley contains the ruins of the most elaborate centre of the first period, that of the Chavin culture. The site is composed of a number of construction units arranged in a somewhat symmetrical pattern. High stone-faced platforms on the north and south flank a square sunken court, about 157 feet on one side. On the west is a raised terrace which serves as a base for the Castello, the main building whose external appearance is that of a great solid block, but actually the interior is a honeycomb of three floors of galleries, rooms and ventilation shafts. All very damaged by recent landslides. (From Ancient Arts of the Andes, Wendell C. Bennett.)

** 1. Huella (Traces), p.25. Privately Published. Courtesy of Dr. Courtenay Mayers vividly described in their works. Chavin was a land of the living; all that is left is a message in stone. Their deity was Viracocha, eternal Master and Sun of the Sun. Viracocha is the Civiliser and Benefactor God who incarnates the fecundity of life in the triumph over nature, Sun of the Sun. A beautiful hymn to Viracocha is as follows:

'O Creator! O Conquering Viracocha! Ever-present Viracocha!
Thou who art equal unto the end of the earth!
Thou who givest life and strength to mankind, saying let this be a man, and let this be a woman; and as thou sayest so thou givest life, and vouchsafest that men shall live in health and peace and free from danger!
Thou who dwellest in the heights of heaven, in the thunder and in the storm-clouds, hear us, and grant us eternal life!
Have us in thy keeping, and receive this our offering, as it shall please thee, O Creator!'*

We had beautiful weather for all this. The gods of Chavin welcomed us, we felt, and cared for us on our passage to see them.

However, we had an adventure coming back. Our car stalled completely on its way up the mountain, with miles of hill ahead of us and no other traffic on the road. It also started to rain. I shall never forget our car at an angle, Indians camped opposite us in a sort of wigwam; an Indian lady offering me two raw potatoes, an incredible courtesy as it was all she had to eat; rain pouring down, and our conscientious Ralph moving heaven and earth to get us started. Over an hour dragged by; we tried to make plans, but there were none possible, and a night on the cold mountain side would have been unimaginable under the circumstances. However, suddenly the car started, and our world became possible again. But only just! We still had many miles of uphill zigzags to gain the Pass of Cahuish, where we could probably coast down to Catac and get help. But would the car stall again before we reached the top? We sat firmly in our seats and willed the thing to go on. Fortunately we finally reached the tunnel, and paused for a few moments before beginning the slope down.

We insisted that Saint Rafael must have hot coffee (we had a flask) and change his dripping shirt before we proceeded. He had been outside working on the car in the drenching rain and refused to do

* 2. Thomas Joyce, South American Archaeology, p.160. Hymn translated by Sir Clement Markham.

anything until we reached the top. He also thenexplained to us, confidentially, that he had just been in hospital with heart trouble. But, he said, all right for a man to be on the mountain all night, but not two ladies! We thankfully coasted downhill, through Catac and home to Huaraz. We were approaching the hotel when the car, literally, fell through the road. We were stunned but quite unhurt, and several workmen nearby rushed to lift us out. They had been working on the water pipes, and presumably the recent rain did the rest.

The following Sunday we motored north to Trujillo, which is a fair-sized old-fashioned town, rather nice at first with its pleasant, large open hotel. There was an interesting museum whose curator was very kind as he sent a boy to show us Chan Chan, a huge and hot Chimu city with extensive and tumbledown buildings outside the modern Trujillo. We also saw the site of Moche, and the Huacas of the Sun and Moon, the former an immense, very damaged, pyramid in adobe brick. Enormous populations must have lived here in the old days and one imagines the whole valley fertile and well watered.

Finally we took the long trip back from Trujillo to Lima (about 550 kms. as I remember) with its massive desert stretches, mile after mile, broken only by a few green patches where the rivers are. Certainly IRRIGATION, in capital letters, is the only solution.

I must record the great Paramonga Fortress, built by the Chimu people. This was a comparatively modern culture, conquered finally by the Incas, but the stories of the fantastic Court of the Great Chimu were well-known, even in Europe. This fortress represented the lower boundary of the Chimu Kingdom and stands out magnificently for all to see.

We also paid a visit to the Museum of Don Rafael Larco Hoyle at Lima. Augusto Alderaz-Calderon, son-in-law of Larco Hoyle, whom we had met through our Subud contacts, showed us around. I have never seen such an extensive collection anywhere of gold and jewels and examples of the Mochican and Chimu art of the country. We had a long talk with our guide, who wanted to start a branch of the Institute over here and use the Museum as a study of Ancient Man. Unhappily this has never come to pass.

The southern coastal cultures of Ica, Paracas and Nazca seem to have a curious link with Chavin, although they are presumed considerably later in date. The link is assumed mainly through their type of pottery, as almost nothing appears to be known about the people themselves. In the case of Paracas, pottery and wonderfully woven grave clothes come from the Paracas Necropolis and Cavernas, their graves, which the extraordinarily dry climate seems to have preserved indefinitely.

Nazca, rather further inland, boasts the extraordinary Lines or Signs, which cover a large part of the desert nearby; a desert which has been unchanged for thousands of years, owing to special climatic conditions. Very little, in 1961, appeared to be known, or even mentioned in the archaeological books about these curious drawings of lines, animals and bird figures, strangely stylised like the pottery on the desert. We had learned from Maria Reiche, on our earlier trip to Peru in 1956, something of these phenomena, as she herself was the only person who had been continuously investigating them. All appeared to have been made by the same method, merely by removing the suntanned stones of the desert to reveal the lighter ones underneath. In other words, 'the prehistoric "draughtsmen" simply scraped away the dark surface layer and left a shallow depression, along the edges of which they deposited dark stones'.*

Miles and miles of straight lines branching in all directions, figures, spirals, circles, and some extraordinary geometrical angles and rectangles on the top of the Andean foot hills are the results of this treatment. It is practically impossible to pick out any pattern if one is on the ground. Miss Reiche worked from a stepladder. The lines on the foot hills can only be seen when one flies over them. Nothing was known of them until our "aeroplane times", an astonishing thought.

On account of bad roads and considerable distances, we ourselves hired a small Cessna plane, whose pilot had the wonderfully suitable name of Gonsalo de Solar. We made for the south towards Paracas and Nazca, and landed almost anywhere we felt inclined to at intervals: roads, desert, beach, small air clubs and, once, someone's estate where the owner rushed out and greeted us most warmly. At Paracas Bay we looked at the local museums and then took to the air again to fly over the foothills and their strange marks. What did the early inhabitants use them for, these curious "burnt-in" angles and rectangles? Our pilot repeated again: "We never knew they existed until 1942 when pilots began to fly over here."

Was this some sort of air strip? Did men know how to fly on some sort of disc, as is rumoured in early myths? Or are these myths early warnings of flying saucers, or Unidentified Flying Objects, as they are now called? Present-day man is constantly boasting that he is the first to fly and land on the Moon, and many other things. I wonder whether he knows anything about this? Or were the lines astronom-

* Maria Reiche: Prehistoric Ground Drawings in Peru.

ical instruments, like the Mayans used for their huge pyramids? Or were they both? As usual we had no answers and no-one seemed to be worrying about it.

We went back to the Lima Museum to look at the wonderful pieces of weaving, needlework and pottery. How elaborate, exquisite and colourful they were, utilising practically all known stitches in embroidery.

Who were all these unknown souls, and are we likely, some day, to dig up some more marvellous cultures, which even we do not know anything about?

I would like to mention that we flew on to Santiago in Chile and had some interesting meetings with the little group who wished to work with Gurdieff there and who had sent up an emissary in England to ask for our help. My sister continued to write to them for many years afterwards.

Part 3

In 1961 we made another excursion in Mexico, rather similar to the Chavin one in Peru, to the mysterious beginnings of things. The dating map of the continent shows strange similarities between past events in Peru and Mexico right through their history until the Spanish conquest. Even the latter they both shared, unfortunately for them.

Our excursion this time was from Mexico City to the east, the Veracruz district. We actually stayed at Jalapa, the capital of the province, as we wished to see the New State Museum recently built there to house the Olmec heads from Tres Zapotes, and the Totonac and other remains from the area. The Olmec, or rubber people, appear to be, according to the experts, the earliest culture to appear in this part of the world along with Chavin in Peru. Like Chavin, little is exposed of its beginnings, and what there is, is very hard for the traveller to reach, as the great heads, without bodies, were until recently in the middle of the jungle. However, the Mexicans are very far-sighted. Instead of making copies, which never give the flavour or feeling of these old pieces, they built a modern but simple Museum, part outdoor and part indoor, and hauled all the contents from the jungle. This could not be done in one piece, as the rest of the Olmec remains were at La Venta, in another state, and their owners would not agree to it. So the heritage had to be divided: some going to the new Jalapa Museum, the others being housed in La Venta Park at Villahermosa in Tabasco.

Arrived at Jalapa, we went at once to see the new Museum, and found three great Olmec heads on the grassy part outside it. About five feet high, they make a startling impression upon the onlooker, which tends to increase (we saw them three times) each time one looks at them. They are all individualised heads, not as in Easter Island, standardised. Again the usual mystery. Have they always been without bodies like this? If they did originally have bodies, they must have been enormous. They have curious fitted caps on their heads, like football guards or flying helmets. Are they players of the sacred ball game, which we find in nearly every ceremonial centre, or aviators from another world?

We went into the museum proper, and found more huge heads, some badly damaged, one a large negroid one, and a most wonderful piece of sculpture, which it was suggested was the god of the animals. This latter piece, although damaged, still possessed some magnetic force but not at all savage or primitive, as one might expect.

The museum also contained much Totonac pottery and sculpture. These are jolly, simple people whom one sees all about their ceremonial centre El Tajin, near Pampantla. We had a lovely time exploring this delightful and unusual place, enormous and mainly unexcavated. The main building is called the Pyramid of the Niches. It has a character all its own, with the use of niches all over the building, a device not found elsewhere. These are 'architectural devices based on chiaroscuro - in other words, on the inter-play of light and shade, mystically connected with life and death. The interior of the niches was always painted red, the frame blue'.*

We liked the Totonacs, who appeared at intervals in groups, in spotless white clothes, and beamed at us in a most friendly way.

On a later visit to Mexico (in March 1966) we managed to visit the other half of the Olmec collection, although in an unsatisfactory way, as we struck a holiday period when all the parks and museums were officially closed. As we had planned a visit to Palenque, a fine ceremonial centre nearby, we went by plane to Villahermosa, the capital of Tabasco, where the other Olmec finds had been taken. Our time there was limited, and we never managed to see inside the Tabascan Museum, but we did manage by bribery to get into La Venta park for a few moments, and saw a few more of the unique Olmec sculptured pieces.

The further trip to Palenque was a real adventure. Our scheduled

* El Tajin: Official Guide, Instituto Nacionald De Anthropologia e Historia

plane was grounded, so after a good two hours' wait (we had arrived there at 7 am) we were given a small Cessna which took a young Dutch couple and ourselves safely and efficiently to Palenque Airport in about 40 minutes. From there we took a taxi and bumped about ten kilometres to Palenque proper. Then we climbed laboriously up the hills in hot scorching sunshine and arrived at the gateway to the site. It is really a most beautiful place; very hot but with a cooling breeze blowing all the time, and the lovely smells of herbs and orange blossom. Above all such a wonderful air of peace. Although the buildings are not really so interesting as those of Tikal and Copan, I would not have missed it for worlds.*

We arrived back at the airport just after four o'clock to find no plane there! We waited and waited on the field, with nothing but one long log on which to sit and still no plane came. When it was nearly dark, we sent a desperate message via a taxi driver through the Palenque village phone, but at the last minute, as darkness came on, the plane appeared.

I must not forget to record the 'pigs episode'. Whilst awaiting our plane, a similar one of a different colour appeared. Some yokels were standing around obviously expecting something to emerge. It did: in the shape of three large squealing sows carefully tied up. In due course they were untied and went wandering off contentedly with their new masters!

It was in 1956, when we first visited South America, that we heard unexpectedly about the great dig of the hitherto unknown Mayan city of Tikal, the largest, and probably the oldest, of all the great classic Maya cities in Middle America. Hidden in the roadless Guatemalan jungle, it would have been practically impossible until the coming of the transport aeroplane to mount any large expedition there.

We had stopped in Guatemala City on our way to reach, if possible, another jungle Mayan City (Copan), which had been excavated some years previously by the Carnegie Foundation. We had been able to get almost no information about the journey, and even what we had was wrong. For some reason we could not reach it by plane from Guatemala City. We had to fly to Honduras to a

* Palenque - Temple of the Inscriptions, which contains an interior stairway leading to a funerary crypt. In this was discovered a large tomb covered by a sepulchral slab nicely carved and decorated, covering the sarcophagus where the body of a man was found. The curious position of the man sculptured on the slab has caused much speculation. He would appear to be driving some type of complicated machine. Could this be a UFO?

capital I had never heard of 'Tegucigalpa' (known as the air conditioned city because of its beautiful climate), and continue our flight from there. Pan American sold us tickets for a plane journey from Teguci, as it was affectionately called, to Copan airport. But this was much too easy. We found that no official planes went there, and we ended up taking an air taxi from Teguci, which floated perilously over the jungle hills to our destination, a most fascinating place lying undisturbed amongst its green trees and sunny peaceful paths. The only living being there, in charge of the site, jumped on his donkey, galloped off, and returned fairly soon with a small English guidebook of Copan. But this is another story. I will only say that it was frightfully hot, and when we finally returned to Teguci after many hours, my sister consumed three large bottles of Coca Cola at one sitting. All the same, it gave us the 'itch' to see more jungle cities in the future.

At our Guatemalan hotel, during our struggles to find out how to reach Copan, we were suddenly approached by a very pleasant American gentleman who had heard we were interested in archaeology. He introduced himself as Edwin Shook, the Field Director of the Philadelphia University Museum's Expedition to Tikal. He explained to us that he had recently completed the first preliminary season of work at Tikal, and the second one was just starting. It was to be a ten-year dig in all; a big undertaking for which the government of Guatemala had constructed a special airfield the previous year, and the President and others had given their full support. The area was declared a National Park. As well as the inaccessibility of the place, there was no reliable supply of water in the Peten area where Tikal was situated, and in the dry season, the only time excavations were possible, the supply dwindled to practically nothing. However, even with these makeshift arrangements, they hoped to have visitors from the first, and he invited us to come. Unfortunately, at that time, this was quite impossible. We were already chasing another jungle city, and had most detailed and complicated plans for several further South American countries before returning to New York. But we said that if we ever came again to this part of the world, we should certainly accept his invitation.

So now in 1961 we were able to go there, when excavations were in full swing, and visitors comfortably catered for and housed. In early days, it had only been possible to come for the day and bring one's own food. A large group of archaeologists were working there under the leadership of Dr. Shook and Dr. and Mrs. Kidder, who had all three worked on Mayan sites previously under the Carnegie Foundation.

One could go for a day's excursion, or a three days' one. We chose the latter. We wanted to stay in the jungle. We had never forgotten our trip to the top of Macchu Picchu on our earlier visit to South America, and how we wished we had stayed longer there. We started all agog at the crack of dawn. The flight was a fascinating one and although it was rather cloudy for sight-seeing we passed slowly over dense jungles with masses of vegetation pushing up in all directions. We landed on a very slight airstrip to discover we were in Tikal. From silence suddenly to noise! Everyone met us. Archaeologists, Indians, children, jeeps and barking dogs. I remember the largest of the latter was an Alsatian, the smallest a tiny puppy who rolled around the Alsatian's feet. A pleasant-looking stranger suddenly shook hands and introduced himself as Ed Shook; I simply had not recognised him, the leader of the expedition who had invited us to come and view it several years before. A gallant soul in a peaked cap, who turned out to be one of the celebrated Ortiz brothers (they had guided many visitors around Tikal for years before the coming of the present 'dig' and knew more about the place than anyone else) greeted us also, and piled our luggage into a Land Rover. He obviously had an eye for ladies of any age!

We bumped up to Jungle Lodge, an arrangement of three straw-thatched buildings in the native style. The rooms were all in one with partitions, comprising a samoan-style dining room, where all the visitors ate with the archaeologists, and a lounge. A remarkably good arrangement considering jungle difficulties.

Ortiz and his jeep, which could just go through the trails, took us on a guided tour the first afternoon. Afterwards we were given a map of all the trails, and warned not to go outside them. It would have been difficult to do this, as the jungle was very dense. On our first expedition Ortiz suddenly stopped his car, pointed to a very slight opening in the forest, and murmured something about 'the old road to Washington', or at least that is what it sounded like. I could not believe my ears. How could anything called Washington be over here? What I realised later he was referring to was the old road to 'Uaxactum', the very earliest of the classical Mayan sites, some few miles away from Tikal.

The wonders of Tikal are the immense pyramids, three or four of which are the height of a modern 20-storey building, and one even higher, corresponding to 22 storeys. They are similar in design to other Middle American pyramids we had seen, with huge staircases and temples on the top. They are grouped around the Great Plaza, where most of the ceremonies must have taken place. My sister's Tikal ambition was to get to the top of the largest monster - Temple

1 (of the Great Jaguar) - to see the beautiful wooden temple gates on top, which according to report had been specially copied from a genuine set in the British Museum. There was a small mechanical lift to the top, which the workmen were using but somehow she never achieved her ambition. Perhaps it was not thought safe for a lady to go flying up and down like that!

We climbed many of the smaller temples and 'palaces' as some of the other buildings were called, and the same old questions asserted themselves. Who were these people who built them, and what were they doing? Studying the stars? They must have been great astronomers at least.

Two interesting points came up in our researches during the next two days. Many of the stelae and altars had fallen and been excavated. This meant they were far better preserved thaan the upright stelae which had weathered. They were most beautifully carved in a light pinkish stone. Many were not damaged at all, except for a large crack, usually through the head of the main figure. Was this deliberately done? Was it because someone wanted to destroy the power of the beings who lived here? Was this the real reason for the abandonment of so many of the Classic Mayan cities, which has never been explained?

My deepest recollection of our second Central and South American trip was of the number of groups that had formed since our first trip around the Continent, inspired by Rodney Collin Smith in 1956. At first only a few, mainly around Mexico and Peru, sometimes working on the lines of Ouspensky, in other cases (such as the one in Caracas) under the aegis of Mr. Gurdjieff's pupils. To these, were added the Subud groups, sometimes only a very few people in each, but many of them. To some of us it seemed as though a new chapter opened with each leader, and we would not willingly have missed any of them.

CHAPTER 24

Travel in the Far East and Australia

In December 1958 Marjorie and I took up again our plan for a trip to Australia and New Zealand. We had hoped to do this in 1957 but had been persuaded to postpone it by Mr. Bennett. The main reason for this was the coming to the West, in early 1957, of Mohammed Subuh and his wife Ibu from Indonesia.

We now had a great deal more purpose in going, as we were flying to Djakarta first, for instructions from Bapak as to the opening of the women in the Perth group in Australia and other matters he wished us to carry out.

We left London on Tuesday the 30th and were seen off by a cheering party of friends and Subud companions.

Our plane flew first to Bahrein and on to Bombay where we were greeted by our first Subud member abroad, Pat Gillibrand – a B.O.A.C. pilot, who greeted us at the bottom of the gangway. Down we came into a hot, mellow land with palms, and brown people walking slowly and gracefully about. All our Subud friends came to greet us and we spent a happy New Year with them.

On January 2nd we had dinner with an interesting couple, Harinder Singh and his English wife whom we had been introduced to earlier by the Gillibrands, and who was interested in Subud, himself a Sikh who had just joined the B.O.A.C. staff.

Our next trip was a pilgrimage to Elephanta Island, to the caves which had impressed my sister some thirty years previously. Marjorie tells us that she went with some misgivings this time, wondering whether the great effect the Trimurti had made upon her would somehow seem nothing now.

The caves, hollowed out in the 7th Century A.D., have wonderful carvings. The central figure approached by a long avenue is a three-headed bust of the Trimurti, Shiva in her different aspects and meant for us the Law of Three, the great creative power of the Universe. It is wonderfully placed making a continuous impression upon the visitor as he or she approaches.

Although much of the sculpture had been damaged by Portuguese artillery, its effect is almost intact and my sister felt the Trimurti to be more wonderful than when she had last seen it. The sculptures of Shiva, dancing with apsaras, and divine figures, make a sort of 'heavenly host', similar in idea to many Christian paintings of God and Christ with the Angelic Host. It was a true "Symbol". We had hardly realised the depth of this word before then.

Our last view of Bombay, before we left for Colombo, was a visit to the home of Indu Bhavu, a little Indian Lady Subud member, where we were welcomed by the whole family (sister, three brothers, mother and father) and given fantastic and wonderful things to eat.

At Colombo a large delegation was there to meet us, including Mr. Gerson, Mr. Tarsi Vitachi, the editor of some English newspapers, and several others. We were taken to the beautiful Subud House at 20 Torrington Avenue, where we were given two large and cool "open air" rooms. The silence was wonderful after Bombay, nothing but bird sounds at night and no-one to disturb us. We had five days real peace, with a pet monkey next door, hopping up on the communicating wall when we called and gentle little people dropping in at intervals to see us, taking us out during the day, and Mr. Gerson and Irina Lowe looking after all our wants.

We did not do much sightseeing, but put ourselves at the disposal of the "Subud" group there as much as we were needed. They asked questions about Subud matters in England, life at Coombe Springs, and much else. We also met again Vagira, her husband Brian, her mother-in-law, Mrs. Cook and her two small sons, Haisha, now an elegant grown-up boy at boarding school, and Arjuna, her son by Brian, a sturdy lad.

Another day, we had a strange mixture with a visit to the zoo and a visit to the "Buddha of the Sapphire Eyes" of which Mr. Ouspensky wrote in 'The New Model of the Universe' "a huge recumbent image highly painted, in which the gleaming eyes seem to be watching one from every angle."

We had several "Latihans" with the ladies' group and talks with many of them. We enjoyed dinners cooked by Irina, with Mr. and Mrs. Gerson and just as we were about to take our plane for Singapore, Mr. Tarsi Vitachi took us briefly to see his family.

We arrived in Singapore, at the Raffles Hotel, late at night and found two large and magnificent suites reserved for us, which unfortunately we were never able to enjoy, the first night because we arrived so late, and the second because we left so early!

But Mrs. Emma Allen appeared the first morning of our visit with elaborate plans for a shopping and sight-seeing tour, after which she took us to her house for lunch and later we went to a Latihan.

Too quickly we left for Djakarta, where Bapak, his family and group were the most important part of this trip for us. They never disappointed us. We were charmingly received by them all, and felt a nearness and sweetness in them which was quite out of this world.

Bapak took us, in his new car, on a long drive to the Bogor Gardens and to a hill station, Puntjah, higher up for cooler air. I shall never forget our walk through the gardens; our feeling that some deeper understanding of the flowers, plants and the whole world of Nature had come to us through Bapak's presence. We talked (with Ismana as interpreter) of many unusual happenings and occurrences of the times. "All this and Heaven too" – I quoted.

We had two large Latihans. Both men and women collected together in a spacious hall, and while the women had their exercise, the men waited on the balcony and afterwards vice versa. Bapak also gave a short talk. The Latihan proved much more powerful than anything we had previously experienced: there seemed to be an enormous upsurge of force. We also had a small Latihan with Ibu at Bapak's home in a very small space with all the family chores going on around us.

The size of the group in Djakarta did not appear large, although we believe that more experienced groups were situated in Djakdjakarta and another place where Bapak had previously lived.

We had several meetings with Ismana and Rahaju. Altogether, the situation was a very unusual one, and we felt the amazing rightness of Bapak in every situation in which we saw him. We had further talks with Bapak about the work and the "openings" he wanted us to do in Australia and also about his coming tour to Central and South America.

The other side of the coin could not have been more different. We had remembered this island and its capital – then called Batavia, when it was under Dutch rule. We had stayed at The Hotel des Indes, the most beautiful hotel in the far east, with perfect service and food. Again we were staying there, but alas, though the good old skeleton of the hotel was still there, the place was a shambles.

We were late in arriving owing to our visit to Bapak, and our reservations had been given away. One charming Indonesian couple living there themselves and appointed to look after us, tried to arrange for another room, which was constantly refused, while we stood and sweltered.

However, we found our feet after a bit. Our Subud friends introduced us to the head cook, Fritz, who instructed us to always ask for him directly, or, indeed, to walk straight out into his kitchen, otherwise we were subject to awful pieces of meat with flies on them. This worked and we were soon regularly able to obtain American breakfasts with orange juice, filtered coffee, eggs and toast.

Our plane to Australia was running late, but eventually we were once again in the capable hands of the Quantas "boys" and safely packaged on our way to Perth, Australia. We arrived there at 3 am on January 17th, a dreadful time to arrive, and for our unknown hosts to receive us, but they were gallantly at the airport – Keith Ewers and Mr. Fisher, all ready for our further travels.

Keith Ewers was one of Australia's well-known writers, and his wife, Jean, who was our hostess, makes beautiful pottery.

As we drove through the silent, balmy streets to the Ewers home, just outside Perth, we could so far see very little of this new continent.

We were glad to meet the Perth group, as my sister had been corresponding with them for a couple of years or so. No one looked as she had expected. We were asked together with three lady helpers (already in the Perth Group) to open twenty more ladies – so we spent all week at it. Latihans on Monday, Wednesday and Friday and in between friends took us for drives and we explored Perth. We saw many specimens of almost unique fauna and flora: lovely blossoms, the flowering gum trees, the Kookaburro birds and so on. We went on one expedition to Bridgetown by car. There were six of us in the car, a two days drive, but we enjoyed again the new flowers that we saw, especially the flowering "gums" which have a lovely scent and beautiful pink and red blossoms.

We left Perth on January 20th for Melbourne. We had hoped to make a stop in Adelaide, but due to the cricket "Test" match we were unable to book reservations and so regrettably we had to skip that lovely city.

After an overnight flight and some much needed rest, we made some phone calls to various introductions we had been given and were delighted to receive a call from Donald Neil, who had quite disappeared out of our lives four or five months previously. We had both known him well at Coombe Springs, and also at the Subud Nursing Home. Mr. Roberts, the Subud representative in

Melbourne, also called. We wined and dined frequently with Donald and had a pleasant supper with Mr. Roberts and Gamini, a Singalese student, whose wife we had met in Ceylon.

Altogether, we spent a week in Melbourne and took two excursions, one to the Blue Dandenongs, a lovely mountain route with views, interrupted by an excellent "Devonshire" tea and an aborigine throwing a boomerang for us.

The other trip was a day one to Phillips Island, where we saw penguins, seals and koala bears.

One last visit before leaving for Sydney by air on February 5th was to Balaarat and the Villiers works there. My father was Managing Chairman of the Villiers Engineering Company at Wolverhampton, England. Mr. Douglas Ramsden, the Director, came to fetch us and we had a most delightful day, including a pleasant lunch with his wife and children and an afternoon visit to the factory.

In Sydney we telephoned the Sandwiths, and almost at once they invited us down to Bowral (60 miles south) to stay as long as we liked. We did actually spend two weekends with them. Although we did not know them well (they were friends of Mr. Bennett) they were very kind and made us welcome.

I want to add here that Mr. Bennett and Elizabeth with her children had already preceeded us to Sydney and they had "opened" quite a number of people there. Among them were Dr. Philip Groves and Mrs. Marcia Thompson. The weather in Sydney was not settled. There were fierce rain storms and after a nice day with Dr. Groves and the Thompsons, we were able to see for ourselves the degree of difficulty this could cause in the streets of Sydney.

On Wednesday February 25th we flew to Auckland, a five or six hour trip. Blue sea and sky and a mass of gorgeous cloud formations that delighted us.

CHAPTER 25

New Zealand, the South Seas and New York

We arrived late at Auckland Airport on February 25th and went toward the city by bus across much water, and a silent land for several miles. By then, it was midnight and as usual we had not been given the hotel we asked for – the one we were given was a noisy affair on a very busy street and appeared to be rather rough and ready.

When we tried to register for our rooms, money was demanded in advance and also 'key money'. You paid for your key and when you left this was refunded when you handed in your key. As we had arrived so late, we had not the New Zealand money in hand; but fortunately my sister had enough to pay for the key deposit they demanded. We slept fairly well and next morning went straight to our travel agents, the Bank of New South Wales, to protest. The Bank's travel agents were appalled at our treatment and moved us to a charming hotel called 'The Star', where we were given the Bridal Suite and were most happy. The real joke, we found out later, was that the manager of our first hotel was a Subud member, and the Latihan exercise was held at that hotel!!

We were able to telephone our cousin, Diana Gerzon, living outside Auckland. She came with her husband, Phillip Gerzon and had dinner with us and then we were able to spend the weekend with them and their two daughters at Holland House. We visited their weekend cottage by the sea as well, and actually achieved two bathes, the first we had had in Australia and New Zealand!

Auckland is a queer town, built almost entirely on small hills, presumably extinct volcanoes – it is a much quieter town, especially at night, than the Australian cities, and there is much less strain in the atmosphere. One feels how magnificent the country really is, but how insensitive most of the inhabitants are to its wonderful environment. We applied for our New Zealand Drivers' License from a pleasant officer who told us about the traffic laws of the country and we looked around generally before taking on a Holden Special for 1958 for our New Zealand tour.

We set out from Diana's home for Rotorua about 150 miles away, where we stayed for three days at the Grand Hotel there. Rotorua is the centre of the 'thermal' area, as it is called, and has many geysers, mud pools and hot and coloured springs. It really makes one understand something about the mineral forces of the earth. The climax, for us was when we arrived at Wairakei to see the Karapiti Blow Hole. This enormous Fumarol is illuminated by night by the guide, who burns two large sacks which ignite with the steam pouring from the Blow Hole and forms showers of sparks, but this is simply a rattle for the tourists, because we felt the Hole was awe-inspiring enough without decoration and we were told it is a 'safety valve' for the North Island against volcanic outbreaks in other places. It gave us a queer feeling to see what must go on under the earth, and how thin in some places the top crust seems to be. Much of this underearth activity is being used for man, and the government is actively engaged in using the geysers at Wairakei and the steam vents in the valley of the geysers there.

It is quite unbelievable, as one goes through it, to hear all the thundering noise they make. We visited Orakei Kirakie, another thermal area, which is much more beautiful, with charming coloured terraces, pools and a Maori sacred cave. Unfortunately the government are planning to destroy much of this in a dam building scheme. We drove on to Lake Taipo and stayed at the Lake Hotel. The hotel, a nice modernized one, was situated in the middle of the town instead of by the lake, where it could have views of its superb environment which we felt could easily rival Lake Louise in Canada and other world beauties.

We left for Napier on the east coast and Hawks Bay, and we drove over two high passes in the nearby mountains to get there. It was our first taste of driving on 'dirt' roads. They slowed us down very much, were very rutted at times and produced either much dust – if the weather was dry – or mud – if it was wet. All the bay area was lovely and Napier, a pleasant little town. We drove along the coast to picnic and looked for our friends, the Christopher Baynes house – and then drove on to North Havelock to see some friends of our cousin Naomi Griffith. Mrs. Williams was at home and welcomed us most charmingly. Then we motored on past Clive Lodge, a large house which

Christopher Baynes told us had been auctioned recently, but not to him!

From Napier we drove on to Wellington – a long way – to put our car in the docks for the inter island steam boat, then we went by cable car to see the view of Wellington from the mountain.

The following day, we joined our car on the steamer, and made for Picton on the South Island – the weather was windy and cold, but there were beautiful views, especially when we came into the Picton fjords.

Our hotel in Picton, painted bright blue, was rather indifferent; bad beds, usual trouble with 'key deposit' and a habit they have of lumping everyone together at meals, which we presumed was because the waitresses (who seemed scarce) had less to do. We also noticed the daily 'bottle parties' (men only) which took place every evening between 5 and 6, and the morning tea, which always came round at 7 am.

The scenery on the South Island made itself felt at once, providing the weather is good in the sunshine it is simply superb everywhere. We left Picton for Nelson, a town which holds the record for sunshine, and which we hoped we might come back to for our Easter break later, but we were disappointed. It reminded us of an old fashioned wild west film when the hero would come out with pistols and the heroine would be swooning on the balcony. There was, indeed, glorious sun, and we found a bathing beach nearby with golden sands, but no decent place in which to stay or even undress. We reluctantly cancelled our Easter reservation here.

The next day we took a long drive, about 300 miles over the Buller Gorge and Lewis Pass to Christchurch. The roads we took were of the dirt/mud kind. We had difficulty in seeing the gorge, as we were so busy keeping the car going on the slippery roads, and to add to our difficulties it began to rain. However, we finally reached our destination to find most of the inhabitants of Christchurch out on the streets celebrating Friday night (the beginning of the weekend).

We had some difficulty finding our Hotel and somewhere to park, but with help from the hotel staff, we were installed in two nice bedrooms with baths. We liked the place very much, a good sized city, and it has a river named the Avon running through it which gave it a more leisurely and relaxed air. We saw a good 'movie' here, and the Museum, and there were lovely views over the sea and mountains and we arranged to return here for Easter. Then we set off once again toward our South Island trip proper. Our first overnight stop was at Timaru with a pleasant hotel – unfortunately the weather worsened and we were advised by the A.A. man to take a good coast road to Dunedin and from there another good road to Queenstown via the lovely Lake Wanaka. Scenery again gorgeous – mountains, lakes, bush and tussocks of grass everywhere, all bathed in the very bright light into glorious shades of purple, blue, red and gold and lighter shades of beige with tall poplar trees with their dark green leaves already changing into their autumn colors of gold and beige. All this is the wonder of New Zealand and it has to be seen to be believed.

Queenstown itself was a rather shoddy little place set on a most beautiful lake. We liked their launch – named 'The Meteor', and took some lovely scenic trips on their Lake Wakatipu. Unfortunately, the air trips which take one over the fjords and glaciers were not operating the day we were there.

Our next destination was to be Milford Sound in the fjord country. We had felt rather alarmed about this trip, as the famous Milford highway was supposed to be unique. We stopped for lunch at Te Anau, another charming lake due west, and a short piece of shocking road by Lake Wakatipu. We came upon an excellent tar-sealed road which took us to our destination in about three hours, the ascent to the famous 'Homer Tunnel' (about three miles through the rock). It is supposed to be a one-way affair – half an hour from Milford and half an hour in the opposite direction – but this rule is not adhered to. We saw many cars and trucks charging through at the wrong time.

After passing through the tunnel, one descends precipitously to the 'sound' in a very short time. There was a pukka hotel on the sound run by the Government Tourist Board and an A.A. hostel, some garages and the inevitable ice cream and chocolate shop, a cafe, as well as a small wharf for the steamers. The air was magnificent and the colours around and over the Sound incredible. We woke up next morning to a beautiful day and we took the launch trip down the sound toward the sea where we saw waterfalls and fish, porpoises, I think. There was also a small airport nearby, but not then in use. We were sorry to have to leave the next day on account of the beautiful air and the peace and quietness of it all.

Up again by the Milford Highway, we retraced our steps, feeling like old hands now at dealing with the road – back to Te Anau to the excellent little hotel where we went on an improvised evening launch trip to some glow worm caves recently discovered. We drove by easy stages back to Christchurch to claim our reservations and to spend

Easter there, but before we came into Christchurch we had seen Mt. Cook in all its glory, with the sun full out. It is called 'Aorangi' to the Maoris, and the lakes Pukaki and Tekapo.

After a beautiful Easter service at the Anglican cathedral opposite our hotel, we spent a quiet few days with some friends in our hotel, and when the holiday calmed down a little, we retraced our steps by Picton and Wellington. On the way, we had a perfect siting of Mt. Egmont with its snowy peak, and paid a visit to the Waitomo Glow worm caves. We returned to Auckland on April 3rd and handed over our car to the appropriate authorities. We also made plans for our ongoing trip via Fiji and Tahiti, across the Pacific to Honolulu and U.S.A.

One must not forget when writing about New Zealand to speak about the Maori people who lived in New Zealand for hundreds of years before the white man came. The immigration of these people from Polynesia took place about A.D.1350. Their remarkable feats of navigation and seamanship in open canoes earned them the description of 'Vikings of the Sunrise'. As a people they have been remarkably successful in their adaptation to the new life. They hold strongly to their old tribal affiliations and still employ the Maori language. Their arts and crafts have survived, they form a colourful group, and have united well with the so-called 'pakeha' or non Maori people.

We left Auckland for Fiji (Nandi) on April 20th. We were booked to take the 'Coral Route' trip, from Suva, Fiji to Western Samoa (Apia) Airutaki (Cook Islands) and Tahiti. We had the opportunity to go by seaplane to Tahiti and return and we were glad that we did take it. After five days of rest in Suva, we liked Fiji very much. The sturdy Fijians are much darker in colour than their neighbours, the South Sea islanders we saw: i.e. Samoans and Tahitians. We will always remember the Sunday service at the Methodist Church. All the people were dressed in white, looking very newly scrubbed with their short fuzzy heads in their lava-lavas – the garment both men and women wear. We were able to find an excellent chauffeur to take us drives round Suva and its environs and we made a lovely boat trip on the 'Oolooloo', a smart little launch with a glass bottom, so that passengers could see the corals, fishes, etc. below.

Early on the morning of the 16th April, we were marshalled on board the Teal Flying Boat – a rather slow start, for our trip to Western Samoa. After having come down to refuel near the Cook Islands the passengers all alighted from the flying boat to bathe on a nearby beach. As we crossed the international date line, it was still April 16th and when we came down again near Western Samoa, the coastline struck us as incredibly beautiful with palms, sea and foliage plants and their people, much lighter in skin than the Fijians, seemed to us, by their looks, dress and hairstyle like ancient Greeks. We never saw a trace of negative emotion in their features and they seemed a radiantly happy and friendly race. They live in most original homes, with charming straw roofs and no walls. In winter, we were told, they hang straw around the house for warmth, and the cooking is done in a smaller hut at the back. Lavatories are also most original. They have straw huts placed on the ends of piers, built out into the sea.

We were able to visit one of their homes and sat cross-legged on the floor, admiring the attractive decorations and portraits of the family. Outside, they had a small and colorful garden. The houses are arranged in groups with a large or several larger houses belonging to the Chiefs.

We stayed at the 'White Horse' Inn belonging to the local couple. The owner was partly German and partly Samoan, and his beautiful wife. We had a form of natural 'air-conditioning', a row of rooms with a common opening near the ceiling – so that everything could be heard, and everyone was concerned if an individual light was turned on. It was very hot, and it certainly helped us all to sleep at night. We spent thirty six hours here at Teal (Seaplane) expense and managed to get a very clear glimpse in that time of the island and its serene and wonderful atmosphere.

We took three drives in Samoa: To Robert Louis Stevenson's house 'Vailima', now the Governor's House, and around the island by the sea, and another to a cocoa, coffee and rubber plantation inland. Finally, a drive back to our flying boat to take off for Aitutaki in the Cook Islands for refuelling. Here, we unceremoniously came down on the water, and a launch took us to a nearby atoll, where we all had a good swim in excellent warm water before again going back to our flying boat.

In the middle of the same day, we flew in to Papeete and found it terribly hot, not cooler and drier, as we had been told. All our luggage was held for "fumigating" on account of 'Rhinocerous beetle', but we retrieved it later, apparently unharmed. On arrival at the port, we were promptly garlanded with perfumed flowers and driven off in a large and imposing taxi to the Royal Tahitian Hotel, where we had booked rooms. We had heard conflicting rumours about Tahiti – some said "It was cheap and dirty" others that "it was out of this world" and yet more told us "It was a man's town". Actually, we found it the most beautiful island with perhaps the most perfect nature aspect of any place I have seen. The combination of the roar of the waves on the reef outside the bay, the swish of the waves on the beach, the night sounds of the crickets and humans, and the luminous summer light with the sun setting in vivid yellows and greys, and a full moon coming up, are quite indescribable. We took full advantage of this in our bungalow hotel – a rather ramshackle affair on the beach with almost everything open. Bathing at any time we chose was ideal from the black sands below the bungalow. As usual in French lands, no plumbing worked properly and there were many deficiencies. It was all rather run down, but we preferred it to the smarter hotels in less luscious surroundings.

Papeete – a small place – is a rather Eastern edition of the Cote D'Azur, a sort of 'poor man's Cannes' with a South Sea island flavour! We drove round the island, which had no other towns, merely small villages of untidy bamboo huts, nothing like so colourful and elegant as Samoa. The people seemed to be a mixture of types and it was difficult to see what a real Tahitian was like. Ladies with long dark hair, mainly crowned with flowers and very little else, except a skirt – the lava lava – which they wear all over from their breasts downwards. We heard that there were many so-called 'vahines' or ladies whose sole purpose was to entertain the men, and one festive night, when an American ship put into port, we felt the local Tahitian girls were pretty bored by the tough and insensitive attentions of the average Anglo Saxon men on holiday. We rather sensed that the whole beautiful island and its people are under unlucky stars, and that the forces here are wrong, but it is very difficult to say more than that.

We took an excursion by launch over to the beautiful island of 'Moorea' – perhaps the most exotically lovely of all the islands we visited – where an excellent small hotel in native style had been built. We lunched there, then lazed about and finally had a swim, in limpid water; so warm, with little cold bubbles at intervals, that it was like a 'thermal' bath. Later, we had a Tahitian dinner with sucking pig cooked native style amongst hot stones, with their own vegetables and sweet potatoes, followed by native fruit – all eaten on 'leaf' plates with the fingers. Afterwards, we all took to the buses and bumped along for several miles with some boys playing their native instruments, to a nearby village where an elaborate dance was staged with both men and women in gorgeous 'grass' skirts and flowers. For a time this was most impressive, but it was broken up too soon by the dancers turning into ordinary mortals and changing into European style dancing. We soon left and returned to our hotel and slept soundly. Moorea has strange jagged peaks and is obviously volcanic with its huge craters – Tahiti appears to be similar from a distance, and one is reminded of the legends of Mu and Lemuria and the lost continents which were the home of 'Man'. They may not be just wild stories!

We spent several nights in a better hotel – 'Les Tropiques' nearer the town and we were particularly amused at the dancing band there and the little waitresses with long flowing hair, who seemed to understand when you needed them without being told, and particularly the singing of their native airs. Somehow, these songs grow on one the more they are heard, and I may add one hears them most nights. They do not annoy at all, they are so gentle, naive and truly sung. The dancing, too, of the mixed Tahitian and French young was also most refreshing.

The Teal Flying Boat left with almost all the foreign visitors on board on April 26th and we retraced our return flight to Samoa and then to the Cook Islands to refuel and bathe while the refuelling took place, and back to Suva. We were glad to be back in Suva at the comfortable Club Hotel, but we always sigh for Tahiti, for, abuse it as people may do, it has a rare charm which comes through all dirt and disadvantages! The 'Bures' at the 'Hotel Tropiques', the amusing 'hulas' of the dancers, especially the boy and girl who mimicked them perfectly with complete indifference! The sunsets, too, were too glorious for words. The lovely open-air dining rooms built right out over the water. We still sigh for Tahiti and remember its paradise.

On May 8th we left Fiji for Honolulu on our return trip home. It was to be a long trip across the Pacific, but we made a stop over at Little Canton Island where we enjoyed delicious iced drinks before flying on the last lap to Honolulu, where we were garlanded with sweet smelling flowers on all occasions and frequently kissed by our guides and others. We drove in our limousine to Waikiki Beach where we were to stay at the Edgewater Hotel, a rather humble brother of all those lordly palaces overlooking the sea. Honolulu is a most fantastic place, fundamentally an elaborate 'Blackpool' on a rather grand scale. The people are so mixed with Chinese, Japanese and American it is hard to find a true Hawaiian. We never saw the proper 'hula' dancing: only some small girls at the International market aped the hula, a silly business, put on for the tourist Americans who looked bored and very tired, although they were surrounded by sunshine and gorgeous food at all times. We were able to visit their Bishop Museum and to take another three days visiting other nearby islands, Maui and Hawaii proper, before flying on to San Francisco and via the Golden Gate.

Under the Subud flag, we had met many interesting and unusual people on our travels and realised the immensely unifying and happy process that the Latihan brought between different creeds and races, at least at first. When we finally returned to New York we met again both Bapak and the Bennetts and were called upon to take a large opening Latihan of ladies. It was now summer in New York, and piping hot. The new Subud rooms were not yet ready for occupation and their air conditioning had failed. About a hundred excited and hysterical women who had had no experience (or very little) of the Latihan were milling about in the hall, and the newly appointed American helpers had no idea how to manage. We were able to sort out the various sections, and we started the opening speech to the new people and told them to close their eyes. The atmosphere was still so agitated and conditions were so hot and noisy (heavy traffic crashing down a main road with all our windows open) that I could not imagine anything working. But I was wrong. Gradually, people became calmer and, even in the traffic, seemed quieter. I opened my eyes for a moment and caught a quick glimpse of the radiant face of a little Negro girl near me, concentrated and aglow with some new force within her. We did not have to worry on these difficult occasions, and there were plenty of them. The Great Life Force, as Bapak called it, will always come to one's aid.

CHAPTER 26

The Right Life

My sister and I went on working for Subud as "helpers" until 1962. There was an excellent and varied group of Women Helpers in Kensington who did manage, my sister felt, to put their various capabilities together constructively. But it was difficult to see that the results were always beneficial as a whole. People came and left very rapidly so that there was always a core of enthusiastic supporters. Certainly, to those who were moved by it, were very stirred up (sometimes very negatively) certainly that was evident. But whether this made people more sensitive or understanding of themselves and others when it came to the test? Rather, in the domineering type – they became more domineering, and more certain of the rightness of their interpretation.

Both my sister and I had been appointed to Subud Trusts in 1959 following the Subud Congress when several other welfare activities were put forward, but in 1963 we resigned. We both felt that the Subud enterprises up to date had been dismal failures, we felt that the Subud "force", if one can put it that way, seemed to make the lack of unity even worse in practical affairs. We both put a direct question to Bapak about this at the time of the failure of Brookhurst Grange, with which we were associated at all levels of the negotiations, and never had a real answer from him.

Actually, Bapak's only answer to all such questions was that all would come right in the end if we continued the Latihan and "the working from within". Perhaps because of our former background with Ouspensky – Gurdjieff work, this way did not seem to be entirely right, and the beginning of the end, as far as we were concerned, came when we gave in our Helpers cards, as Bapak had indicated that we should do unless we were willing to follow the Latihan and give up our previous work.

There was, at that time, a strong movement amongst some of the Subud people, certainly approved of by Bapak, to "take over" Coombe Springs as the main centre for Subud work over here. At this time, many of us rallied to the Gurdjieff – Ouspensky work – but first, where could we find someone with the authority to answer our questions?

This took Mr. Bennett, Marjorie and myself on a trip in April, 1962 from England to Delhi and then in a comfortable small plane to Kathmandu in Nepal over the Himalayas. Unfortunately, the mountains were not visible as they were covered by mist, but it was very different travelling from a few years previously when hardly anyone went to Nepal, and then one had to be carried by bearers over the mountains. Kathmandu struck me as a dear little place, nestling in the heights looking into the main village like any village in this sort of position. I was reminded of Huaraz in the Peruvian Andes though houses, temples etc. are quite different in style. The same straight streets looking out onto snowy high mountains and sturdy, simple mountain people with practically no comfort, all looking very happy.

So this was the land where Buddha was born. All through our visit there, from watching the people, I felt I understood more and more what he must have looked like, rather slight, exceedingly graceful in his movements. The place, of course, is all shrines, temples and statues dedicated to him. But we had not finally come to sightsee, enchanting and unusual as it was.

Near the airport, in a small house in a wood lived a wonderful old gentleman known as the Shivapuri Baba (simply – the old man of the Shivapuri Hills). Coming from a high caste Brahmin family in South India, he was reputed to be 136 years old, although an advanced age in the East is not so uncommon. His life had been totally different, however, from that of the usual Brahmin saints in that he had been instructed by his grandfather, a great astrologer, that when he had completed the many years of his training, he was to make a pilgrimage throughout the world. The old man left him some jewels in order to enable him to accomplish this purpose.

Mr. Bennett had visited him the previous year and had known of his existence for a considerable period before that, so we were, in some sense, well prepared, but I wondered when the little gate to the wood was opened by a young boy, if I would make contact with such a being. He welcomed us while lying on a chaise longue in front of his little house with trees and flowers around and the sun blazing through – a slight figure with white hair and beard and sparkling, kindly intelligent eyes. We sat down on stools in front of him and had no difficulty in asking questions and talking directly to him. His English was excellent, and his hearing good: nearly all our conversations with him were recorded. Incidentally, he took a most animated interest in the whole proceedings and use of modern methods and we filmed him as well.

My sister relates: "As we were talking, I felt again that I was on firm ground. He reinforced for me all my Ouspensky and Gurdjieff training and made me see, not in words, but inwardly, where I was going wrong, particularly in the way the mind develops and embroiders on things it does not understand, and yet all parts of it must be developed in their proper spheres. What he said was probably Hinduism as presented in the Bhagavad Gita, but he made it appear as pure, simple reality." I suppose he knew and had himself experienced it all. When he said " the first thing is to reach God, by seeing God everything is known," and we asked "how can we do this?" he replied: "Think of God alone. Dismiss every thought from your mind and you will see God in a flash and all your problems will be solved."*

She had heard similar things from all sorts of religious folk, but never have the words carried such conviction before. With him, they did. Somehow, the ground was explored and he really knew. There was a road to this – we might not be capable of going over it, but it was there. She thought of the well-known saying: 'Now we see through a glass darkly, but then face to face.'

I asked Shivapuri Baba "There is always the feeling, perhaps more in the West than the East, of not really knowing why we are here. That our life is passing and that I am not sure of using it as I might. The Shivapuri Baba had been listening carefully to all that was said while lying on his chaise longue holding a rose in his hand. We were sitting in front of him on low stools. He smiled, held out the rose and said:

"Now – so to say – there is smell in this flower. Can I explain this smell to you so that you will smell it yourself?" I replied rather dubiously – "No, I suppose not." Then Shivapuri Baba explained, "You cannot know the smell. If I give it in your hand and you smell it, you know what the smell is. Is that not so? In the same way, I cannot answer your questions. Your question will be answered only by God. See Him first. Every mystery is solved. Before that, whatever answer I can give you, it will not solve your problems. The

* A Way of Living – Marjorie Von Harten

first thing is to reach God. By seeing God everything is known. "But" – I answered "how can we do that?" Shivapuri Baba answered: "Think of God alone. Dismiss every thought from your mind. You will see God". I parried: "This is very difficult". Shivapuri Baba replied thoughtfully: "Difficult, but not impossible. It is difficult – I do know. But if you will take enough trouble to remove that difficulty, all other difficulties of life will vanish. Unless we see God, we cannot know anything. Before the sun comes, we can see nothing on the ground. When the sun comes, we see everything. Before that, a simple explanation is no explanation at all. I can say, this is sweet smelling. But how many flowers there are that have a sweet smell! What is the nature of this smell? You cannot know. One can experience it, but it can never be explained. Let the thought of God be alone in your mind, destroy every other thought. You will see God before you and all your problems are solved."

Then Shivapuri Baba went on to explain the duties of life already noted.

At this point, Shivapuri Baba introduced a notion that clarifies not only much that is written in the Gita, but the whole problem of consciousness, its nature and limitations. Shivapuri Baba: "Now your body is covered with this cloth. If the cloth is removed, I can see your body. In the same way we are covered by consciousness. God is beyond consciousness. Forget this consciousness a moment; you will see God. In a flash! First what we have to do is: discipline this life, then meditate on God. When you see God, every problem is solved.

When asked by Mr. Bennett what was the fundamental principle of life which man should follow on earth, he spoke to us about the three disciplines, the right activities towards our body, the proper training of the mind – "Mind is wild", he told us – and the right activities towards our home and society, our profession and towards the nation. He stressed that to reach God, everything we did must be rightly undertaken. Naturally, we should fail over and over again, but we must simply try until we reach perfection in what we are attempting to do. "By experience reason comes." When asked about meditation and God, he replied – "One should cultivate the whole of creation as the image of God, the manifestation of God. One should be humble, humiliated before that. When such thoughts are established, anger will not come. He asserted constantly that anyone could reach God if he truly wished to do so. If he did not wish, he had no hope.*

*.V. Harten "A Way of Living – Ch.7 Right Life – The Shivapuri Baba".

We had four visits with him, and our talks ranged over many subjects, including his world pilgrimage at the end of the last century. He went everywhere, mainly on foot, apparently, and met many of the great people of the period. He went to Mecca and he even travelled to South America and the Andes – probably from his description to us, to Lake Titicaca and Tiahuanaco. As we had recently visited this part of the world, we could recognise his descriptions, although he had forgotten many of the names. Few people must have known about these regions at all in such early days. After a considerable stay in South America, he took ship for the Pacific Islands, passing through New Zealand and Australia and coming to Japan in 1913. The outbreak of the First World War found him in Sinkiang. He followed the ancient Pilgrims' Way to Nepal discovering, as he told us, that the ascent of Mount Everest should be made by the route finally taken by Sir John Hunt and his party in 1952.*

He had several names, but he gave up his Brahmanic family name. He had taken the name of Govindananda Bharati, which he had been known by throughout his world travels. When he returned to live in Nepal, he was known simply as the Shivapuri Baba after some local hills. Apparently, he always refused to be considered a Mahatma or Messiah and did not appear to expect any homage or special respect.

During our drive to the airport after our last visit to him, I recall very well that the great snow-capped mountains around us which had been completely obscured by mist during our whole visit, quite suddenly – in a 'flash' as it were – appeared in all their majesty. They had always been there, but we could not see them. Was this somehow an analogy to man's blindness about which we had talked so much? My thoughts on writing this came to something else. We remembered Ouspensky's rather prosaic definitions of the different levels of man of which we represent only one, two and three. He speaks of the highest type possible for man.** "Man number 7 means a man who has reached the full development possible to man and who possesses everything a man can possess. That is, will, consciousness permanent and unchangeable "I". individuality, immortality and many other properties which, in our blindness and ignorance we ascribe to ourselves. It is only when, to a certain extent, we understand man No.7 and his properties that we can understand the gradual stages through which we can approach him. That is,

* J.G. Bennett "Long Pilgrimage – p.28. This book gives many more details about this extraordinary saint.
** Tape of Shivapuri Baba.

178

understand the process of development possible for us." Had we finally met such a Being, I wondered?

The Shivapuri Baba died in January 1963. It had been hoped to get him to Benares for the winter period to avoid the very cold Himalayan winter, as he was now so frail. We tried to help financially from England, but for some reason it was not possible to find the right place for him. Perhaps the journey there would have been too much, also. He died conscious to the last moment, sending this message to humanity – 'Live Right Life – Worship God – that is all – nothing more'*

* The quotations here are from J.G. Bennett's Book "The Long Pilgrimage". This book gives many more details about this extraordinary man. The quote of P.G. Ouspensky is Page 71 – "In Search of the Miraculous."

CHAPTER 27

Africa 1963–1964

I went with my sister Marjorie to Africa in January 1963. Our main aim in visiting Africa, besides getting in touch with our Subud friends there, was to make contact with its nature, its peoples, its animals and its flowers; indeed, the whole vista of nature there. We went from the Cape to Cairo, although naturally it was not possible to go everywhere in this vast land.

We sailed from Southampton on January 2nd with some difficulty, as England was covered in snow and ice. However, we had decided to take the boat train from London, as we felt the Union Castle liner, the R.M.S. Pendennis Castle, would not go without it. As it was, the boat train only reached Southampton with difficulty. It was snowed up twice in "the wastes of Basingstoke" and we were nearly an hour late, to the consternation of the Stewards, who thought we were lost!! By the 7th we reached Las Palmas to refuel: it was a lovely morning, warm sun and heavenly bright blue skies.

Eventually we docked at Cape Town and found that Mr. and Mrs. Rath of the Cape Town Subud Group were there to meet us on the dock. We were very pleased and touched to see them there, and to be taken by car to our stately hotel, the Mount Nelson.

It was high season in Cape Town, with the opening of Pariament the following day, and that was followed by the races, which I gathered was a kind of 'Ascot'. Glorious people swarmed up to the hotel afterwards, the women dressed in their out of date finery and the men looking as if they felt themselves uncrowned kings. We felt much more in rapport with the non-whites: Indian, Cape-coloured, Malay and African. We walked down into Cape Town, a lovely city surrounded by its hills, and were quite fascinated by our explorations. The whole area seemed to belong to the Mediterranean both in looks and climate. The sun was extremely bright all the time, and the sky a vivid blue. There were pleasant homes and beautiful flower gardens, and long green avenues lined with flowering gum trees full of pink and red blossom. There were also many old and lovely colonial houses left from the days of the Dutch settlers. We went out to Wynberg, a suburb, to call on Sir John and Lady Maud, the British Ambassador and his wife,, and found him most interested in the idea of Subud. We were also greatly helped and had fine hospitality from the Raths, who could not have been kinder to us. We went to a Subud Latihan, and met many very friendly people, also a couple called Dennis, who took us out driving. We were sorry to leave, but we had already booked our seats on the 'Garden Route' trip, so on Saturday, 26th at dawn, we set out, having made our proper farewells at the Mt. Nelson Hotel before leaving.

We were to go to the Railway Station, where we were given books of tickets, and then we were very promptly and efficiently stowed with our belongings in a large Mercedes bus. We started off bravely enough for the open road, when suddenly a gale blew up (as it often does in Cape Town) and off sailed our emergency escape hatch, which bounced along the road and broke. There was consternation in the bus, with one conductor rushing up and down beside the bus and shouting in Africaans. We were on our way in an hour, however.

It is nearly 1,300 miles from Cape Town to Durban. One is dealing with a vast continent, and for miles and miles there is no human habitation at all, only high mountains and plains everywhere covered with dense green foliage, and over all this, heavenly sun and bright light, although occasionally a dark cloud brought us some fairly heavy thunderstorms. Set far apart in the landscape were the white farm houses.

The next five days were very similar. Around mid-morning, the coach stopped and we had some tea and light refreshments – we enjoyed the local grapejuice, the unfermented juice of the red and white grapes, which were being picked along our route. On one occasion, a large branch of fresh grapes were handed around the bus as a gift from a vineyard owner; a most delicious treat. We stopped for about half an hour for lunch and again for tea, ending up at about six for our night's resting place.

Our first night was spent at Oudtshoorn, the centre of the ostrich feather industry, although trade was not then so good as it used to be in the Edwardian days. We toured an ostrich farm and spent two hours learning about the anatomy of the bird. They do not attack, but their flying kick can be extremely vicious; their eggs are so hard that a man weighing 250 lbs can stand on one without breaking it, and yet the chick breaks its way out safely. We were shown the various types of feathers on one unfortunate ostrich!! We felt extremely sorry for the bird and wondered whether we, too, were at the mercy of a superior force manipulating us to our disadvantage. It is only the male that has beautiful white feathers; females are grey. Ostriches can live for forty years, but are usually killed when they are about 15 years old.

We also visited the Cango Cave, the second largest in the world, with its extraordinary formations of stalagmites and stalactites. We had only a short drive that day to our next stop at the Wilderness Hotel for the night stopover. The Wilderness is a most beautiful holiday resort on the seafront. I wanted to bathe, but as no-one else was there, I did not go in. Later, we were told: Beware of sharks!

The Garden Route passes through marvellous land, with sparkling sea, and long, sandy beaches to the south and lovely green primeval forests, some as dense as the Guatemala rain forests, with wooded mountain slopes all round, and one is always driving over medium high passes with pleasant expanding views. We passed many seaside resorts, but inland there are huge expanses of land with nothing except for the occasional farmhouse. There were beautiful coloured flowers in trees, flamboyant, and something like the Royal poinciana – and bushes – hibiscus in all colours, Canna lilies, bougainvillaea, and later the ever present frangipani, yellow and pink. Also, there were great masses of our late summer flowers – roses, asters, stocks, hydrangeas of immense size, and dahlias. It seemed strange to see them after we had so thoroughly finished with them for the year at home. Everything seemed to grow over here. Mealies (Indian corn, like maize) is the staple Negro diet, also a delightful squash, something between ours and the American species, and all our vegetables. A wealth of fruit too, although we could only get fresh fruit in season; peaches, sold everywhere for 4/6 for a full-sized box, bananas, grapes, fresh figs, plums, paw-paws, heavenly melons and passion fruit. We missed the snow we had seen in the high mountains such as the Andes, Alps and Himalayas, but it was the summer season here.

Our passengers had now dwindled to about 15, who were going the whole way to Durban, mainly English, with a few South Africans. We became quite a close-knit group. At Port Elizabeth we changed buses, and were rather sad about it, as we had so liked our drivers, but we had equally good ones for the second leg. We found that the South Africans take special care of tourists.

We passed through some of the native homelands, the Transkai-Ciskai, and spent the night at a little place called Umtata, where the African Parliament meets. The African reserves, as they are called, stretch for 16,000 square miles, and have an enormous black population with a few whites administering government hospitals, Trading Posts etc. Much of what we passed through was beautiful territory.

The Africans nearly all live in rondavels: small brown round houses which look like mushrooms from a distance. Some Africans wear European dress, but in their own territory they hardly wear a stitch except beads, belts and loin cloths. Several times, parties of young and old people rushed out to greet us, and a group like this is full of vitality and quite overwhelming. They are always laughing, moving, waving and full of smiles, and the young people, especially the girls, are really extraordinarily beautiful. But we wondered how were the sophisticated whites and these bubbly children of nature to get on together? Well – if we blow ourselves up, I at least could console myself that the South Sea Islanders, the American Indians and the Africans will still, one hopes, be left to produce totally different types of civilization, possibly much better than ours.

One day, our conductor took us to visit an African multi-millionaire who had, we were told, fourteen wives, but actually we saw only nine women of all ages; the youngest was Sylvia, a really beautiful girl of about 18 with such stillness and repose about her features. Our host said that he was about 80, but he was as spry as possible and literally full of life. I must say that in some ways, he reminded me of Mr. Gurdjieff! We heard from our guide that he was supposed to be the son of Kruger's coachman, but no-one knows where he got his wealth – though there are rumours....

Our last stop was at a seaside town called Margate (we had just passed Ramsgate) and from there we drove into Durban without further delay. Durban is a large industrial city with beautiful beaches and pleasant suburbs. We were installed at the Beach Hotel on the Marine Parade in two big apartments.

We soon found our feet, and went on a long drive through the Zulu Reserves. This is the hereditary land of the great Zulu tribe under Shaka, who opposed the white man so bitterly. It is called the Valley of a Thousand Hills: beautiful country again, with rondavels and vital black people of all ages. We were invited into one of their houses, a brown mushroom affair, and were very impressed, in spite of the rather uncomplimentary remarks of our guide. A very neat round room, very cool (I believe they are warm in winter), no furniture except a cooking pot, and mats to sleep on. Beautiful young girls and bright vital children. One cannot judge them by the white man's standards, and all we seem to be teaching them is to hold out their hands for pennies and sweets. The women appear to do most of the general work around the house. They also fetch water from the river, sometimes a long way off, carrying the cans on their heads, where, indeed, they carry everything – stacks of wood and all sorts of parcels. The menfolk are at work, mainly in the towns or factories, and do not come home except for special visits. The men build a roundavel for each wife and also probably for their sons and daughters-in-law. There are no real villages, just clumps of family rondavels all over the place, mostly situated on the hills.

A feature of Durban are the Zulu rickshaw runners. Dressed in feather headdresses, beads and all sorts of oddments, they take people for rides down Marine Parade and back; trotting, loping and jumping high in the air as they go. We did not try this: I think the combination of both of us would have been a bit too much for them!

All this time, we had considerable contact with the women of the Durban Subud Group, as well as with Victor Gebers, his charming wife, Nellie, and their baby son, who came over from Eshowe in Zululand to see us. They invited us to visit them, and we left Durban with considerable relief to go with them to the country. Durban was terribly humid, and the heat was sometimes hard to bear. Victor belonged to one of the original sugar families in the district and lived in a delightful house near the small town (really only a village) of Eshowe, the capital of Zululand. His parents were then still alive, and old Mr. Gebers told me many stories of the old times, saying how much he loved the Zulus. He really did; it was good to hear.

Again, I was impressed with how lonely Africa is for the individual family. We went out one evening to visit a young couple and their children for a Subud exercise, in a charming farm with no one else near; the nearest neighbour was a mile away at least. The husband was called out during the evening to fight a sugar cane fire and probably would return only in the early hours of the morning. The wife would be quite alone with her babies.

We returned to Durban in a friend's car – Mr.Hilton Heard, a Subud member, who reminded us of our Father's old friend Colonel Garton from Glastonbury, and trans-shipped, or rather trans-carred, to an African Safari vehicle, with driver, for our trip to Johannesburg via the Drakensburg Mountains: about 500 miles or so. We spent four days over this, driving beside the main line of mountains with their magnificent table mountain type of hill, all marked horizontally and shaped by erosion into fantastic peaks. The endless green of everything continued to surprise us. It was, of course, the rainy season, but this only meant an occasional drizzle or sharp thunderstorm. After that, back comes the endless sun.

Our third night was spent at the Mont-aux-Sources, a most beautiful spot overlooking the highest part of the range. In the Natal National Park nearby, the film 'Zulu' was being made.

Our car finally left the mountains and started along a vast plain. We were now in the Transvaal, rather monotonous, with immense sunflower seed plantations, rich crops of mealies, and many kinds of vegetables. Small towns at intervals, many of them with Scottish or English names (Dundee, Glencoe, etc.) Finally we were approaching Johannesburg, but first came the enormous spoil heaps from the gold mines which spread practically into the city itself.

There were two Subud groups in Johannesburg and many old friends, so we did not have a moment to ourselves.

We saw a lot of the two groups and they were quite different from those in Cape Town and Durban. We answered questions one evening and that seemed to go well.

Several rather thrilling experiences took place here. We made a visit on Sunday to the mines, or rather to a gold mine, to see the native dancing. There is an exhibition of this dancing every Sunday morning at one of the mines. It is as competitive as football and, to my mind, a great deal more interesting. Teams from the various tribal groups compete with their costumes, bands and traditional dances. There is a special dance called the "Gum Boot Dance" in which the miners dance in their gum boots and mining costumes. This gets loudly applauded.

We never tired of watching the negro, always so individual, so full of movement, song and laughter. The dancers were magnificent specimens of young men, dressed in all sorts of bits and pieces, and showing much dignity nonetheless. They danced for their own benefit, not ours; visitors were tolerated. I filmed them at length, but this was very difficult, as the dances are so original and changing that one invariably starts filming just as they suddenly fall down!

In Johannesburg we also had two fascinating interviews: one with Mrs. Klarer, a charming woman of quite unguessable age with lovely auburn hair. We were taken to her flat by Richard Lacey, a Subud friend, and met there Mr. and Mrs. Abraham. Mr. Abraham had been the photographer for Laurens Van der Post's Kalahari films. All present were interested in U.F.O.s., Mrs. Klaren claiming to have been inside one, and carried into space to Venus! I felt, like Adamski, that she had somehow touched something Cosmic. We would have liked to have had another talk with her, but there was not time then. (At another time, later, we were able to do this).

The next day, Basil Van den Berg, the young man who was said to have invented a non-gravity machine, came to call. Surprisingly enough, he was also a healer and, from the little I know of spiritual healing, I would feel that he started where most other healers leave off. He described it as a "scientific field" and that one could find what power to use on which disease for a cure; he did not ascribe the power to himself, but to others beyond. He also said he had been shown just how to create a most complicated engine from the hieroglyphics on the feet of Adamski's space man, these glyphs having many levels of meaning.

Basil was also intending to produce a much simpler machine which made use of natural forces and perpetual motion. To the best of my knowledge, the general public is still waiting to hear more about this!

Some years before this, when we made a trip to Mount Palomar in the U.S.A. to see the renowned Observatory and telescope there, we had been able to meet and talk with the late Mr. Adamski, who then lived nearby. He seemed to us to be a simple person, reminding us of our old and very wise gardener we had as children. He was a man possessed of a most unusual force. I do not think necessarily of higher inner development as we understand it, but certainly of another kind of development. Perhaps it is better to say that he had been in contact with other types of beings than ourselves. I came away feeling that his story was true – that he had met beings from other planets, and that one day we will know more about it all, and probably accept this miracle quite casually as we have wireless, television and other marvels!

Rhodesia – now Zimbabwe (renamed Zimbabwe)

I think it is hardly realized what a wealth of fascinating scenery there is in this beautiful country. There are the Victoria Falls, some of the great waterfalls of the world, the Zimbabwe ruins, certainly one of the most mysterious ruins of the world, as well as a wealth of Prehistoric Rock Art which, although hardly known about or explored, can compare with the best of its kind elsewhere. Animals and birds of every kind are plentiful, particularly in the national parks, as well as an enormous collection of tropical flowers and bushes.

When we arrived there from South Africa, it was at the height of the rainy season, and we were still under the spell of the beauty of the Cape and the Garden Route, Durban and the Drakensberg Mountains and apartheid, and we longed to sit firmly on "non European seats" whenever we saw one.

We arrived in Bulawayo, a town founded by Cecil Rhodes on the site of the old Matabele village or Kraal, but we saw nothing much at this time but a hot airport and then went straight on to Livingstone and took a bus to Victoria Falls Hotel, a magnificent place, a long building with a large terrace overlooking the Falls, some distance away. There was also a wonderful view of the spray, which rises continuously from the immense chasm into which the mile wide Zambesi falls.

The first thing our eyes lighted upon on the half-filled terrace was an extremely intelligent coal black girl talking steadily to a young Englishman with whom she was having a drink. No fuss over European or non-European seats here!

The falls are so immense, it is impossible to see them all at once (except from a plane – which we did coming in) but from this height one gets no real idea of their size. One can go to the Eastern Cataract at one end, with the glorious view of the falling water framed like a picture in trees from the other bank and one can also go to the Devil's Cataract at the other end, where the water swirls away at one's feet over an immense drop, and one gets glimpses here and there of the middle falls. But the best view of them all, as a piece, is from the rain forest on the opposite bank, where one is usually able to walk in mackintoshes and waterproof boots, about three quarters of a mile along a path covered with an immense volume of spray. 'The Smoke that Thunders' is the African name for them, and both the 'Smoke' and the 'Thunder' are most awesome.

We had intense tropical storms at least half the time we were there, with devastating rain, great rolls of thunder and flashes of lightening. The Zambesi River was already very high, and the spray more and more immense, so although we made some brave attempts in mackintoshes, etc., it was really impossible to see anything after these deluges.

However, we did return the following year in the bright, sunny weather, and went through the rain forest, which gives a superb view of the main falls. Nevertheless, we came out of this experience very hot, with clothes soaked through. A feature of this second visit was the beautiful rainbow over the falls by day and the exquisite lunar rainbow we saw at night. This was a pale colour, but a perfect arc over the falls of a most unearthly quality. The sad thing we found on our second visit was the new 'customs' barrier between Northern and Southern Rhodesia (the former now known as Zambia).

On our first visit, we also took a delightful launch trip up the Zambesi River, away from the falls, to an island about eight miles away where we saw both monkeys (a small grey kind) and hippo, as well as many kinds of birds and a tame crocodile who looked very evil indeed! We surprised a family of hippo in a cove, and they all submerged quickly, looking at us with their heads, ears and snouts above water. Never had a hippo at a zoo looked at us like that. Then two emerged a few feet away from our boat and quickly submerged again. They looked for all the world like the horse's head on the Acropolis in Athens!

Although there were signs up everywhere that 'wild animals can be dangerous', most people with whom we talked declared that usually they are not, unless molested. It is said that the game parks have made a great difference, as the animals are protected and rapidly get used to man. Charming little grey monkeys appeared when we had tea, taking bits of biscuit gently from our hands, but when my sister was trying to photograph them, another monkey leapt smartly into her seat, which she had vacated, and grabbed her biscuit – a neat piece of work!

The famous baboons round the hill still make raids on the hotel garden and there is a special 'boy' to keep them in order. He constantly goes about with a couple of stones in his hands. But he was caught napping once at lunchtime, much to our delight!

We returned to Bulawayo by air, and found ourselves in a pleasant, sizeable town with enormously wide streets. We were told that Rhodes insisted that a full ox-team of sixteen could be swung around them. There are also steep gullies at the cross-streets, and we wondered what these were for, as they made it rather rough for cars to cross. We were soon to know.

We had several friends living in this town (Sidney Legge, whom we knew from Coombe Springs, and Mr. and Mrs. John Brett, sister and brother-in-law of Miriam Bryans of the London Subud Group) who wished to show us the sights, and we started out next morning for the Matopas, the strange hills nearby with huge craggy boulders poised as though they would fall at any moment. This is called the 'World's View' where Cecil Rhodes is buried, a simple, impressive grave among the boulders. We had imagined there would be high hills, but although very impressive they are really quite low. We were now in the Matabele country, and the kraals of the great chiefs.

The weather was beautiful at first, with lovely sunshine, but as we climbed up to the second of two caves nearby to look at Bushman paintings, drops of rain began to fall, and it was obvious that the best of the day was over. On our way back to the hotel, the heavens opened and the rains fell. Never had I seen such rain. All the streets in Bulawayo were running deep with water. We soon saw the purpose of the cross-street gullies, which were raging torrents difficult for small cars to cross. In blinding rain, we reached our hotel and watched at the hotel door as the young people had a whale of a time jumping the torrents to get where they wanted to go.

The next day, we hired a car to take us to Zimbabwe, around 200 miles to the east. The day did not look too bad when we left Bulawayo. However, it simply became worse and worse as we proceeded. We left the good tarmac road, and took one of the 'strip roads' to Fort Victoria. Then the rain started again. The danger points were the rivers; they look mild enough streams when the sun shines, but become raging floods when the rain comes down, gradually washing right over the low-lying bridges. One can easily get stuck in the middle of such a bridge, and this can be dangerous, as great bores of water come plunging down and can carry cars and their occupants along with them. We did not know this until later!

We were then told by another driver that Fort Victoria (our destination) was cut off, as a further river was impassable. However, our chauffeur decided to go on, as there was no other road we could take at that point. The rain became worse and worse, and at one point there was such an immense deluge we had to stop as we could see nothing. Finally, we came to the debatable bridge; it was not too bad, and we were able to cross. It was still raining when we turned off for Zimbabwe and we were downcast, as we could not see how we could walk and climb over ruins if this down-pour continued.

However, we decided after lunch to go to the museum and put in our introduction to the curator, Mrs. Lilian Hodges. Unfortunately, our driver, a delightful chap called 'Saturday', decided to try a short cut with the result that we stalled in a huge pool of water. Saturday peeled off his shoes and socks and waded into the pool to try to start things up again, but we were only finally able to get out when a female help appeared and volunteered to push. Women appear to be far stronger than men here. With me steering, we managed to get out of the pool on to dry land and our engine finally started. Rain still pouring, we arrived at the museum to find that the curator had fled to her own house in the village. So we again set out and finally arrived with a rain-sodden and unrecognisable introduction at a delightful little house which would have had a lovely view if we could only have seen it. Mrs. Hodges welcomed us most sweetly and said she could give us her services the whole next day.

All the evening and most of the night, the downpour went on, but we woke to realize that the sound of the rain had ceased. In no time at all, the paths were drying in the sun and when we returned along the road the following day, the rivers had shrunk to little streams again.

At the museum, Mrs. Hodges was waiting for us, a slight, grey-haired and very capable lady. Zimbabwe is in its own National Park, and the two people in charge of the area were herself and the Park Warden. She mothered and bossed everybody, settling all their problems, and the Africans loved it.

We scaled the Acropolis by the ancient way, although it was specially stated in the guide book that elderly people should take the modern way! Mrs. Hodges was making a tour of inspection to see that no stones, rocks or bricks had fallen in the rain to make the ruins unsafe, and we were very glad to have her as our guide. Her museum henchman and Saturday, who seemed most intrigued with it all, followed at a distance to repair the damage, and she was constantly calling to them to repair this or that.

The Acropolis is an astonishing collection of boulders on the top of a hill to which the builders, in Inca style, have added huge walls and narrow stairways between the rocks and buildings. The guide book remarks that this and the Great Dwelling House not far away with immensely high walls, were as great a feat for the Stone Age as the Kariba Dam is for ours. The Acropolis was a sacred enclosure, some wonderful soapstone birds were found. They reminded us of those equally mysterious figures in ancient Chavin in Peru, which we took such trouble to reach. Some of it also seemed like Macchu Picchu in the Andes and we also arrived at some equally dizzy heights with lovely views over the surrounding countryside.

Zimbabwe is very mysterious because one cannot see the reason for anything the builders did, and there seem to be no traditions about it. No-one knows who built it. It was at first thought to have had some connection with Solomon and the Queen of Sheba, and certainly some very early connection with the coast and over the sea. Modern theories put Zimbabwe at a much later date, although the site has been occupied since early A.D. The present buildings were probably erected by the native African people over a period of 800 years from the 11th to the 19th centuries before the widespread European colonisation began. It was, of course, important as a trading centre with India, Portugal and the Far East, and also as a sort of Church of very ancient standing. At the time that it was built, there appeared to have been some very able people, the 'Mwenye', descendants of the Moors, who were the craftsmen and the 'Rozwi', who were excellent organisers and builders, who were blending the large numbers of tribes into federations. Again, like Angkor in Cambodia, a blend of mixed races appears to have produced works of genius. A community of the court of the Mambo or ruler lived on the plains nearby, and their chiefs were probably buried on Zimbabwe Hill. The eight Zimbabwe sacred birds were thought to form a register of deceased chiefs for use in this ceremony.* There were a number of smaller ruins in the style of Zimbabwe nearer Bulawayo such as the Khami Ruins etc.

In the afternoon we started off again, first to the temple (wrongly named, as it is actually the living quarters). Immensely high double walls with passages in between and high towers, apparently quite solid; chevron patterns around one part of the wall only, huge standing stones rather like a small Avebury. What do they all mean? And why were they built so beautifully and carefully? We never saw a more mysterious place, and even our extensive knowledge of ancient buildings could not help.

We returned to Bulawayo the following day only 24 hours before we were due in Salisbury, the capital. My sister spent the rest of her time there visiting the African Townships with Mrs. Brett, who had been mayor of the town. It was a fascinating experience. Everybody knew Mrs. Brett and simply adored her. We were pleasantly surprised with our quick glimpse of Salisbury. The city looked attractive and new, but on this occasion we continued our trip to Nairobi and our game park experiences. But we looked forward to another visit the following year. There was a great deal more that we wished to see in Salisbury.

On our second trip to South Africa, we approached the country by sea via Beira and took the train. It was the worst railway trip we have ever been on. It is actually about 400 miles between Beira and Salisbury, but we bumped, stopped and meandered all through a night and a day, stopping at practically every house.

At Umtali we breakfasted on the platform on real bacon and eggs, which tasted wonderful after arid continental breakfasts. We reached Salisbury at about five o'clock, and were thankful to relax. Warned by our train experience, we took to cars and our own feet in the future.

This time, we wanted to see some of their celebrated rock paintings. These we found, are exceedingly hard to find even with the best of directions. One of the reasons for this is that the people who find them destroy them, for no apparent reason at all. One authority who was taking us around a hill near Umtali, said that however hard he tried to prevent this, he could not help this happening. Umtali is a charming little town with a small but quite fascinating game park.

We went to the lovely districts of Inyanga and later the Vumba Mountains, or rather hills. The former look rather like Scotland without any heather, and contains the old country estate of Cecil Rhodes (now a hotel) and many ancient dwellings of the Zimbabwe type, but on a much humbler scale. Some excellent orchards, fish hatcheries and waterfalls are all around. We took a trip to the Kariba Dam, an awe-inspiring place we could not begin to describe here.

We have long wanted to write something about man and his relationship with animals. In a Mexican Museum near Vera Cruz in the early Sixties, we saw an ancient figure which came, apparently, from the land of the Olmecs, the oldest known civilization of Mexico, and was called by the curious name of the 'God of the Animals' !. Its power was not savage and primitive as one might expect, but gentle and sad, as though needing help. Perhaps if one could have a taste of the qualities of all the animals, this might be the end product.

In our world, the ordinary human has less to do with animals than ever before. We see the unusual species in zoos and circuses performing for our pleasure and amusement. But we seldom see them in their free, private lives. Our African trip gave us many examples of these animals running free in their game parks, but even these preserves create unnatural problems. Too many animals eat too much food and it becomes necessary to cull them. Many people want to do the right thing, but how are we to understand and value animal life, so that everything can find its right place? What is the course we should take? Frankly, we do not know. But surely, we who are more than animal should be able to care for them properly, not sentimentally, and try to understand their purpose in life, even as we should try to understand our own.

Uganda

The nicest part of this visit was a launch trip on the Gazinga Channel, connecting the two great lakes (Lake George and Lake Edward) where one is only a few feet from the game on the bank. Two elephants surveyed us with interest, and one large beast put his

* From Vanished Civilisations by Roger Summers.

trunk in the air and a foot in the water. He looked as though he would dearly like to charge us. But as there were some eight feet of water between us, he thought better of it. Here, too, there was wonderful bird life: many eagles, beautiful coloured herons, storks, including the hideous marabout variety, vultures, cranes and many small birds such as kingfishers, the black ibis, and also the sacred ibis, the Egyptian one.

Our last visit in Uganda was to the colourful Murchison Park and falls, older and better known than the Queen Elizabeth, but not so interesting except for the Victoria Nile and the crocodiles on it. We went there by launch and saw enormous crocodiles, "gators" as my Californian lady friend insisted, sleeping on the banks. They usually woke when the boat drew near, and slid rapidly into the water. I had an excellent view of several of them – such evil prehistoric-looking beasts! There were many hippos everywhere too, the crocodiles do not seem to worry them at all.

We returned again to Nairobi from the Murchison Park expedition, and then next day, took a car out to "Tree Tops" – an expedition that I was looking forward to above all others.

Tree Tops is in Nyeri in the White Highlands, and is literally a hotel in the trees of the Aberdare National Park, overlooking a most beautiful pool with the forest glades all around it. Its origin was a brilliant idea by Eric Sherbrooke Walker and his wife, Lady Betty, to build a place where people could observe the wild animals as they came for water and salt.

The original Tree Tops was burnt down by the Mau-Mau, but was rebuilt in much larger and better style. When we were there, it could take twenty two guests at a time; there were small and well fitted bedrooms for all, and a dining room with a telephone!

One leaves "The Outspan", the Nyeri Hotel starting point, after lunch in three Landrovers under the guard of a "White Hunter" with gun, and arrives near Tree Tops. We walked a few hundred yards only, with the Hunter in front. There are ladders against many of the trees en route, and some stockades in case of sudden appearance of wild life.

No-one had told us how beautiful the scene was at Tree Tops: a large pool surrounded by chestnut trees, and animals of all kinds grazing, drinking water or licking salt. There was a continuing change of scene. Our old friends, the wart hogs, were about, also the buffalo, water buck and charming little bush buck, and large birds of all kinds, including the sacred Ibis, and two very beautiful golden crested cranes with two small chicks; not to mention the baboons, who climbed up to the balconies, where we were sitting (especially when tea was served) many with small babies riding on their backs.

Watching animals is the most extraordinary and restful thing to do. They are so individual in their movements and behaviour. As a rule, they do not bother each other, except for some of the bigger ones who, like the rhino, come later in the evening. He is a regular bully and will leave no-one alone.

At dusk, all the animals disappear and the night prowlers appear, such as rhino, buffalo herds and elephants. Unfortunately, we did not see any elephants, but as we had already seen many herds, we could well imagine their presence. The Tree Tops people had arranged special lighting, which comes on so gradually that the animals do not notice it, but we humans could see the animals as clearly as in the daytime. It is a continual shifting of scene: a herd of buffalo will silently come forward – one does not hear them, but they are suddenly just there, then an old rhino, grunting and guzzling water, just under the balcony, apparently quite oblivious to the presence of humans upstairs. He immediately starts to bully the buffalo, and charges right through a group of them. When they have departed, back come the little bush buck family stepping daintily along to their salt lick, only to take to their heels instantly if a buffalo or rhino looked in their direction.

Watching animals like this is quite different from rushing around in a car trying to photograph them. We really have no conception of what man has lost, by losing connection with the animals.

After our adventures in the National Parks, we decided to continue north through Ethiopia, although we had at one time thought of going direct through Khartoum to Egypt.

The airtrip from Nairobi to Addis Ababa was perfect, the captain giving us graphic descriptions of the country we were passing over. The flight took about an hour and a half and we landed safely at Addis Ababa (which means 'New Flower'), on a handsome but unfinished airport. 'Unfinished' was the word for all air and tourist affairs in this country! Asmara, the second airport we landed at in this country, had runways, but hardly any airport. At Addis we were given visas, and we took a taxi to the Ghion Hotel, standing on high ground just below the Emperor's Palace! At one time we were told, part of the Ghion Hotel was the Emperor's Domain, and there were still rows of stables nearby where the royal horses had been kept.

We tried to get in touch with our Ethiopian agent, whose headquarters were in Asmara, but no-one seemed to know him, and the car we had ordered for the next day never came. However, we finally went out to explore Addis with an American lawyer, whom we had met at the hotel, driven by (we were told afterwards) the King's detective. We also introduced ourselves to Mrs. Acock, to whom we had an introduction. She was living in the hotel. Two energetic American ladies went sightseeing with us the following Monday and we visited Coptic Churches and the Emperor's Palace. We also saw the Emperor's pet lions in the park, with two families of cubs, one very small one being brought to us to stroke. We also saw monuments, some markets and the European quarters of the city.

Our two days passed pleasantly enough and we continued to Asmara as planned. Asmara is the capital of Eritrea and from it, we were told, we could visit all the most ancient sites. So far, the answer to all questions about old sites had been the same: they – all of them – would take us days to reach. A large notice prominently displayed at the Ghion Hotel desk – 'Visit ancient Lalibela' – intrigued us, as we knew these old churches were famous. We pursued the matter further, but were only told: "Oh, there is nowhere for ladies to stay!"

The hotel at Asmara was a good Italian one. Our agent appeared at last, Mr. Tozzi, a delightful Italian, who had been trying to find out our whereabouts for days.

Asmara was a charming town, very Italian with many European shops and gorgeous flowers, especially the purple jacaranda trees lining many streets.

The next day, we had a lengthy talk with Mr. Tozzi and his friend Mr. Cotti about future plans. We wanted to reach Aksum, a sacred town and reputed to be very old, which it was possible to do in five hours driving according to our guide book (we actually reached it in three hours) and Gondar to which we were supposed to fly. Lalibela had to be abandoned, as it was not reachable in the time we had to spare. We finally decided to set out the following day (luckily with Mr. Tozzi himself) to do both Aksum and Gondar by road, a very lengthy and extraordinary trip, mainly over the Italian military road, built by them for the conquest of Ethiopia.

First, we went to Aksum, a rather dirty little town, but very interesting as the old religious capital of Ethiopia, and connected with the Queen of Sheba. In fact, Ethiopia is steeped in impressive Biblical tradition. According to the Chronicles, the present Emperor 'Conquering Lion of the Tribe of Judah', was the descendant of Menelik, the son of King Solomon and the Queen of Sheba, and the Tablet of Moses, brought from Jerusalem after the founding of the dynasty, was carefully perserved in one of the sanctuaries of Aksum. The Ethiopians cling to the origin of their royal house and have returned to the descendants many times after other kings. Even at the time of our visit, the present Emperor was building a new church there, although it seemed little needed. As well as the wonderful pre-Christian obelisks or stelae⋆ of great height still standing, we found some standing stones not far away, reminiscent, on a small scale, of the Carnac Menhirs in France, as well as our own Avebury.

Probably there is some tradition of real knowledge here, although the present Ethiopians obviously have no understanding of this. But it was curious, nevertheless, to see them clinging to the Solomon story as though they sensed it was something immensely valuable. Ladies were not allowed inside the principal church (on account of the bad behaviour of some queen) but the jewels and crowns were brought out for our viewing, by special dispensation of the High Priest. We also viewed some other royal tombs (whose, I never gathered) which had been recently excavated. They looked rather Egyptian. It is a pity all this history cannot be properly recorded, as it should bring forward some interesting connections. No-one seems to care, and the old things are being cheerfully destroyed.

En route, we saw many of the poorer Ethiopians who waved gaily to us. They were dreadfully poor and their land was in a shocking condition: erosion everywhere and no hope of proper cultivation. They were a graceful and polite people and Christian for centuries. They apparently did not want to alter their way of life and had even pulled down the fine houses, farms and public buildings put up by the Italians. Naturally, they hated the Italians, but I was reminded of the 'Stupid saint' and the necessity for 'knowledge' as well as 'being'.

All this I gleaned during one of the hardest trips we have ever had. On the journey out, we had two tyre blow-outs and five more on the return trip! There was no shade and the sun was very hot indeed in the valleys, especially in the middle of the day.

We spent two nights in Gondar, an interesting town with curious royal palaces of a period in Ethiopian history when the court was

---

⋆ The first thing which impresses one about Aksum are the relics of the earliest period, namely the gigantic obelisks or stellae. According to the medieval book of Aksum, there were originally 58 stelae of different types in the holy city. Present day archaeologists have counted a good many more. But the seven great monoliths impeccably hewn from the hardest granite-like stone, one measuring sixty feet high (the only one now standing) another hundred feet, with nine sets of windows timber framed, one above the other over a bolted door with a sacrificial table in front, are a complete mystery. No monuments resembling them have ever been found elsewhere, either in Grecian, Eguyptian or Roman structure. Speculation as to why these monuments were built ranges between a house for a dead prince which contains precious relics, to monuments to the Planets (as there are seven).

isolated from the rest of the country. There was also a Coptic church on a hill with curious Christian paintings. It was interesting to see the Ethiopian countryside and way of life, although we were not sure that the very hard trip from Aksum to Gondar was worth the effort. We returned rather wearily to Asmara and took our Khartoum plane one day later than expected.

We liked the Ethiopians very much. They are obviously of quite a different blend of races from the other parts of Africa and we were told that they are mainly a Semitic people. The men, particularly, are upright, tall, slender and handsome with a very pleasant atmosphere about them. They frequently carry a long stick which they hold between their arms held high above their heads. We suppose it is cool and restful, but it looked rather a strain to us.

Unfortunately, owing to a change of plane, we were never able to see the confluence of the White and Blue Nile at Omdurman, as we landed at night on Tuesday, April 9th and had to take a very early plane to Luxor the following morning. Khartoum was exceedingly hot, though we found a hotel with air-conditioning and large lime juices in glasses to greet us there.

At Luxor, the delays and lack of explanation one has always associated with Egypt, or rather, the United Arab Republic, started. All our affairs were in order, luckily.

We were tired and wanted to rest, but were disturbed and told that our guide was downstairs. However, as often as we went downstairs, he never seemed to be there! After some diversions we managed to find out that our Cairo agent was, in fact, calling on us. He was trying to make arrangements to visit Abu Simbel* on the fast boat, the hydrofoil, but it was most difficult to come to any practical arrangement and several times we despaired of the whole thing.

Meanwhile, we went to Thebes, which was rather difficult to see as there were so many tourists there. It was almost impossible to relax and study the columns and hieroglyphs and the atmosphere. It was interesting to see King Tut's Tomb again, on a small and rather heavily painted place, but the great tombs of Seti I and Amenophis III were impossible to view properly for the crowds who gathered there. It was very hot, I suppose 80° to 100° all the time we were in Luxor and Aswan.

The next day we were able to see Denderah, about 60 miles away, to see a temple built to honour Hathor the Cow Goddess, which is

* We wished to see this famous monument before it 'was moved' to another location owing to the danger of destruction from the new Aswan Dam.

associated with Cleopatra. Its famous Zodiac was taken out by a French archaeologist and a replica put in, but there is an interesting climb to the roof up the old steps, with figures pointing the way, up and down. There were also a few tourists with us that day.

By this time, we had reached Easter Sunday, and our planned stay in Luxor was almost over. Still no news of our much awaited hydrofoil trip, but tickets were eventually produced that Tuesday and early in the morning we went to the harbour of Shellal. We had excellent seats in the main cabin of the Italian-made boat and soon we shot firmly through the water cheerfully saluting the other craft on the river. It was a long trip even then, five hours until we sighted Abu Simbel, which looked from a distance rather smaller than we had imagined. One should try and see this site next to the water and at sunrise when the sun strikes directly inside. We landed. It was unbearably hot, well over 100°.

Inside the main temple, which is hollowed out from the rock, are three huge compartments running into each other. The last one is the Holy of Holies, and graced with three sitting figures. Much colour is left on these bas-reliefs which we had not expected. These are, of course, beautifully done, but mainly of Ramases 11's warlike deeds and conquests, of a rather late and imperialistic period.

The other temple was dedicated to the Goddess Hathor, for Nefertari, his wife, in a graceful, charming and feminine style.

The five hours' return journey was rather wearisome and hot, but we felt that we had accomplished what we wanted to do although it was a tiring business.

As we had another day at Aswan, we went sailing to Kitchener's Island and made a visit to the high dam in the evening where work was being carried on day and night under arc lamps, and it was a hive of activity.

Next day, we returned to Luxor, picked up our luggage and flew on to Cairo. Our last evening was spent sitting out in our silk dresses in the desert watching 'Son et LumiËre' on the Sphinx and pyramids. We also had a fine visit to the Cairo Museum, which had been quite changed since our last visit there. We specially enjoyed the Old Kingdom Sculptures and the wonderful Tutankhamen exhibits.

We left Cairo on April 22nd and returned to London non-stop. It seemed to us incredible that one could travel so quickly.

CHAPTER 28

Trips with Mr. Bennett

Turkey 1966

We left from London Airport on August 31st heading for Istanbul; there was quite a party of us: J.G. Bennett and Elizabeth, Harry Stubbings, Olga de Nottbeck, John Bristow, my sister and myself. Tony Blake also joined us for part of the trip.

We arrived at Istanbul Airport to be met by Mr. Bennett's friends the Tozans, and after the usual preliminaries went to the Pera Palace Hotel, a solid and very ancient of days type of place. We dined quietly and then went for a short walk on simply ghastly pavements. I had to keep my eyes on the ground so much that I missed the real sights and Istanbul is a fine city lit up at night.

The next day we went out in the town for general sightseeing: Suleymaniye Mosque and the Topkapi Sarayi (Palace of the Seraglio). The treasures of the Sultan were quite incredible, enormous jewels and gorgeous pottery from the East. In particular, gifts from China from all periods, with particular reference to the lovely bright yellow porcelain only used by the Emperor, and scarce in European museums. There was also an interesting collection of pictures of Ottoman monarchs.

We lunched in town and then drove to the Golden Horn where we could see nothing but factories. As Mr. Bennett said, no doubt it was lovely in earlier days. Home to rest and then to dinner with the Tozans. It was a relief to get out of the endless noise of Istanbul. Mrs. Tozan, an Austrian who spoke good English, was a most charming hostess; but I fear we were a flop with the master of the house as, according to himself, he only spoke French and German; and we could not start a flow in either of these languages.

On September 2nd we took a whole day's boat trip up the Bosphorus. This started with a real adventure. Mr. Bennett and Elizabeth decided to walk down to Galata Bridge, where the boat started, with instructions for us to follow in two taxis. All seemed clear, but it wasn't, as King Faisal of Saudi Arabia was in Istanbul on a State Visit, and got absolutely and completely in our way. In consequence it seemed impossible for us to reach the boat before it sailed. The Bennetts did their best to delay its sailing, but it was only our heroic taxi-man who saved us by somehow wriggling his car to the right side of the road, so that we could sprint in at the very last minute. We called out to Mr. Bennett, who did not see us at first. When he did, he went back to the boat and forcibly held onto the thing until we panted aboard! There was no other boat that day, so this was just as well.

The views were beautiful, especially of the lovely old aristocratic wooden houses along the straits. They must have been very damp and cold in the winter, but wonderful for bathing and water sports during the summer. There were numerous castles, villages, people, small boats, and everything else to see as we went along.

Later we had dinner at an Istanbul restaurant which Mr. Bennett had known for years and years. But I fear that, except for country bread, I don't like Turkish food. Yoghourt and the local fruits in season are very good, especially the grapes, melons and peaches.

Next day we went sightseeing at Santa Sophia and the Blue Mosque in the morning. This was my sister's third visit to the former, and she was tremendously impressed as she had never been before, at this first massive effort of official Christianity to establish itself. The force the early Christians felt must have been terrific, and the church itself, with its great square covered by a cupola, quite beyond their building efforts at the time. Actually, the cupola fell twice, but was restored both times. The first time my sister saw it, in 1933, it was a Mohammedan Mosque, and all the Christian frescoes were covered up. As it has now been made into a Museum, many of the frescoes which have survived, have been uncovered. They are most beautiful. Many of the pillars used were taken from the earlier 'heathen' temples, from Baalbec and the Temple of Diana at Ephesus etc, and this annoyed me greatly at my first view. But I see now that the Christians wanted all the spiritual help they could get in their efforts. One felt it was still a place of worship, and should not really be a museum. We felt the same way about the Mevlevi Tekke in Konya. The Blue Mosque is spectacular with all its effects and very harmonious, but one should not see it after the great Hagia Sophia.

Lunch was at the hotel after which we went by boat to see Professor Mellaart's home* on the Bosphorus. We met his charming wife and had a delightful tea and talk with him, which Olga recorded.

On Sunday we started for Konya. We took the ferry first, cars and all, to the Asiatic side. The sellers of dark glasses appeared, and some members of our party had much fun in beating them down in price from astronomical heights. Everything here had to be bargained for, even Istanbul taxis, which actually all carried perfectly good meters.

It was a most beautiful drive, but oh! it was a long, long way to Konya. We actually took 12 hours, and arrived there at 9.30 pm feeling very weary.

Our hotel, the Turistik Saray, was almost noisier than Istanbul, and that was saying quite a lot. There was so much noise in Turkey, car horns used incessantly, animals' hoofs, every kind of human making as much noise as possible all the time. However, me with my pillows and my sister with her earplugs, managed to survive it all. In Konya, even Mr. Bennett was disturbed. He started to count the intervals of silence in the din, and got as far as eight seconds once! The muezzin calling from the Mosque** usually broke through the comparative silence of the early hours around 4.00 am but that, we all agreed, if genuine, and not a recording, was rather nice, and sent us off to sleep again.

We spent the first day sightseeing in Konya. It seemed strange that when my sister first met Mr. Bennett, about 1933, and told him she was going to Turkey, or rather, through Turkey to Damascus and Jerusalem, he recommended that she go to Konya. It certainly would not have been possible then, but here we were at last. The ancient name was Iconium, meaning the city with an image, and according to legend it was here that Perseus cut off the head of Medusa and hung it on a pillar. St. Paul preached here, and it seems to have been connected with everything historical in these parts, starting with the Hittites.

The main centre of interest nowadays is the so-called Museum of Islamic Art, really the sacred centre for the Whirling or Mevlevi Dervishes and the burial place of their founder Jalaluddin Rumi, his family and other dervishes. Although officially now a museum and

* Catal Huyuk, excavated by James Mellaart in 1961-63, ranks with Jericho in Jordan as one of man's first known attempts in the development of town life. Before 6000 B.C. it was a town, or even a city, of a remarkable and developed kind.
** Muezzin calling from the Mosque: in the Mohammedan religion prayers to Allah are made every few hours from the tops of the mosques by the Muezzin Minister in charge, sometimes simply in a recording.

the dervishes banished, it still has its feeling of worship, and one can see people come here for that purpose. Although false walls, and doors, have been set up to facilitate the museum idea, one can see how the prayers and dancing were carried out. We also saw, through the courtesy of the Director, the Mevlevi kitchens, where the novices learnt to turn as well as cook. There are metal studs in the floor where candidates whilst doing their ordinary work had to learn to keep the foot fixed for the turning.

We also saw some of the other local monuments, notably the Mosque of Allaeddin on Allaeddin Hill. He was one of their local monarchs and, I suppose, the origin of our magical Aladdin.

September 6th, the famous day we went to see the site of Catal Huyuk. We started out in good time with picnic baskets filled from the hotel for our lunch. It was a most beautiful drive of around 30 miles.

We were received at the site most cordially by the Turkish guard, but very severely warned that nothing was to be picked up. My sister secreted two bits of obsidian all the same. Most of the interesting pieces had been moved to the Ankara Museum. But the site, like most ancient sites, was well worth visiting, especially the layout of the inhabitants' houses. Much remained to be excavated here; Professor Mellaart spoke of a further thousand years' occupation, and this is just one 'Tell' or hill. So far they have got back to around 7000 B.C., an incredibly early date for this type of ordered living.

We took our picnic lunch to the 'barrage' or dam, nearby where there was a lovely view. The Turkish farmer on whose land we were, promptly treated us as his guests (a charming custom here) and brought us tea, melons and a rug to sit on. His wife even gave us some rose water to wash our sticky hands after lunch. They would take no money, and only very tentatively asked Mr. Bennett whether he could get the lady some medicine which they were not able to buy in Turkey. (This was later sent on to her.)

The next day we left Konya for Kayseri and Urgub, which we reached at lunchtime. We spent the afternoon exploring the strange Byzantine rock churches in Goreme. These rocks already eroded into strange shapes were carved out into churches and homes with some quaint and rather beautiful Christian pictures, notably those of the Last Supper and the Kiss of Judas.

When we started the trip, the great Hittite fortresses in the north seemed too far away, but neither Mr. Bennett nor my sister and I had seen them. So we decided to see at least one at Bogazkale, on our way to Ankara. Elizabeth remarked that she thought Mr. Bennett would regret this decision, and it did look like it, since this put a great many miles onto our route, and our cars always seemed to be in a shaky condition, particularly if we had a good deal of ground to cover. One or other of them was always collapsing, and cost us a good deal of much needed time. We finally arrived at Ankara about 9.30 in the evening, very tired indeed. However, the Hittite site was really wonderful. Much of its choice bits were in the Ankara Museum, but the superb bas-relief of the God Sharumma protecting King Tutalia from Yazilikaya nearby was simply wonderful, so were others there, the Lion Gate at the fort and the extensive walls everywhere. Once again I should like to go back in time and see what it all looked like in its prime.

On September 9th we went calling and sight-seeing in Ankara, first to the Archaeological Museum where the Catal Huyuk and Hittite remains from the sites could be seen. There is not nearly enough exhibited of the former, both because of lack of room and also the difficulty of preserving the ancient paintings. The Hittite remains were much more extensive and well-known. The many ceremonial standards are very interesting. They are always of a bull with a varying number of horns, sometimes only two and sometimes more. It is difficult to see why this varies, unless some idea such as Gurdjieff's is correct, that the number of horns are a key to the person's wisdom.

We then went to call on Mr. Michael Gough, the Director of the British Institute in Ankara, and had a pleasant talk with him. We also went to the Unesco site already being developed outside the town for a gigantic commercial university for students from all parts of the Middle East.

Next day we went on from Ankara to Bursa, a very noisy town which turned out, rather disastrously for us, to be in the middle of some local festival. We went first, before going to our hotel, to see the Green Mosque and an Ottoman Emperor's tomb; beautiful tile work here, the most famous in Turkey, with very special green tiles. We were sitting having tea afterwards when the rest of our party, having been delayed on the road by one of the frequent punctures, joined us to report that the hotel had no rooms for us, having reserved them for the previous day. Mr. Bennett valiantly went into the rather hopeless battle of rooms for eight on Saturday night and it all turned out wonderfully. We were suddenly transported from the noisy overfull town to the heights of the Asiatic Mount Olympus, some 20 miles away, to the inn belonging to the sanatorium there. It was rather coolish for our thin clothes but otherwise marvellous with its pine forests, gorgeous air and silence. The doctor in charge welcomed us most pleasantly in impeccable English, and was quite overcome when he heard Mr. Bennett's wonderful Turkish.

On September 11th we left the mountain heights and went on to Istanbul where the Pera Palace opened its doors to us again. Here we stayed for two nights, leaving Istanbul for home, this time via Athens, on the 13th.

I have forgotten one episode, which gave us much fun and real pleasure: our purchases in the markets of Konya and Istanbul. We much admired the countrywomen's huge full trousers, so Elizabeth, Marjorie and I bought some material at Konya and a little shop made us up three pairs. We intended to use them as fancy dress (and as an antidote to mini-skirts) at a special party when we got home. The price, with material, was two pounds each. Marjorie and I also bought carpets, small prayer rugs, painted wooden spoons and some tiles.

Iraq and Iran

After our last trip to Africa in 1964, I decided to move my home to a bungalow in Guildford. I had heard that there was a buyer for my home on Pitch Hill, Ewhurst, and as my sister and I were making so many trips abroad, I decided that a smaller home would suit me better. Robert Whiffen came to help me redesign the bungalow and he found another expert to help me terrace the garden. The bungalow was on the side of a hill and had lovely views of the Cathedral and University and of a large part of the town. It also enabled me to travel more easily to London by train or car to be with my sister or other friends in Kingston or Richmond. Judy Macleod came to help me move and continued to come to take care of the bungalow.

Mr. Bennett at Coombe Springs wished to go to the east to explore his contacts there, and we were glad to go with him. I have previously mentioned our trip to Nepal to see the Shivapuri Baba, but now we were to fly on to Iraq and Iran where there were so many famous ruins. We hoped to see Babylon and go to Ur of the Chaldees and even the site of Nineveh, and we could not imagine a better escort.

Nearly always, we have found that the most sacred events go hand in hand with the most bizarre. Our Indonesian visit to Bapak was one example. We had another example after our trip to Nepal. We had planned to go from Delhi to Baghdad and then into West Persia

(Iraq) for two or three days only, as Mr. Bennett was eager to make a visit to the small village of Kerind and also to the larger town of Kermanshah. We were very thrilled with this idea, as we had never been to Iraq, or to the 'Conqueror's Road' from the East with the famous Darius Inscription at Bisutun and other sites already mentioned. Unfortunately, owing to the disturbed state of Iraq and the shortness of our stay, the latter never materialized, but we did manage to make a remarkable visit to West Iran.

In Baghdad, we started off with a taste of "revolution" the first afternoon of our visit. The wife of the British Political Attache had taken us out to tea with some enthusiastic young people and it was during our drive back to our hotel when we ran into a local riot. It was the rush hour, lines of cars formed a block and people started suddenly to run. They were waving some banners and there was some shooting. Our driver was practical and never lost her nerve. She merely edged the car into another queue, shot across the nearest bridge over the Tigris River, saying that we could not go home just now, but must go to our next engagement early!!

We were under the most respectable auspices, namely The British Council and the British Embassy, but it took all the strings we could pull to get us over the border. Iraq was in ferment and the dictator terrified of assassination.

Permission was necessary for every possible move one could make, and no doubt it looked suspicious from an Iraqui official's point of view for a tall, blue eyed Englishman with his 'harem' of two ladies to be crossing and recrossing the Iraq-Iran border for three days only. What could we be up to? Mr. Bennett was, as usual, quite undaunted, although it took three and a half hours with Ali (The British Council's most wily courier) to get all the exit and entrance permits necessary.

Nothing daunted, we started out the next day in a big De Soto car for the Persian border through a flat and very dry country originally covered (so Mr. Bennett told us) by forests in which the inhabitants hunted leopards, tigers and lions! In due course, we came to the border, where we had the usual delays before we were all allowed to pass. As we were accustomed to fight our own battles in strange lands, we found it a pleasant change to be sitting quietly as 'harem' with nothing to do except smile.

In Persia (Iran) the scenery became much more beautiful, and it was a good deal cooler. We were entering the land of the nomadic Kurds. We arrived at the village of Kerind, our first stop, about teatime to discover Christopher Weightman, an English student studying Persian, sitting patiently beside the inn. He had come by bus from Tehran to meet us, and had already been waiting since the previous day!!

There was some trouble about accommodation, as the inn was not considered suitable for ladies, so we had to make our choice between going to the police or the doctor's residence. We chose to go to the latter, and were taken to where the young doctor and his wife lived. In Persia, doctors have to serve their 'intern' work in these small villages throughout the countryside. He spoke fairly fluent English, but his wife - not a word.

By this time, we only longed for a rest and to be alone, but this was not to be. The men departed for an unknown destination and we were left in a small square room with almost no furniture, except a card table and chairs, with a beautiful Persian carpet on the floor and our hostess. We had no language in common, but she chatted in a mixture of French and Turkish and gave us biscuits, sweets and tea at intervals. A restless small daughter and a little puppy and kitten completed the party.

This went on for hours until our two men returned, and the doctor appeared from his surgery. Our host insisted that we stay there for dinner, but for a long time nothing further appeared, except several small drinks. At last, scrambled eggs and a very green salad came in. The doctor anticipated our unspoken thoughts and told us he had already washed the salad in permanganate of potash, and he observed further that he was giving us some yoghurt to follow as dessert.

It is Persian custom not to serve the meal until the end of the evening, as it is etiquette for the guests to leave immediately afterwards. So the evening ended fairly rapidly, and we were escorted to our quarters for the night. This was to be in the surgery! A bed had been made up for Marjorie on the operating table, and I was to sleep beside her on a truckle bed. Apologies were made and we were advised not to use the water from a tap in the room. It was a hard night! I remember I tried to clean my teeth next morning out of the window, I hoped unobserved. When I looked down, I saw a queue of interested people, all lined up waiting for the surgery to open.

After some breakfast at the inn (made possible by our own oranges and coffee) we were able to drive on to Kermanshah for the second part of our expedition, where there was at least a proper hotel and a European bathtub.

The country meanwhile became more and more beautiful: lovely snowy mountains, red soil and deep green vegetation. The whole covered at intervals with flocks and herds of black and white goats, sheep, cattle, horses, donkeys and some mules. The wealth of the land is in these animals, not in unsound paper. Their owners are mainly Kurds who migrate from place to place with their animals. The movement of these groups as they migrate is most lovely. It gives the impression somehow of a new being. This was the special period of migration, and we saw one whole tribe of Turkish Kurds on the move and managed to photograph them as they came toward us. They surrounded Mr. Bennett laughing and shouting as he spoke to them in Turkish.

We were passing palaces of Sassanian and Persian Kings on our way to Bisutun where high on the rocks off the main road is the famous Darius Inscription! This was cut by the order of Darius, to give a description of his conquests, so that all passers-by might see and read it. We, too, scrambled up the rocks to try and photograph it and to see more of the details of the inscription. Darius must have been a statesman and organiser, a follower of Zoroaster, and the true successor of the great Cyrus.

Afterwards, we sat by the wayside amongst riverlets, drank hot tea and watched the local ladies carrying tin cans on their heads. Mr. Bennett tried to make friends with one of their little babies by picking it up, but a howl of terror came forth and he was not a success. We spent the night at Kermanshah, after saying goodbye to Christopher Weightman, much to our regret.

After the fuss that we had had in crossing the frontier, we wondered whether we should have further difficulties on our return, but this did not happen. It seemed as though the authorities were relieved that the big Englishman and his 'appendages' would behave as they said they would do.

One pleasant little interlude remained in my mind: we visited the Persian police (although this appeared to be then unnecessary, as we did not then require exit permits) but one policeman appeared to be intrigued with our status. He knew very little English, and wrote down on a piece of paper, which he handed to me, what he considered 'tourism' to be. He had written 'Walking in the World'. We have thought often of this since then. What a poetic and exact description of a tourist, and an excellent title for our book.

The rest of our stay in Baghdad was as upside down as the first part had been! We visited ancient Ctesiphon (also Sassanian) with its mighty arch of small bricks and many storks nesting on the top. At another time, we visited Babylon, under the guidance of Professor Lenzen, a local expert on the place. Our poor escort was feeling far from well, and we were not too well either, but what spoilt everything were a couple of Iraqui armed guards who insisted on accompanying us everywhere. We were not allowed to take pictures, and were herded together all the time. Principally, one felt it was to insult the foreigner, as one could not imagine anything dangerous about Babylon. It was a pity, though, as the atmosphere of the place is fascinating, and one could have felt much more if one had been free to roam about.

Our final call was to Bonsippa, south west of Babylon, and known in the past as its 'sister city', to view a mount on which a queer shaped object, apparently partly blown away, showed itself.* Professor Lenzer told us this was supposed to be the remains of a Ziggurat connected with the legend of the Tower of Babel. A great explosion appeared to have occurred there. As I was the only one with a camera, I photographed the ruin with great care, as it was a quite unusual interest. But when we later tried to have the photographs enlarged, the film was completely lost by the firm doing the work.

Next day, Mr. Bennett left for home. We had planned to spend a few days in Cyprus, but just as his plane roared overhead, we received a cryptic telegram from B.O.A.C. to the effect that 'No carriers were allowed to leave Beirut for Cyprus. Were we on the brink of international war? It appeared later that it was simply a petty dispute between airports and no international crisis! But bang went our Cyprus trip where we had intended to rest and be on the beach for our extra few days.

* Encyclopedia Britannica - 'Borsippa' The Birs proper is probably the most conspicuous and striking ruin in all Iraq...Here arises a pointed mass of vitrified brick, some as much as 15 ft in diameter, and also single enamelled bricks, Generally bearing an inscription of Nebuchadnezzar, twisted, curled and broken, apparently by great heat.

CHAPTER 29

Sayed Idries Shah and
the Sufis

Both my sister and I were still members of Mr. Bennett's Council at Coombe Springs and therefore were very closely in touch with developments there. As well as Mr. Bennett's travels in Turkey, Iraq and Iran, which were to seek for the real source of our work, there was an unexpected development during 1962.

From one of Mr. Bennett's oldest and much trusted friends came a letter, enclosing a newspaper cutting, describing a visit made by the author to a sanctuary in central Asia in which he had found a teaching that was unmistakably of the same origin as much that we had learnt from Gurdjieff. This letter prepared the way for the announcement that this friend of Mr. Bennett's, Mr. Reggie Hoare, who had shared with him many of the ups and downs of Gurdjieff, Ouspensky and Subud, had met Mr. Idries Shah, who had come to England to seek out followers of Gurdjieff's ideas, with the intention of transmitting to them knowledge and methods that were needed to complete their teaching.

For some months, Mr. Bennett states that he was wary, but having had several more conversations with Mr. Hoare, he was convinced that he ought to see Mr. Shah for himself.

Accordingly, Mr. and Mrs. Bennett went to the Hoares for dinner to meet him. He turned out to be a young man in his forties, speaking impeccable English, and but for his beard and some of his gestures, might well have been taken for a public school type, but half way through the evening, Mr. Bennett recognised that he was not only an unusually gifted man, but that he had the undefinable something that marks a man who has worked seriously upon himself.

For several months, Mr. Bennett did not follow up this contact, but then Mr. Hoare persuaded him to see Mr. Shah again and assured Mr. Bennett that Mr. Shah's credits had been examined by him and they were impeccable, and that he was convinced that Mr. Shah had been sent to the West by an esoteric school in Afghanistan, probably the same one which Mr. Gurdjieff descibes in the last chapter of his book "Meetings with Remarkable Men". Mr. Hoare further attached special significance to what Mr. Shah had told him about the enneagram symbol and said that he had revealed secrets about it that were far beyond what he had heard from Mr. Ouspensky. Reggie Hoare was a cautious man and was trained by many years in the Intelligence Service in assessing information, and Mr. Bennett accepted his assurances and also his belief that Mr. Shah had a very important mission in the west which he should help him to accomplish. Mr. Shah never claimed to be a teacher, but he did claim that he had been sent by his own teacher and that he had the support of the "Guardians of the Tradition", and he produced a document authorising Mr. Bennett to make it known to his pupils and anyone else Mr. Bennett thought fit.*

Due to extreme pressure from Mr. Shah, Mr. Bennett understood that Mr. Shah not only wanted the use of Coombe Springs, but he wanted the property himself, not only access to his (Mr. B's) pupils, but the right to take under his own wing any that could be useful to him. This could be a chance for Mr. Bennett to liberate himself from his attachment to it – he had lived there since 1941 and expected to die there, and he was deeply attached to it all and especially the Djamichunatra which was his own inspiration. Nothing could be harder than for Mr. Bennett to walk out and leave it all.

By June 1965 Mr. Bennett had to convince his council that it was right to let Mr. Shah have Coombe Springs, and later that summer the last seminar was held and Mr. Shah came to talk to the students, where he conveyed to them the importance of his mission and created a sense of urgency. In October of that year, an Extraordinary General Meeting of members was held to give away their most valuable asset, Coombe Springs. There were, of course, some members who wanted to compromise, but Mr. Shah insisted that it should be all or nothing. Finally, the decision was taken and preparations were in hand for its inhabitants to move out. Mr. and Mrs. Bennett found a small house at 23 Brunswick Road, Kingston.

On the 13th January, 1966 there was a great feast at Coombe Springs to celebrate Mr.Gurdjieff's birthday, which included a

---

* "Witness" – J.G. Bennett p.356.

display of Gurdjieff's movements in the Dyami.* Mr. Shah took possession soon after, and the only invitation Mr. Bennett received was to "Midsummer Revels" lasting two days and two nights which were primarily for the young people whom Mr. Shah was wishing to attract around him. We later heard that Mr. Shah had decided to sell Coombe Springs for the development of twenty eight luxury houses. Mr. Shah and his family moved to Langton House, near Tunbridge Wells in Kent, a place much more suitable for his purposes than Coombe Springs.

Mr. Bennett himself became fully absorbed in another educational project.

* "Witness" – J.G. Bennett p.361.

CHAPTER 30

Our Topsy Turvy World

Our work with Mr. Bennett continued, but now we had the wonderful Sufi books to help and guide us. Many of our old friends joined Mr. Shah and lived near to Langton House. It was again a new epoch and as in Subud, a new era of work. My sister and I did, of course, come to meet Mr. Shah. He came to many of Mr. Bennett's public lectures in London. He needed a secretary and I was able to suggest one. We were asked to Langton House to many public gatherings, and spent a day alone with Mr. Shah there, when he showed us his home and introduced us to his family, but we were not drawn to ask if we could join him.

The world of "All and Everything" and Mr. Gurdjieff and the Sufi World certainly seemed complimentary. The situation in which we find ourselves "Humanity is asleep", concerned only with what is useless, living in a wrong world. Believing that one can excel, this is only habit and usage, not religion. This "religion" is inept..." Do not prattle before the People of the Path, rather consume yourself. You have an inverted knowledge of religion if you are upside down in relation to Reality. Man is wrapping his net around himself. A lion (The Man of the Way) bursts his cage asunder." This is our situation (as quoted by The Sufi master of Afghanistan in the "Walled Garden of Truth" written in 1131 AD) and quoted by Mr. Shah in his authoritative work entitled "The Sufis".★

Life was not always like that – once there was an ideal community – members had no fears – instead of uncertainty and vacillation had purposefulness and a fuller means of expressing themselves. Lives changed by trying to escape a terrestrial calamity. Perceptions

★ Quotation from "Sufis" and "The King's Son"

became coarse and values dimmed so that when the time came to return, they had become lazy and forgotten the means of doing so. (This was beautifully illustrated in the story of the "King's Son" and other Dervish Tales).

People for the most part only live in a very small part of themselves – but with right development they can and must evolve new complexes of organs to transcend time and space – an essential if we are to survive. (Story of "How Man is Sustained", "The Most Ancient Masters", "The Three Deaf Men and the Dumb Dervish").

Man must try to awake – he does not know he is asleep – to try to develop his real 'I' when he already believes he has this – (Story – "The Sufi Quest").

Also, examples of wrong work in television and newspapers. Mankind involved in weapons of war instead of weapons of peace. Emphasis upon the forces of 'egoism', 'vanity', brutality', instead of 'love', 'charity', 'humility' and 'faith' in a higher power.

Mr. Gurdjieff, in his book entitled "All and Everything" suggests, perhaps, in more detail, the downfall of Mankind:

A. Attainment of objective reason proper to three-brained beings as aim of their existence.

B. Circumstances, not ripe here on earth for it, so organ Kunda buffer implanted in three-brained beings to delay their development.

C. Although organ later destroyed, certain consequences became crystallized in them and remained.
    1. First consequence: periodic destructive wars – decrease in population and then noticeable increase – ours the only planet in universe where this happens.
    2. Certain being-functions in people inappropriate to them, such as 'egoism', 'self-love', 'vanity', 'pride, suggestibility', 'wiseacring', etc.
    3. Destroying wisdom already placed in certain ways on earth for future generations.

D. Only cure for the unsuitable manifestations – conscious efforts and intentional sufferings or 'Being – Partkdolg – duty'.
    1. People have little knowledge of the importance of this, and so nature is forced to alter certain laws.

2. People living most of their life in the wrong part of themselves. No longer possibilities of being 'sincere' with themselves and others or to be able to criticise or judge another part of themselves impartially.
3. Importance of 'hypnotism' to help people to rid themselves of false values and restore 'health'. (Real consciousness only manifesting in their sleeping state). Therefore, remaining chiefly in a very primitive state.

Another subject for consideration was the job which the earth people should be doing i.e. supplying vibrations to help the expansion of the Moon planet and Anulious. This was known and understood by the early Samliosian Civilization of Atlantis and was called "Help for the Moon". However, when an artificial organ was implanted within each individual called "Kundabuffer", to prevent the inhabitants from developing too quickly toward objective reason, this was quickly forgotten, and this special organ had a property such that first they should perceive reality topsy-turvy and secondly, that every repeated impression from outside should crystallize in them which would engender factors for evoking in them sensations of pleasure and enjoyment. But when it was felt by a thorough investigation of a third most High Commission that there was no longer any need for actualizing these measures, they were deliberately destroyed together with the organ "Kundabuffer" and all its astonishing properties.

Time passed and the process of existence proceeded there as on all other planets. But Beelzebub noted, after looking into his spyglass closely, firstly that the numbers of people on this planet "Earth" were increasing, and secondly that it was possible sometimes to observe very strange manifestations of theirs, that is from time to time they did something which was never done by three-brained beings on other planets; namely, they would suddenly, without rhyme or reason, begin destroying one another's existence. Sometimes, this destruction of one another's existence proceeded there not in one region alone, but in several. Sometimes it was noticeable that from this horrid process of theirs their number rapidly diminished, but on the other hand, during other periods, when there was a lull in these processes, their numbers also very noticeably increased.

To this peculiarity of theirs, Beelzebub remarked: "We gradually became accustomed to it and explained it to ourselves that obviously, for certain higher considerations, these properties must also have been given to the organ "Kundabuffer" by the Most High Commission with aforethought, in view of the necessity that they should exist in such large numbers for the needs of the maintenance of the "common-cosmic Harmonious Movement."*

Gurdjieff mentions that he visited nearly all the planets of that solar system, both populated and unpopulated, but he liked best of all the beings breeding on the planet bearing the name of "Saturn" whose exterior is quite unlike ours, but resembles that of the being bird "raven" which Beelzebub notes exists and breeds on almost all the planets of the whole of our great universe. He remarks further that the verbal intercourse of these ravens is, in his opinion, the most beautiful he had ever heard. "It can be compared to the singing of our best singers when, with all their Being, they sing in a minor key."**

Beelzebub remarks further that these birds have hearts like angels nearest our Endless Maker and Creator. They exist strictly according to the ninth commandment of our Creator, namely "Do unto another as you would do unto your own."

But to return to the History of our own planet "Earth", Beelzebub told Hassein and his old servant Ahoon that although the horrors of war and the destruction of each other's existence runs like a crimson thread through all his tales, when Hassein pressed his grandfather to tell him whether earth people "never ponder on the disposition of theirs – phenomenally terrible and exclusively inherent in them alone" ***

Beelzebub answers them: "Of course they ponder, of course they see – but because of their abnormal existence there, the inhabitants there can neither 'think sincerely nor see and sense reality'." ****

When Beelzebub was leaving Planet "Earth" for the last time, people there were already hoping that the new society "League of Nations" would help curb this malevolent tendency of theirs. Many times before on the Earth, important power possessing beings had formed similar societies. One such society Beelzebub mentions "first arose there in the town of Samonika in the country Tikliamish (Asia) just at that period when this country was regarded as the chief centre for culture of all the three-brained beings of this peculiar planet. "This society of beings had as their motto the following sentence: 'God is where man's blood is not shed'. But its members very soon quarrelled amongst themselves and went home without accomplishing

---

* "All and Everything": p.92.
** "All and Everything": p.92.
*** "All and Everything" by G. Gurdjieff – pp.1057 and 1058.
**** "All and Everything" by G. Gurdjieff – p.92.

anything."* Further societies were formed by these power-possessing beings in time, but always with the same result. The effects of "Kundabuffer" proved to be too powerful for the inhabitants of "Planet Earth" to become real "MEN".

Mr. Gurdjieff says: "Messengers" from "His Endlessness" were sent from time to time to help to rectify these faults – one such was "The Most Saintly Asheata Shiemash" – but the results of his labours were very quickly destroyed by his followers who had not yet attained objective reason. Furthermore, many objects built to remind its people were destroyed by them during these periods of reciprocal destruction or wars – which were constantly being waged there.

Further messengers were sent to help the people toward their spiritual goal, one lived in Tibet and another was a "Sufi" who was in Asia, but the results of their labours were again of little worth to the people of the new generations.

The importance of the cosmic truth, however, that they are made in the image of God, not of that God which they have imagined" but the real God, by which word we still call our Common Megalocosmos. Each of them, to the smallest detail, is exactly similar, but, of course, in miniature to the whole of our Megalocosmos and in each of them there are all of those separate functionings necessary for the "exchange" of substances maintaining the existence of everything in the Megalocosmos as one whole.*

* "All and Everything" by G. Gurdjieff – p.92

CHAPTER 31

The Inauguration of
the International Academy for
Continuous Education
Part 1

In February 1971, Mr. Bennett announced a new and novel experiment in group work in which everyone who wished could participate. Four projects were suggested, each of which would be concerned with understanding and verifying one important element in the Teaching.

1. Transformation of Energies
What is understood by saying that man, like everything else that exists, does so for the transforming of energies and by means of the same transformation? What is 'reciprocal maintenance? Can we not only grasp the idea, but recognise and verify its working in our own lives?

2. Man is a Three-brained Being
Have we verified this idea for ourselves? If so, what does it really signify? What does Gurdjieff mean by 'separately spiritualized parts'? Does the idea influence our daily lives?

3. Why do we talk?
Study the impulses that make people talk. What is talking and what could it be? Useful, useless, destructive and creative talking. What can we learn about ourselves and others from the study of talking?

4. Man sees Reality upside-down
The idea is that we suffer not merely from illusions but delusions as to what is real in ourselves and the world. Have we considered all the implications of the suggestion that reality may be the opposite (i.e. upside-down) to what it appears to our minds? Can we do anything to verify or disprove the assertion.

These projects were further explained at general meetings in London and Kingston. On April 21st there was a Jubilee Conference and dinner held at the St. Ermin's Hotel in London and Mr. Bennett explained that the above objects were especially important in view of the inauguration of the International Academy for Continuous Education to be opened in October, 1971. He explained that they would help in designing projects for the Academy in which members could participate in even if they could not join the basic course.

Nearly three hundred members and guests met in the ballroom of St. Ermins Hotel and the dinner was preceeded by an all-day conference on "the whole man" – Mr. Bennett spoke briefly, announcing that the Academy was founded that day.

Then, by a peculiar set of circumstances, Mr. Bennett was invited to give lectures at various centres in the U.S.A. He went first to Boston where he was met by his friends Paul and Naomi Anderson and members of their group and lectures were hastily improvised at the Students' Union in Harvard and Clark Universities, Worcester, Mass. at which Mr. Bennett invited those students who were prepared to commit themselves to come to England and work very hard for a whole year. Within two days he had thirty good candidates.

I knew about this new venture and hoped that a sizable house near me in Surrey might be selected for this venture, but Mrs. Bennett had already found a suitable place, Sherborne House in the Cotswolds, which had been a school, and had beautiful gardens and a meadow and was much cheaper than the estates round here, whose prices are higher due to the popular proximity to London.

By the time Mr. Bennett had lectured in New Hampshire and California and New York, the academy was fully booked with seventy two candidates. When Mr. Bennett returned to England, he had already enough money to buy Sherborne and ninety students for the first basic course. This time, Mr. Bennett said "The impossible was made easy." *

The academy was inaugurated on the 15th October, 1971. They went into Sherborne House on September 7th when repairs had to be made to central heating, renewing a derelict kitchen and buying and installing furniture and setting up a secretariat. Everything went well – Mr. Bennett had a wealth of experience of 75 years from writing his books and particularly the "Dramatic Universe" and seminars and summer schools at Coombe Springs. The state of

* J.G Bennett: Witness, p.302, 1997 edition.

Sherborne House created the conditions for which determined the students to succeed. For sometime all the cooking in the kitchen for a hundred people was done on an old broken down stove bought for a few pounds, until the big new cooker arrived. The central heating was constantly breaking down and the smell of paint was everywhere.

Nevertheless, the students worked hard on Gurdjieff movements, cleared the kitchen garden of weeds and planted vegetables which were promptly eaten by rabbits and pigeons. Many of the students combined their zeal for higher things with all kinds of prejudices connected with food and living conditions and one of Mr. Bennett's first talks to them was entitled "Like and dislike". He said that unless one was free from one's own reactions of like and dislike, desire and aversion – one could not possibly begin this work, and all struggled manfully with these unaccustomed demands. But in trying to show the students how to dig in the garden, Mr. Bennett had hurt himself, and a hernia operation was needed, and the necessary leisure to follow gave him some much needed time for reflection. During this period he was able to review his ideas of the message he would give to them on his return and he felt confident he would succeed. In the New Year, they celebrated Gurdjieff's 95th anniversary on 13th January, 1972 with a great feast to which we drank toasts to the Idiots as was done in Fontainebleau forty nine years before. They also began Visiting Saturdays at which the students demonstrated the Movements and learnt to tell visitors what they thought they were doing.

Meanwhile, entries for the following year were coming in steadily. They tried to buy the magnificent stable block, a gem of mid Victorian architecture. Lord Sherborne would not sell, but leased them a large area and also gardens and cottages that greatly increased the available accommodation. The building work was undertaken by a group of students who acquired astonishing skills in stonemasonry and other building arts.

In the final weeks of the course, Mr. Bennett sent all the students to teach one another what they had learnt at Sherborne. He said that they could only truly share what they possessed with others, and that giving is the necessary completion of receiving. He wanted them to go back and collect around them small groups to whom they could transmit the ideas and methods that they had learnt. "So long as we remember", he said, "that we could do nothing and understand nothing in our conditioned nature we shall be protected from the stupidity of teaching that we are better than those we teach."

Mr. Bennett's nephew Pierre Elliot and his wife Vivienne were already at Sherborne and helping him with the Movements, as was Anna Durko, an old student of his. There were Gilbert Edwards, who was helping to co-ordinate the work and Dick Holland and, of course, his wife, Elizabeth Bennett helped him on every hand, and they were joined by Tom Pearson and his wife Edith. Tom was to be their bursar. The Rev. Val Rodgers and Mrs. Rodgers also joined them for the course as did Lord Thurlow and his wife and family.

International Academy Part 2

In the early 70's Mr. Bennett asked my sister and myself to come to Sherborne to talk with him. We both knew that he wanted us to come nearer so that we could help with the work there. We had already spent some time in the neighbourhood as we came regularly for Council Meetings, but we were not at all sure that we wished to move there permanently and we also rather worried about Mr. Bennett's health. If anything happened to him – who would take over?

I happened to have received from my stockbroker a year's review of my stocks and shares and this I took with me. It was possible that Mr. Bennett would wish us to see the architect he was employing to draw up plans for a house for us in a field near Sherborne – we had already heard of other members who were being urged to come and live there. We drove up to Sherborne with some friends. We both felt uneasy but realized also how much we owed to Mr. and Mrs. Bennett and the work that they were pursuing with their students there. I was not particularly happy in Guildford – my bungalow was situated on a steep hill and an acre of garden was all on terraces and steep slopes. I already had trouble with my back and was told that it would not improve until I moved from there, but could I afford to build a new home?

Mr. Bennett greeted us affectionately as always and enthusiastically showed us plans for new homes drawn up by his architect – so we had to tell him of our misgivings. Who would carry on his work if anything (God forbid) should happen to him? He said immediately that his sons, George and Ben, were being trained for just such a situation. They were both young men very much taken up with the problems which face young people growing up in an uncertain world and we were doubtful of their ability to teach others at that time. Then we turned to the question of finance – I showed Mr. Bennett the stockbroker's report of my finances, and he saw immediately that I was unable to finance a new home such as he had envisaged, and so the plan was dropped.

Mr. Bennett also had the help of Hasan Shushud, a Sufi, who came from the East. Mr. Bennett was greatly helped spiritually by him and he, in turn, helped the students and Mr. Bennett wrote in his autobiography, "Witness" 'Hasan was strong meat for them, but his presence produced a deep sense of the reality of the Unconditioned World'.*

Mr. Bennett had planned to give five yearly courses at Sherborne up to 1975-76 and in 1976-77. He intended to invite those students who had shown themselves capable of transmitting what they had learnt and were ready to make a step forward. Meanwhile, Mr. Bennett was also active in other fields. He was a prolific writer, especially on Mr. Gurdjieff and his ideas, and in 1972 he was asked by Mr. Gurdjieff's family to help carry out Mr. Gurdjieff's instructions concerning his last book entitled: 'Life is Real Only When I Am' and to help his family to get this last book of Gurdjieff published by the Editions Janus, a publishing agency to which Mr. Gurdjieff had entrusted the publication of his books and music. This new responsibility was a very delicate one, as he was no longer an 'orthodox' member of the Gurdjieff group, but he was happy to renew his friendship with the students whom he had worked with in 1948-49, and when he consulted some of his older pupils in France and U.S.A., he felt that he should agree to edit the work and find a publisher. From doing this work, Mr. Bennett not only helped to heal some animosities amongst the Gurdjieff family and some of his followers, but also led to Mr. Bennett's deeper understanding of Mr. Gurdjieff's mission.

There was to be another very important development to take place at Sherborne. At a Council Meeting in 1974 to which Mrs. Bennett and her oldest son, George, were invited. It was announced by Mr. Bennett that he had asked some of his American students to find a suitable property in the U.S.A. to become "The American Academy for Continuous Education". In due course, a suitable property was found in West Virginia, and only a comfortable drive from Washington D.C. The property had originally belonged to a member of the George Washington family, and was a listed residence built in the Southern style with wide surrounding stoops and high pillars at the main entrance and on either side were smaller houses originally built for the slaves. It was set in a large area of woodland, and there was an immense auction barn included, with a large hall at one end

* Bennett – "Witness" p.377.

where movements could be held or plays performed. One of Mr. Bennett's most competent pupils, Mr. Manfred Blum, was to be in charge there until Mr. Bennett's nephew, Pierre Elliott, and his wife could be spared from Sherborne to go and live there.

Claymont opened its doors to students in 1975 and when my sister and I visited there in the Summer of 1975, an impressive collection of students were already hard at work. The roof of the auction barn needed to be raised to give more space for a further storey, and Manfred Blum was organizing a party of men to do this. There was much activity in the main houses – cleaning, cooking and the necessary space to be created for an office with telephones, etc. A garden behind the house was begun and later a greenhouse was added.

The organization which came to life there was to be known as 'The Claymont Society for Continuous Education'. In 1976, there was a large group of students who had been through Mr. Bennett's course at Sherborne who signed up at Claymont. They ranged from those whose skills were blacksmiths and furniture makers to plumbers and heating engineers, teachers, farmers and gardeners, administration and alternative technology. Something like three hundred students, sponsors and teachers were on their mailing list. Quite an auspicious start for the Claymont Society.

But in December 1974, Mr. Bennett suddenly died at Sherborne of a cerebral haemorrhage. A few days previously, Mr. Bennett and Elisabeth had called on my sister and me at our flat in Kensington, London. They were very affectionate as always, but I noticed that Mr. Bennett's eyes seemed bright and pulsating and I felt that he was already in a different world. As always, his schedule was very full and I felt he was burning himself up. The funeral was to be at Sherborne in their local chapel with the Roman Catholic priest presiding on the morning of 16th December. My sister and I went, of course. His Mass was attended not only by his family, wife and children, his students and Council members, but also by Madame de Salzmann from the Gurdjieff Foundation and by Mr. Idries Shah, Director of Institute for Cultural Research – with whom Mr. Bennett had so many contacts in the past. A student of Mr. Bennett had particularly noticed his arrival for the funeral and said: "I was standing on the upper landing of the Great Hall in Sherborne House on the morning of Mr. Bennett's funeral. Idries Shah had just arrived, and he went up to Olga de Nottleck (one of Mr. Bennett's oldest pupils) and said something like: "Oh, Olga, how lovely it is to see you – you look wonderful." Olga looked him straight in the eye and responded: "You don't expect me to fall for that, do you? What are you doing here?" Mr. Shah said something to the effect: "I am here out of respect for Mr. Bennett who never put himself on a pedestal."

Mr. Bennett was buried in the grounds of the local church at Sparkford, Somerset, close to members of his family who lived nearby, and his grave faces Cadbury Hill, traditional home of King Arthur. He was not able to go again to the U.S.A. to see his newly founded 'Claymont Society for Continuous Education', although his wife Elizabeth went many times to talk to their students.

Both my sister and I went on the final course to be held at Sherborne House after Mr. Bennett's death. We were happy to be again with so many of our old friends and colleagues. We had a very real sense of Mr. Bennett's presence and Elizabeth, his wife, contributed a great deal to our deliberations.

But Marjorie and I were entering a very difficult period of our lives personally. I had been having constant attention to my back for a slipped disc and this grew worse in 1976. I had sciatica as well and my local osteopath was unable to treat me, so it was felt that I should not be living alone and I moved to London to join my sister where we had an excellent doctor and French osteopath to call upon and where my life was much less physically demanding. But I did not know then that my sister, too, had some medical troubles – she went into hospital in London and her condition was diagnosed as cancer of the uterus. She was operated upon, but the cancer spread. The year was 1977, and the Queen's Jubilee, but I was busy driving from the flat each day to visit my sister in hospital. I was greatly supported by our many mutual friends, but after some months in which I had called upon 'healers' and doctors to help, she died on July 14th, 1977. We had been loving companions all our lives, and her death left me destitute, but I recalled how wonderfully she had accepted the death of her husband at such an early age, and I tried to do likewise. Mr. and Mrs. Macleod were always with me, and they helped me to arrange her funeral. She was buried with her husband at Chorleywood Church, near their old home at Rickmansworth, Herts. Later we arranged a memorial Service for her in London near her flat in Kensington. Many compositions of Mr. Gurdjieff's music were played.

Now, with my Teacher gone and my sister too, I had to build a new life for myself. My sister and I had done so much together – we had travelled extensively in Europe, North America, Canada and South America, to Indonesia and India, New Zealand and Australia and across the Pacific, and we had both been to college in the States and learnt our philosophy from Mr. Gurdjieff, Mr. Ouspensky and Subud and had a great friend in Mr. Bennett and his wife Elizabeth. We had both written books together about our experiences with them and about our Father, whom we loved and respected. It was clear to me that I must sell my bungalow in Guildford, but as I am much more fond of the country and not a town girl, I wanted to sell my sister's flat and move back to Guildford or its environs to be near my good friends, the Macleods, who lived then in Cranleigh, near Guildford. So for the time being, I took a small, newly built house in the centre of Bramley village, halfway between Guildford and Cranleigh. The Macleods, who came to me in the week, had found the trip to Guildford very exacting in the rush hour, and Bramley was nearer them and not then so difficult or crowded to drive to. So I divided my time between London, clearing out my sister's flat, and my little house in Bramley for weekends. Both my sister's flat and my bungalow in Guildford were for sale. I enjoyed the "to and fro-ing" between London and Guildford; it gave me time to reflect and to read, and I needed this 'interval' in my life. I had my corgi dog for company and many friends who came to visit me.

The bungalow in Guildford sold fairly easily, but the flat in London was more difficult to sell, partly because it took me some time to empty it, and also because it needed some modernization. I was my sister's sole beneficiary, and so I needed a bigger place to bring all our belongings together. With the help of the Macleod family, we found a lovely modern home near the Bramley Golf Course, with plenty of space to house my large collection of books, and I moved there in October, 1979.

There was to be another unexpected death soon after my sister's demise. Judy Macleod, Keith's wife and my housekeeper, became ill with a heart complaint. I had no idea how serious it was. Her son, James, was not satisfied with her progress at home and insisted that she should go into hospital at Cranleigh. She had a massive heart attack when admitted, and died. Her husband, Keith and son, James were left to mourn her passing. I only heard the news over the telephone from James' wife, Eileen, and was dumbfounded. I went immediately to their Cranleigh home to offer my condolences. Judy had been a faithful friend to me, as well as an employee for many years, and I could scarcely imagine my life without her care and guidance. James' wife, Eileen stepped into the gap and helped me for some years afterwards.

CHAPTER 32

Israel 1968, 1981 and 1987

It was another third of a century before we visited Israel again, namely in 1968. What a change had come over the place, or was it simply in us? We had seen some history made there since our previous visit in 1933: the ending of the British Mandate over Palestine, and the British promise (hotly debated) of a national home for the Jews; the coming of World War II and also the persecutions hastening the return of the Jews to their 'home'; the setting up of the State of Israel, and the conflicts with its Arab neighbours culminating, as far as they have gone at present, in the Six Days' War. The spotlight has now rested on that country and its inhabitants as it never seems to have done before, although men from earlier generations such as my father realised its vital role in their own way.

We became much interested in the details of its extraordinary history. Physically a small piece of land, about the size of Wales, and joining three continents, Europe, Asia and Africa, from the dawn of man's known history it has been the axis of the ancient world, fought over and conquered by illustrious leaders from all sides. From the time the historical Israelites entered and established themselves in the main sites of Canaan, they were attacked continuously: first by the peoples living around them such as the Egyptians and Philistines, the latter a people probably from Greece who had settled on the southern coast of Canaan. Then from the East by the Assyrians, the Babylonians, the Persians, not to mention the Greeks under Alexander the Great, and the Romans from other directions. More Modern conquerors were the Islamic peoples, the Crusaders, and the Turks. Even Napoleon managed to get there.*

* In his Egyptian campaign he captured El Arish and Jaffa in the spring and summer of 1789, and severely beat up a Turkish relieving army at the battle of Mont Tabor. (Encyclopedia Britannica: French Revolution War).

Four successive temples were built in Jerusalem: Solomon's, Zerubbabel's, Herod the Great's and finally the Dome of the Rock and its companion the Mosque of El Aqsa created by the Mohammedans, all on the same site, supposedly that of Mount Moriah. Only the Mosques survive today on the massive platform erected by Herod the Great with its high Wailing Wall. Equally intertwined is the religious life of its inhabitants, principally the three great monotheistic faiths of the Jews, the Christians and Mohammedans. Possibly the inner story really starts from here, from the meeting of Abraham (a sheik of great wealth, not a common herdsman as previously thought, now we have learnt so much more of the culture of the Chaldees (where he lived) with the mysterious Melchizadek, King of Salem (the Old Jerusalem). The latter is described in The Bible (1) as 'Priest of the God Most High', and is further referred to by St. Paul as being 'without father, without mother, without genealogy, having neither beginning of days nor end of life, but like unto the Son of God, abideth a priest continually'. (2) Melchizadek blesses Abraham and the latter is promised that he will be 'the father of a multitude of nations'. (3) His first son Ishmael, whose mother is Hagar, Sarah's Egyptian maid, is also promised that 'I will greatly multiply thy seed, that it shall not be numbered for multitude', whilst Sarah, long past her child-bearing age, is told that she will bear a child and be called 'the mother of nations; kings of people shall be of her.'* In the Old Testament this is about all we hear of Ishmael, except for the description of his appearance and character and the fact that he and his mother were cast out into the wilderness, for here we follow the story of Isaac, Sarah's son, and the sacrifice from which he was saved (supposedly on Mount Moriah, later the site of the historical temples), the death and burial of Sarah in the Cave of Machpelah at Hebron. The marriage of Isaac to Rebekah, herself a near relative, as he was not allowed to marry a Canaanite woman. The death of Abraham, and his burial by his sons Isaac and Ishmael in the same place as Sarah.

It is interesting to note here that the Mohammedan tradition tells quite a different story. 'The Arabs of today claim descent from Abraham, through Ishmael, who, they hold, was the son offered by the patriarch to God. According to them also, Abraham rebuilt the Kabba (at Mecca) in token of repentance for having cast Hagar out in the wilderness. Hence the sanctity of Hagar's Well in the

1. Genesis 14 v.18   2. Hebrews 7 v.3   3. Genesis 17 v.4
* Genesis 17 v.16

Sanctuary, the Zam-Zam, believed to be the same spring which God caused to spring miraculously for Hagar's succour. It is, of course, well-known that the Arabs and Jews are both of Semitic origin, and that their languages are derived from a similar root.* But even to this day the conflict between the two races has not been solved.

So three generations of the family lived in the vicinity of Hebron and, according to tradition, were buried in the Cave of Machpelah, Joseph, the son of Jacob, was sold by his brothers through jealousy into slavery in Egypt, but later by his ability became one of the country's leading figures, and was reunited to his father. Finally Jacob (the third generation) called his sons together and proclaimed them to be the progenitors of the twelve tribes of Israel.

A later member of the family, Moses, was born in Egypt during the period of the Jews' captivity there, and according to tradition was brought up by a princess of the Egyptian royal house, being 'instructed in all the wisdom of the Egyptians, and he was mighty in his words and works.'** Perhaps both he and Joseph knew something of the ancient order of Righteousness Ma'at where 'the Egyptian believed that the good life could be learned.'*** Moses was the man destined to lead his people out of Egyptian captivity, and to the frontiers of the Promised Land. After that, through all the invasions, captivities, dispersions and woes, according to the Bible there is always a prophet at hand to help, advise or upbraid them. Always they are told they have a great task to fulfil, and that their Messiah will one day come to them. Thanks to modern archaeology and study as well as modern communications, it is now possible for the traveller to have a far clearer picture of the Biblical ages, and this will undoubtedly increase as time goes on.

This beautiful little country, literally as the spies told is 'flowing with milk and honey', and certainly now with water, that great need all over the world where hot sun and dry desert conditions exist. Unfortunately, as the world traveller realises, this fact, though so simple, is seldom realised, and vast tracts of land exist as infertile hopeless desert upon which nothing grows. Not so, Israel; modern irrigation methods are being more and more developed, the deserts 'are blossoming like the rose', and no doubt this will increase in the future as further populations come to live there.

The country has the same characteristics as that of Crete, with the

* Idries Shah, Caravan of Dreams, p.46
** Acts 7 v.22
*** Life, 22/7/68 – divine Order radiating from Kings and Gods.

same hills and valleys, bright vivid colours, and abrupt changes of scenery. It is simply saturated with its history in whatever direction one goes, as though by some very intense microscope of light. Possibly this is because so large a percentage of travellers have been brought up in the sacred tales of its history, possibly there is a deeper reason. I have often wondered whether if we had the same extent of ancient knowledge about other lands, we should feel the same way when travelling through them, but I do not think in general this would be the case. A mighty event must leave its special force to be sensed by the traveller who can do so, but the ordinary life of mankind cannot do this, although that too leaves its mark. But so much in the Holy Land we seem to be wandering through the Bible itself, from the southern entrance of the Twelve Tribes of Israel (through the Wilderness of Zin) resolutely following, or not following as the case may be, their Prophets' commands through the lands around the Dead Sea, in particular Moab, to the conquest of Jericho and Ai by Joshua, and the advance to Megiddo in the Plains of Esdraelon and Hazor, north of the Sea of Galilee. The ruthless murder of the innocent inhabitants, apparently by Divine Command, is something we cannot comprehend today, and indeed has turned many honest souls against the apparent barbarity of the Old Testament Jehovah. Perhaps indeed another law was all that could be followed in those olden days for Man. But these conquests gradually gave the ancient Israelites possession over their promised land: Jericho, where the city walls came tumbling down' at the last of Joshua's trumpets; also Megiddo, 'city of antiquity, strategic centre in Biblical ages....looks out over some of the loveliest country in all Israel.....It commands.....the fruitful Valley of Jezreel (Esdraelon)....to the East is Mount Tabor and beyond....looms the snowcapped peak of Mount Hermon.....It commanded the great trunk road Via Maris from Egypt in the south to Mesopotamia and Syria in the north.....It also guarded the east-west road across Jezreel....Egyptians, Canaanites, Israelites, Philistines, Assyrians, Persians, Greeks and Romans were the principal "dramatis personae" in the bitter battles fought at Megiddo in ancient times.'*

Here we are in the land of Saul, David and Jonathan, the first kings and leaders of the Tribes, the Mountains of Gilboa and the conflicts with the Philistines. 'Tell it not in Gath, publish it not in the streets of Askelon; lest the daughters of the Philistines rejoice.' And again, 'Ye mountains of Gilboa, let there be no dew, neither let there be rain

* Quotations from Megiddo guide Book, Natural Parks Authority

upon you, nor fields of offerings: for there the shield of the mighty was vilely cast away, the shield of Saul.'* In prophecy Megiddo 'is envisioned as the site of the last great battle to be fought at the end of time. For they are the spirits of devils, working miracles, which go forth unto the kings of the earth and of the whole world, to gather them to the battle of that great day of God Almighty....And he gathered them together into a place called in the Hebrew tongue Armageddon.'**) Armageddon is a corruption of Har Megiddon, Hebrew for the Hill of Megiddo. The excavations here have laid bare twenty super-imposed cities, and the large scale work, financed by the Rockefeller family, ran from 1925 onwards to the Second World War, and continued from 1958 to the present time. There is considerable evidence that the other two 'chariot cities', (Hazor and Gezer) were built by the same architectural hand which probably designed the eastern gate of Solomon's Temple. Hazor, excavated only as late as 1955 (although some soundings were made in the late twenties) is also seen to be 'a key city of high strategic value.'*** 'Joshua's victory by the waters of Merom marks ....a decisive phase in the conquest of Northern Canaan.' 'And Joshua at that time turned back and took Hazor and smote the king thereof with sword....and he burnt Hazor with fire....But as to the cities that stood still in their strength, Israel burned none of them, save Hazor only.' Solomon rebuilt 'Hazor and Megiddo and Gezer and turned them into royal cities.'**** And so on, through the amazing history of this small country until the great movement for return by the Jewish people in our day.

Our second visit started with an archaeological tour of two weeks, although as some of its members were more interested in general sightseeing, and there was so much to see, we did not get as much archaeology or talks with archaeologists as we would have liked. We went all around Israel in an old bus with guide and driver to see a good slice of the representative sights. As it was not long after the Six Days' War, some of the border roads were still perilous, but our splendid guide Chaim (pronounced Heim), who had been a freedom fighter during the Mandate, knew all the side roads as well, so if the police refused permission for the main road, he always took us by the side ones. Consequently we only missed one bit of our itinerary. One realised the enormous strides that had been made in road building

* 2nd Samuel 1 V.17(3) Revelations XVi vv 14 and 16
** Revelations XVi vv 14 and 16
*** Guide Book, Hazor, National Parks Authority
**** Kings 1X v.15

and opening up the country since our last limited visit. No travelling on donkey-back nowadays, at least not for the tourist.

Our first view of Jerusalem, where we started our tour, from the excellent road to the Mount of Olives, simply took our breath away. Jerusalem with its 'golden' buildings of stone, and the gold and silver domes of the two mosques gleaming in the fitful sunshine, moved us very much. We realised with a shock how beautiful it all was – a thing we had never seen in 1933; the pleasant ordinary little town had somehow taken on another dimension, partly due no doubt to better views and means of access, but also possibly to some development in ourselves. This was not just a 'small Eastern town similar to others', as I had thought previously. It has a strange power spreading over its towns and countryside, quite unlike anything we have felt before. At its present stage Jerusalem is united, and the limiting 'wall' between the former Arab and Jewish sections taken down. One cannot help feeling this is a big advancement on the former arrangement. The Jewish policy is to allow the pilgrims of the three great faiths to visit their sacred places freely. This appeared to work well, particularly from the visitors' point of view. We were handed over by Chaim in the Temple area to the Arab guides to show us the two mosques, and everything seemed peaceful there, except for some slight and quite good-natured banter from our guide to his Arab opposites that they were trying to charge the visitors too much. It sounded more like some routine joke than expressing any violent feelings in the matter. Viewing the great tombs at Hebron (as my father could never do) was also a most peaceful affair. We all – Christians, Jews, Mohammedans and what not – streamed through the Byzantine, Crusader and Arab sacred buildings covering them in an endless line; no one seemed to be causing trouble for anyone else. When we came out, many of us rushed to buy Jaffa oranges from a vendor in the market place.

In Jerusalem the buildings erected by the Jewish people in the new section are both magnificent and modern in style: the Hebrew University, Synagogue (looking like a tent), the immense Medical Centre, and Memorial to the Jewish people who lost their lives in European concentration camps during the last war. Later (on Mount Zion) we saw the Museum, and the Shrine of the Book, where most of the Dead Sea Scrolls, including the Book of Isaiah on exhibition, are being kept. We also visited the Government Centre (the Hakirya) and the Parliament, or as it is called, the Knesset. Many of the buildings in the Old Part of the city are being rebuilt, primarily, of course, the Church of the Holy Sepulchre. It is said that the pulling down of the old Arab houses has caused much offence around the Temple area, which the Jews obviously intend to use for something important for them. Naturally the Jews are over-emphasising their own buildings and creed at present, but surely this is better than the Arabs' policy of simply ignoring the rights of the Jews, and not even allowing them, when the city was divided, to visit their beloved Wailing Wall.

Our gallant bus took us all over the countryside, in a way which would have amazed my father. It was not a question of going to two or three excavations only; we went to most of the main ones in the country, usually to find a busy group of archaeologists working on them. The Jericho excavations have been enormously enlarged since we last visited the place, and the same district also now includes a National Park created for the Qumran Caves on the Dead Sea and the ruins of the old Essene Monastery. We were unfortunate here in getting rainy weather, which is most unusual in this district, and which shortened our trip considerably. From Jericho our bus went north to the Lake of Galilee, and another of our old camping grounds where we had stayed previously. But it all looked different, and there was much rebuilding. We found Tabgha, but Father Teppa, our friend in earlier days, had died, and there was new management. The lake of Galilee still had its storms, and the scenery around, especially the green meadows where Our Lord had taught the multitude, the Horns of Hattin, was supremely beautiful. One could visibly and innerly observe the scene, and feel His Presence was still there with His message through the Beatitudes. Had Homo Sapiens individually learnt anything of what He taught? One wonders.

From here we went to the lovely port of Haifa with Carmel and started the stretch south down the coast with history packed into every spot. We could not go to Gaza (where the late Sir Flinders Petrie was excavating at our last visit) but we went south and east to the Negev Desert where modern irrigation methods are bringing life to the desert. Finally we stopped at the southern end of the Dead Sea and Masada, that wonderful upstanding rock where Herod the Great built his palace and fortifications, and where in A.D.70, after the destruction of Jerusalem, the last Jews defended themselves until they could no longer hold out against their enemy, the Romans. Recently splendidly excavated, it is now possible for the ordinary tourist (even old ones) to climb to the top or to take the lift, and muse over the people who had lived there, and their heroic stand. The old Roman camps of the invaders at the base are still visible, and also the Ramp with which they finally conquered the Jews. In fact it is also the means by which we sightseers can now climb to the top. A fitting climax to our trip.

Accompanying our friends back to Tel Aviv Airport, where we said goodbye to them as most were leaving for home or some other destination, we ourselves returned to Jerusalem for the Easter week, where we stayed at the British School of Archaeology on Mount Scopus. Kind friends there looked after us, and supplied all our needs. We wished mainly to find out certain matters connected with the biography which we were writing about our father's life and work in Palestine and what had happened since his death in the distant days of 1946. We also wished to visit Lachish, the Biblical city in which he was so much interested, and on which so little work of excavation has yet been done. It was the one we had never visited in 1933. We were escorted there by Dr. A.F. Rainey who, with Professor Aharoni, had recently done excavations on the Sun Temple there. The green site was covered with bright golden flowers, and we climbed to the top observing its many features. The Hyksos ramparts and the places where the Foss Temples had been found, and the Guardroom with the 'Lachish Letters' and many other features we had often heard our father mention. Lachish had seen many battles too. It was captured by Nebuchadnezzar in 592 B.C. as well as by Sennacherib two hundred years earlier. It has been said that the city would take about fifteen years for its excavation to be complete.

My sister writes: "As we stood on its colourful ground, we felt how deeply we had feasted on the wonderful history and beauty of this small country, and how stupid were the young girls who only wanted to be told 'heathen' things, and saw little in Christianity but deprivation. And yet the heathen things have a meaning too, which perhaps these old devout Christians never grasped.

Petra Tour 1981

Early in 1981 I noticed that the tour company "Swan's Hellenic Tours" were featuring a tour to Amman, Petra, Damascus and Palmyra. My sister and I, while staying in Jerusalem with my Father during his excavations there in the 1930s, had been promised a trip to Petra, a very ancient and famous "hidden" city near the Dead Sea, and then my Father had cancelled it, and we never went. So this was just one of the places Keith and I were able to go to.

This tour also included a tour of Damascus and Palmyra, and a return trip via Jericho to Jerusalem and some visits there to

Qumran/Masada, Arad, Hebron and Bethlehem, and a return via Bethany and the Jordan River to Amman and home.

After an uneventful air trip, we arrived at Amman on Saturday April 4th and stayed the night there, and on Sunday we went sight-seeing in Amman. On Monday, we drove to Kenak to visit the remains of the great Castle there, built by the Crusaders in 1143, as a guardian outpost of their kingdom, and then on to Petra Rest House for the night.

The next day saw all members of the tour mounted on horseback to file through the "siq" for a full day's sightseeing of this "Rose Red" City first settled by the Nabateans in 300 BC, including the Treasury; Theatre; High Place and Monastery. Actually, the weather was so cold that we elected to stay in a well sheltered cave while the others went on tour and then joined them again at ground level to explore the well preserved Roman remains, Roman Street, baths and theatre within the city itself and some of the rock cut tombs.

After a picnic lunch, we returned the same way by horseback to our Rest House. We were glad to have a shower and rest before supper. The following day, we left to drive back via Madaba, the very ancient "Nebo" to Amman.

From Amman, we drove to Jerash, probably the best preserved of all Roman Provincial cities with its Forum, Theatre, Triumphal Arch and Temple of Artemis. Then we crossed the border into Syria to continue to Damascus where we stayed two nights at Hotel Meridien, sightseeing in Damascus all of Saturday. In the morning, to the Archaeological Museum, the Al Tekieh Mosque, built in 1553-54 as a hostel for pilgrims to Mecca; and the "Street called Straight", and in the afternoon, sightseeing including the City Walls, St. Paul's Window, the Ommayad Mosque, Saladin's Tomb and Al Azim Palace.

The following day, Sunday, we drove via Homs to Krak des Chevaliers, a superb Crusaders' Castle which was a stronghold of the Hospitallers in the 13th Century. After lunch, we were driven to Palmyra, situated in the Syrian desert. We stayed at a modern hotel owned by the same company as the one we left in Damascus and called by the same name, "Meridien". Unfortunately, I had a cold and so was not able to go sightseeing there the next day, but Keith was fascinated by it. He remembers a Roman city, with a theatre and arena – ruins now, of course – remains of big colonnades and arches. The hotel itself had been recently built, out of sight of the ruins, there being a small mound between it and the ruins.

We drove back to Damascus for the night and on to Amman the

following day. This tour included a visit to Jerusalem, but we had to be careful not to antagonise the immigration and passport authorities on the West Bank, as the situation was still tense between Jordan and Israel. Having successfully accomplished this, we went sightseeing in Jericho. It was many years since I had visited Jericho, when excavations of the old city were being carried out by Professor Garstang in which my Father was deeply involved. The city had grown beyond recognition, and looked vital now and well cared for. We inspected the newer archaeological excavations at the original site and saw Elisha's fountain and an old palace with interesting mosaic floors.

After reaching Jerusalem, we drove to St. Stephen's Gate in the old city, walked to the Church of St. Anne and the Pool of Bethesda, and many other places including the Church of the Holy Sepulchre and returned by coach from the Jaffa Gate. We stayed at the American Colony Hotel from Wednesday through the following Sunday.

The next day, we continued our sightseeing with a drive to Mt. Zion to visit the Tomb of King David and the Hall of the Last Supper. Afterwards, we continued on to the Israel Museum and the Shrine of the book containing the Dead Sea Scrolls, and after lunch we visited Rockefeller Museum of Archaeology and the Islamic Museum.

On Friday, we drove to the Mount of Olives to visit churches there and to walk in the Garden of Gethsemane before returning to our hotel for another night. On Saturday early, we drove to the Dead Sea to visit the caves of Qumran where the Dead Sea Scrolls were discovered. We then drove along the shores of the Dead Sea to the new cable railway which ascends to the mountain-top ruins of Herod the Great's rock of Masada, excavated in 1963-65 by Professor Y. Yadin. It was here, in 73 AD the Jews made their last great stand against the Romans and committed mass suicide rather than surrender. Visits were also made to the Western Palace, store rooms etc. at Masada and the ramp by which the Romans finally entered.

In the afternoon, we visited Hebron and the Mosque of Abraham. On the final day in Jerusalem, we drove to Dung Gate to visit the Temple area, including the 7th century Mosque of Omar (Dome of the Rock) and the West Wall (Wailing Wall of Herod's Temple). We continued on to Bethlehem and visited the Church of the Nativity before returning to our hotel.

On Monday, we drove back past the site of the Inn of the Good Samaritan and Bethany to the Jordan River and crossed into Jordan and so back to Amman for the night. Back by plane to England soon after.

234

In 1987 I went again to Israel, this time with Keith Macleod. We wished to see for ourselves the excavations being carried on at the Bible City of Lachish, and if possible to participate in them.

After the murder of its excavator in the thirties, there had been only sporadic attempts to excavate the Lachish "tel", but a member of the first "British" excavations – Miss Olga Tufnell, based in London had written in great detail some books on the excavations there in the 1930s, and a very distinguished Israeli Archaeologist, Mr. David Ussishkin of Tel Aviv University had already been in touch with her about those excavations. Dr. Ussishkin, who is married to a wife whose parents live in England, was able to visit Miss Tufnell and they had been able to spend much time together talking about these excavations and the possibility of resuming them.

Therefore, it was possible to resume systematic excavations in 1973-78 under the Institute of Archaeology of Tel Aviv University and the Israel Exploration Society and Dr. David Ussishkin was to direct these excavations.

I was, of course, very interested in all that I could find out about these excavations. Lachish was a city mentioned in the Bible and conquered by Joshua after the children of Israel moved out of the desert on their return to the promised land (Joshua X 31-32) and the excavations there in the 1930s, activated by my Father, Sir Charles Marston in conjunction with Sir Henry Wellcome and led by the Oxford Archaeologist, Mr. Leslie Starkey, had already turned up a number of interesting finds, including the so called "Lachish Letters" found near the Judean City Gate in 1934. These are eighteen ostraca of the first period before the Babylonian conquest of Judah, letters sent to a military commander in Lachish. My Father, who was an excellent speaker, wrote and spoke about these "finds" both in the States and in England and wrote about them in his widely published books.

Therefore it was with great anticipation that Keith and I flew to Israel on July 16th 1987 to participate in the life of these excavations. We stayed in Jerusalem at the American Colony Hotel, where we had stayed on a previous visit. We telephoned Dr. Ussishkin at "The Dig" and arranged to drive to their camp in the Cypress Grove near "Tel" Lachish the following week.

We had considerable adventures trying to find this camp – our driver set off confidently enough along the road south toward Tel Aviv, but we soon found ourselves in difficulties. Keith tried to help, and finally we enlisted the help of a taxi firm to lead us to the camp and the hearty welcome we received from Dr. Ussishkin and some of his staff. We were given a well designed camping site with most of the mod cons, including electric light and water nearby under the cypress trees. After a lively supper, during which we were introduced to a number of learned archaeologists and many of the students, we were allowed a few hours of rest before rising at dawn to drive up to the "tel" a short distance away, where work was already in progress. Although we wished to try to help with the excavations – we were still treated rather like V.I.P.s and shown the areas on the "tel" where work was taking place. One section called in their report: "Area S" was the most spectacular – a long, narrow section cutting through the upper edge of the mound – using a technique and example set by K. Kenyon in the excavations at Jericho.* Dr. Ussishkin planned to penetrate the lower levels of the mound down to bedrock and to extend the trench to the lower slopes. Here we had to walk on sandbags and boards placed across a deep trench to view the work being done. There were further excavation sites already open near the city gate complex and the Canaanite buildings underneath and near the Judean City Gate complex, which had been partly uncovered by Mr.Starkey in the 1930s was considered of prime importance because of the city gate as the focal point of the iron age fortifications and its significance for under-standing the mound's stratigraphy at that period.

Meanwhile, while viewing these areas, we were called to eat a hearty breakfast on a flat area of the mound under a flapping tarpaulin. Very good it was too, with a view of the Moshav Lachish situated on another hill nearby.

Then Keith and I were allowed to take up some trowels and try our hands at excavation work. We were given two baskets and into one went any loose soil we dislodged and into the other any solid article we might find such as stones, bits of pottery, etc. or other articles requiring further examination. Then one basket of soil was removed to the dump and the other taken back to the camp to be looked at in the afternoon session. Everyone met at the camp for lunch and a rest afterwards – later, the "finds" were cleaned and inspected. After supper, while we were there, we were treated to an excellent lecture in another area of the camp given by an old friend of ours, Professor Rainey.

We drove back to Jerusalem the following morning and spent some days lazing in the sunshine and swimming in their pool, and viewing Jerusalem. We were given a guided tour of the Protestant Cemetery on Mt. Zion by Dr. Barkay, where Mr. Starkey is buried, not far from his teacher, Sir Flinders Petrie.

*See "The Bible is True" by Sir Charles Marston.

CHAPTER 33

"Claymont" and a
Tour of the States

Elizabeth Bennett and I left for Washington D.C. Elizabeth was going to Claymont and I was to accompany her there. We flew via New York and had a rather uncomfortable connection which held us up there and we were late in Washington and had some difficulty informing Claymont of our predicament. However, all was well in the end and we reached Claymont safely. Elizabeth was very quickly surrounded by eager questioners amongst the students and then we were both asked to help with group work. The following day, we were able to see for ourselves the work being done on the farm and go to the auction barn. There were also movements to attend in the evening.

Then, we were asked by the Claymont Council to drive to Georgia to inspect a possible Conference Centre which Claymont had been offered as a "meditation" centre. Accordingly, we left early with two students from Claymont and I enjoyed the drive through Virginia very much.

We were certainly impressed with the facilities offered there, but felt it was too far from Claymont to be of service to them and altogether too expensive to keep in order. It was certainly an impressive Conference Centre and we enjoyed its capacious facilities. On our return drive, we visited "Montecello", the home of President Thomas Jefferson, but we arrived too late to be able to see around the inside of the house.

The next day, I was to meet up with Jamie Macleod at the home of some friends. I left Claymont for Washington. We were to meet up at the airport and to drive to the friends' home in Nokesville, Virginia some miles outside Washington. Jamie is the son of my friend, Keith Macleod, and the owner of a garage in Cranleigh, Surrey, England. I wanted to go on an extensive tour of the States and Jamie wished also to sightsee, so he was to pick up a hire car in Washington upon his arrival there and we were to meet together to begin our tour. After staying a few days in Nokesville, we flew from Washington to Los Angeles, California to begin our tour. We called on my old friend, Dorothy Ingham, who lived in Hollywood, and both Dorothy and Jamie came with me to Mt. Washington in Los Angeles to call on the Mother Centre there. While I talked to the receptionist about my need to join the Self-Realization Fellowship, they enjoyed walking in the extensive grounds and admiring the lovely views.

Then Jamie and I took the direct route to Bakerfield and staying at motels en route, we drove via Yosemite National Park and over the Sierra Mountains to Lake Tahoe to visit my cousins Dick and Jean Deanesly who owned a cabin near the lake, but whose permanent residence is in Berkeley, California. Whenever I see them, I am reminded of my youth, when all the cousins of John and Ellen Marston's family played together and Dick, who considered himself a rather superior older cousin, would become frustrated with Marjorie and me, being partly American, and rather "pert". Dick would say ominously to everyone: "One thing I won't do is to go and live in the States!" Of course, when he was old enough, he joined "Shell" and he was sent to the States. Then he liked it so much that he came home, married a bride from Scotland and has lived there ever since. I reminded him of this and he nodded his head in acceptance of it!

Jamie and I had just time to see the sights of San Francisco, the Golden Gate and Fisherman's Wharf before we took off for Chicago to visit some American relatives, the Edges and my old friend from Sarah Lawrence College days, Jane, now Mrs. Jane Rubovits, with her elegantly young and beautiful daughter Audrey. Peter Edge, a lawyer to Sears, was able to show us the Sears Tower and wine and dine us there. Peter is the son of Charles and Rosalie Edge. Rumour has it that Charles and Rosalie met at my Mother's wedding to my Father in New York City. Charles was a successful stockbroker and came from Birmingham, England and Rosalie, a bridesmaid to my Mother, was American. Both were unusual characters and they wedded and quarrelled and then separated. Peter went with his mother and Margaret, Peter's sister, stayed with her father. My sister Marjorie, tells the story that when she first came to the States in her teens, she stayed in New York City with Charles and Rosalie. They showed her, with much pride, their new car, and then Charles told her to drive it round Central Park, although she had had no lessons!

So she complied, but while in Central Park, she thought: "I will teach them a lesson. I will stay here (in the park) for a while, until Charles and Rosalie get truly worried about the fate of me and the car and come out and look for me." So she stayed in Central Park for a time before returning the car safely back to its owners.

Our next flight was to Boston, where we picked up our hire car and with difficulty drove round very crowded Boston and finally stayed the next night at the Royal Sonnesta Hotel on the river near Cambridge, where we were joined by our friends Marjorie and Ben Benfield whom we originally met on a tour through Russia.

The next day, we drove to Newport, Rhode Island to spend a few days near Rev. Marston Price and his wife Sharon and their family. "Marston", as the name implies, was a relative, and his mother a very great friend of my Father, and I had had the privilege of looking after Marston when staying with his mother in Ann Arbour, Michigan many years previously. Marston was by profession an architect, and then both he and his wife became interested in the Episcopal Church, and so he studied and was ordained and was at that time curate at Newport's lovely St. John's Trinity Church. As I knew Sharon had a young family, I had asked her to put us up in a bed and breakfast flat nearby. She recommended us to a fellow vicar living quite close, and we were very comfortable there. Jamie and I went on a boat trip tour of the Harbour and saw some of the magnificent summer homes lining the water's edge. We dined with Marston and Sharon and one evening, Marjorie and Ben came over to have dinner with us as well. Then we drove to West Farm, New Hampshire, to stay with some cousins, Ann and Harry Tyson Carter. Ann's father was the younger brother of Peter Edge's father, and so she was half American, having an American mother. They had lived in Washington DC for many years and I had always enjoyed their hospitality there. Now that Harry Carter had retired, they had gone to live at another of their homes in New Hampshire.

Our final destination was to be Georgetown in Maine, where a very great friend of my sister Marjorie and her husband lived. Aimee von Huene had a luxurious summer house right on a bay in Georgetown. My sister and I had stayed there previously and I knew that Jamie would enjoy it. Aimee was a wonderful hostess, her fresh lobsters a renowned delicacy, and her cooking of them "a dream". We were able to drive around with Aimee as guide, to Indian Point and Jamie was able to do a little sailing before we left again for Boston in our car hire. There we stayed at The Holiday Inn and did some sightseeing and shopping at the Faneuil Market before returning by air to London. We had an altogether successful trip. I was able to go to Los Angeles to check in at my Self-Realization Fellowship and see many of my good friends and relatives and Jamie was able to see quite a lot of the States.

CHAPTER 34

Self-Realization Fellowship

With Mr. Bennett's death and that also of my sister, I was left to consider afresh my spiritual life.

In the 1960s my sister and I had been given a book entitled "The Autobiography of a Yogi" by Paramahansa Yogananda. We had both been very stimulated by it and realised that when we had been in Los Angeles and staying at the Biltmore Hotel, we must have been close to its author. However, while Mr. Bennett and my sister were alive and we were active in "Subud", that last chapter was not possible for me. But I can always remember the Shivapuri Baba's astonishing words when we sat with him in the woods at Katmandu: "When you see God, all your questions will be answered". Was that really possible? My early teacher, Mr. Ouspensky, would not even contemplate such questions and talked us down with great severity when anyone mentioned such a matter – my Father, when I was a little girl, talked of "God" and the Bible when he came to say "Goodnight" to me. I remember so vividly trying to comprehend the age and wonder of such a magnificent character. But how were we to actually try and get in touch with our Heavenly Host. The churches quoted passages from the Bible: Psalm 82.6:
"I have said ye are Gods, and all of you are children of the most high"; and again, in John 10.34: "Is it not written in your law, I said, Ye are Gods?"

Perhaps I needed now to explore this again. It was not enough for me to try and think of these things. I must really discover how to approach this subject. As so often happens, the answer was near at hand.

Two ladies from Germany came to stay with me at my new home. One was my old friend from Germany, Amelie Wilmsen, mother of my Godchild, and the other her sister "Ovi" (Anna Maria V. Brackenhausen). I had known Ovi many years previously; now she seemed transformed. I asked her what she had been studying, and she told me she had become a member of the Self-Realization Fellowship, and when she returned to Germany, she sent me a small book entitled "The Sayings of Paramahansa Yogananda". On my next visit to the States, I visited Los Angeles in California and went to their lovely 'Mother Centre' on Mount Washington. My intuition told me to participate in this work, to follow their written lessons and their Great Teacher toward that goal which the Shivapuri Baba had so urgently, forcefully and eloquently talked to us about in the woods at Katmandu. May I quote from "Where there is Light" by Paramahansa Yogananda: "I tell you truthfully that all my questions have been answered, not through man but through God – you think you want human love and prosperity but behind this it is your Father that is calling you. If you realize He is greater than all His gifts, you will find Him." (p.177).

For some years now, I have been a believer of this spiritual way, of meditation and a new relationship toward God and my fellow friends. Many years ago, Mr. Bennett gave his students an exercise, to try and understand that each person had a spark of the Absolute within them, and I remember the difference it made to our relationship one to another. Now, once again, this test is before me. This is what self-realization is all about. It is the way of Yoga Meditation. Again I quote from the excellent little book "Where there is Light": "Through Yoga Meditation we can know that we are Gods." (p.5.)

From the very ancient Sufi sources comes the story of the "King's Son" and the "Hymn of the Soul", "The Sufi Quest", and from the Gospel of St. Thomas, "We are his Sons" and from others, Father Zossima's Creed, "The Lands of Immortal Youth".★

Organized religion seems reluctant to talk about this wonderful fact and only emphasises our faults. Faults we certainly have, and each one of us in our learning process must see and correct those faults, but what a wonderful aim we can have in our lives. Paramahansa Yogananda states in this little book "that Man has come to earth solely to learn to know God, he is here for no other reason". (p.177).

This statement is certainly in accord with all that I have understood so far in my life.

★ "The King's Son": compiled by Robert Cecil, Richard Rieu & David Wade, pp.2-14.

I asked the Mother Centre on Mt. Washington, Los Angeles in 1985 to send me the lectures of Paramahansa Yogananda, and this they did at regular intervals. Then, when I came back to England, I went to a series of lectures at their London Group in Notting Hill Gate and when some of their staff came over from the States, I eagerly joined their meditation and other activities.

In the summer of 1988, Keith and I flew again to the States. I wished to attend the Self-Realization World Convocation held annually in Los Angeles at the Westin Bonadventure Hotel there for a week, while Keith stayed in Hollywood with a mutual friend, Dorothy Ingham, a friend of my oldest, dearest friend Nancy Gluck.

Keith, Nancy and I met up at the Westin Bonadventure Hotel during that Saturday afternoon of August 6th when our Self-Realization literature told us to check in. Keith was eager to see me settled in comfortably before going on to Hollywood, but we were somewhat dismayed by the queues of applicants stretching all round the hotel lobby. We were advised to have a cup of coffee and then present ourselves later. This we did, but the queues had not diminished. However, I found that there were a number of young men who seemed to be organizing them and so I stepped boldly up to one of the men, who fitted me into a nearby place, and I was given a room number after having signed my application form. Then Keith and Nancy departed and I was left alone to get on with it. I had been given a very clear programme of the week's events, but I needed to further explore this huge hotel to become familiar with its facilities.

It was already clear to me that there was an exhibition of books, tapes and other memorabilia on the ground floor, so I made my way there and introduced myself to one of the staff for directions. I had not yet recognised anyone from the London Group, but I understood that there would be an informal opening and welcome in one of the big air conditioned halls on the first floor that evening, and there I would probably find some fellow friends. There seemed to be a permanent coffee shop, also, on the ground floor, and I was later to discover that there were no end of grills, bars, coffee shops etc. on the many floors above and a big open air roof garden where we could all gather.

The same procedure of queueing went on for every event with young men ushering us along and helping us with their advice for each class listed in our written programme. I quickly discovered that there was a permanently "quiet" room which was open for meditation at all times.

There were classes given on different aspects of Paramahansa's teaching and also pilgrimages to the Mother Centre, Lake Shrine and to Encinitas Temple and Ashram Centre, and to these were added videos, classes for devotional chanting, college (Kirtons) and Questions and Answers (Satsanga). Classes were given by staff monks on meditation techniques for new students, and yoga.

On the last day, direct disciples whom Paramahansa Yogananda personally chose and trained to carry on his work would join with Convocation participants to share thoughts and highlights of the Master's life and teachings, providing an inspiring conclusion to a week of spiritual renewal.

Another highlight not already mentioned is the appearance of Sri Daya Mata herself, President of the Self-Realization Fellowship (Yogoda Satsanga Society of India). She is truly a "Mother of Compassion" as her name signifies, who has inspired those of all faiths and from all walks of life with her great love of God, and with the humility, wisdom and divine joy that radiates from her being and illumines her words. In India, they speak of Darsham – the blessing that flows from the mere sight of a saintly soul.

On another occasion, I attended a weekend retreat at their beautiful Encinatas Ashram, where we were shown the actual study where Paramahansa himself wrote so many of his books and papers and where he lived for many years. I shall never forget the magnificent views overlooking the Pacific Ocean and the peace and majesty of those gardens lining the shore and coast as well as their church service on Sunday at the nearby Temple.

Since that time, I have regularly attended "meditation" weekends in England and have also gone to weekends organized by the London Group to welcome "monks" sent over from the Los Angeles Mother Centre.

I have found it difficult at home to "meditate" as much as I would wish, and so these weekends – where we all "meditate" together and, indeed, live together for a period, are greatly appreciated.

CHAPTER 35

Trips to Russia

Keith and I went on two separate trips to Russia. In 1979, Swans Hellenic were offering an art treasure tour to Moscow, Central Asia and Transcaucasia; this included a visit to Samarkand, Bukhara and Tashkent, as well as a flight over the Caucasus Mountains to Erevan and Tbilisi in Georgia. Neither my sister nor I had been to Soviet Russia, although I had had two Russian mentors; Gurdjieff (whose book – "Meetings with Remarkable Men" was being shown in many good cinemas in London and elsewhere) and Ouspensky, who lived and worked in St. Petersburg. From my archaelogical side, I was very glad to obtain a view of Mount Ararat in the Caucasus. So this was an opportunity not to be missed.

There were about thirty people in our party that met at Heathrow Airport on 28th September, 1979, mostly like ourselves – middle-aged and keen to learn all they could about Russia. The majority were from the United States. We had an uneventful British Airways flight to Moscow. How thrilling to be circling over the Red Square and Kremlin, with St. Basil's favourite onion shaped domes to one side.

My first "brush" with the Soviet authorities was over my passport; it was in order, but when I marched firmly through their barrier, I was detained briskly because my friend Keith had mine as well as his own, he was behind me. However, this was quickly resolved and we were all led to a most enormous Hotel near the Red Square. We had requested and paid for single accommodation but, as it turned out, we were so far apart from each other that it took too long to walk the corridors to get together again, to be practical. There were very large alcoves on each floor where a portly Russian lady sat with steaming samovar at the ready. Our lady guide escorted us up to the restaurant on the top floor for dinner, where we had magnificent views over the Moscow River and University. We were told that this hotel had at least two thousand bedrooms.

The food was good when it came, but service was rather slow, however, they got used to us in the days that followed, and the service was speeded up. There were bus tours each day, and so we had to stick to our times of departure pretty rigidly.

Our first tour in Moscow was to Red Square and the Kremlin Museum in the morning and to the Novodevichy Convent after lunch.

In the Kremlin area, many of the religious monuments such as St. Basil's Cathedral and the Cathedral of the Assumption were closed and under repair temporarily, but we were taken to see the Tsar Bell on its plinth. This bell was intended to be the biggest in the world. Originally cast for Boris Gudonov for another bell tower, it had no sooner been hoisted into position than it fell to the ground and broke to bits. Recast a century later, disaster struck again. A fire broke out in the shed where it was being kept and water was accidentally thrown over the red hot bell, cracking it in two places. Since then, it has remained on the ground. Another relic nearby is a sixteenth century cannon with its cannon balls, which was also doomed to idleness and silence and serves now mainly as a background for holiday snapshots. We were taken to the armoury, part of the Kremlin Museum, where we saw a number of decorated coaches and figures in costumes. We were taken to the Alexandrovski Gardens nearby and shown the monument to the Unknown Soldier, with its eternal flame, upon which newly married couples with brides in their wedding dresses, deposit their wedding bouquets.

The Novodevichy Monastery lies further away, near the Moscow River, with its cluster of sparkling domes behind handsome turreted walls, and full of history and treasures. Many well known people lived here and bequeathed their treasures to this monastery.

Its adjacent cemetery is one of Moscow's most prestigious resting places. When walking along its paths, we found the graves of Gogol and Chekhov and some heroes of the Napoleonic Wars and wars against Hitler's army. A much visited grave is that of Stalin's wife, Nadezka Alliluyeva, who shot herself in 1932, and rounding a corner one comes face to face with the white marble bust of the late Mr. Krushchev.

While returning to our hotel from one of these visits, we noticed a high arch near Red Square with the emblem of the hammer and sickle proudly displayed over a globe of the world. Keith remarked to our Intourist Guide: "Is this what the Soviet want to do to capture the World?" She looked glum, but didn't reply.

We had some trouble trying to buy drinks and other produce in Moscow. We had roubles but they did not want to take them, and asked only for U.S. dollars. We had not thought of this, and found them hard to come by in Russia!!

After just two days in Moscow, we flew to Samarkand in Uzbekistan. This famous town contains the tomb of Tamerlane , is very ancient and was at one time part of the Kharak of Turkey, until it fell to the conquering Arabs. Thereafter it was under the Samanids until the 10th Century and later it belonged to the Seljuk Turks. In 1220 the Tartars of Mongolia, under Genghis Khan, having pillaged Bukhara, arrived at Samarkand, where they broke the resistance of 100,000 men, destroyed the town and deported part of the population. For a century and a half it was practically a dead city.

Thus, when in 1360 Tamerlane became the ruler of Transoxiana and established Samarkand as the capital of his state, it is no exaggeration to talk of the "resurrection" of Samarkand and from that time the town started to grow into a magnificent city, with innumerable mosques, palaces and gardens. Later, Ulugh-Beg, Tamerlane's grandson, built a famous observatory there. During this period which continued until the assassination of Ulugh-Beg in 1449, Samarkand with its prosperity, its culture and its university, the Kalinder-Kani, was the centre of the Moslem civilization of Central Asia.

In 1500, the town fell into the hands of the Uzbeks under Shaibani Khan and thereafter the capital was in Transoxiana so Bukhara and Samarkand lost their importance and were exposed to attacks of pillaging nomad tribes.

A new period opened up for Samarkand when the Russians advanced along the Syr-Darya river and took the town and later as it grew up again, a new town up at the east end of the old one. In 1896 when the Transcaspian Railway linked Samarkand to Krasnovodsk, the economy of the town was given fresh impetus and since the Revolution the importance of Samarkand has continued to increase, especially in the spheres of farming and industry.

We stayed at the modern "Intourist Hotel" which stands at the junction of the old and new towns, where Gorky Street and Registan Street meet. From the top of the hotel there are magnificent views of the town and its chief buildings, particularly the Gur-Emir Mausoleum, close to the hotel.

Having settled in at our hotel, the next morning we were taken to see the Bibi Khanym Mosque and the Observatory of Ulugh-Beg.

Bibi Khanym, one of Tamerlane's wives, was, according to a legend, a daughter of the Emperor of China. This building, although ravaged by time and earthquakes, is still able to display its quality. A majestic building, erected by Tamerlane and thought to commemorate his campaign to India. The booty he brought back from that war helped to pay for its construction.

Of the original minarets, little more is left than two arches and the majestic dome with its "tile" decoration which is now in a state of ruin, although I was told this was shortly to be repaired.

The dimensions of this mosque are impressive and the portal leading to the main chamber is no less than 41 metres high. The wall decoration, notable for its variety of colouring and pattern, is excellently preserved. In the courtyard of the Mosque is a huge lectern for the Koran, in the form of an open book, 2.50 metres long, made of grey marble and covered with inscriptions. It was originally inside the Mosque.

The other building we saw that morning was the observatory of Ulugh-Beg on a low mound to the right of the main Tashkent Road, after crossing the river. The foundation, 46 metres in diameter, can be clearly distinguished. The total height of the building, which was two storeys, must have been some 30 metres. A modern brick built vault protects the remains of the famous sextant constructed by Ulugh-Beg about 1430 for his astronomical observations.

In front of the building is the grave of the archaeologist V.I. Vyatkin, who discovered the site in 1908. There is also a small museum containing material discovered during the excavations there.

After lunch, we set out again and went to Registan Square with its beautiful blue and green tiled buildings. The square was formerly a forum where the faithful came to pray and the heralds announced important events. It contains three hansome buildings: (East Side) Shir-Dor Medrese of Ulugh-Beg, and on the (West Side) the Tilla Kariand the Medrese of Ulugh-Beg on the North Side. Medrese means school – where the pupils learnt about the sacred book the "Koran", and studied theology and the religious sciences, and such secular branches of knowledge as mathematics and astronomy.

Then we were taken to the Gur-Emir Mausoleum where, in the crypt, were the graves of Tamerlane, Mohammed Sultan (Tamerlane's favourite grandson) and his successor Ulugh-Beg, two of his sons and his friend and spiritual master Mir Sayyid Barka. The building itself is an octagonal structure with a "ribbed Dome" covered with magnificent blue tiles, borne on a massive drum. Onyx and gold were used in the decoration which has been recently restored. Wooden doors inlaid with ivory lead into the main chamber containing white marble tombs surrounded by a low balustrade. On one of them, inscribed in Arabic script standing out in relief, is the genealogy of the mighty ruler of Central Asia, Tamerlane, the date of his death and other information. In the crypt is Tamerlane's grey marble tomb. In the courtyard is Tamerlane's grey marked throne.

That evening, in our hotel, some of the passenger lifts failed to work. As our room was near the top of the building, I, with another friend, went to our Tourist Guide to ask how we were supposed to ascend to our rooms for our night's sleep. Since the luggage lift seemed to be the only one working, we suggested that several of our group who did not have good hearts should be allowed to take that lift, and after some delay, this was accepted by the management – luckily!!!

While in Samarkand, we were driven to see a Cotton Cooperative – very modern – and we were interested to see lines of cotton growing on one side of the road and rice on the other. We had never seen two such different products growing side by side.

Keith also noticed a number of military tanks drawn up in a field beside the road and turned to an American who had already seen them. Later, we understood they were for the invasion of Afghanistan.

Next morning, we were off to Bukhara, which has always been a rival of Samarkand, situated on the banks of the Zeravsham in the lower valley of the river which is soon lost in the sand before reaching the Amu-Darya (the ancient Oxus).

Bukhara was not built directly on the river bank but on a canal which irrigates the land nearest the town, and supplies the inhabitants with water. This was a persistent cause of ill health until the Soviet Government supplied its citizens with fresh, clean water. Despite these rather unhealthy conditions, Bukhara enjoyed a favoured position on the caravan route to Herat and Afghanistan, Persia and India on the famous "Bukhara Road". Bukhara is a very old town and derives its name from the Sanskrit "Vihara", which means "monastery". It was conquered by the Arabs at the end of the 7th Century, then it was exposed to the covetousness of the Turks who invaded Transoxania several times.

In 892, Bukhara fell under the rule of the Samanids and remained so until 999, and as the political capital of a great kingdom, it enjoyed a long period of prosperity, and its trade and crafts flourished.

From the year 1,000, after the fall of the Samanids, Bukhara lost some of its political importance, but under its next rulers, the

Karakhanids, the town remained a renowned intellectual centre, and in the 12th century the town was the brilliant cultural centre of Islam.

In 1220, Jenghis Khan captured this town, whose citadel heroically resisted the Mongol conqueror for twelve days.Bukhara was put to the fire and sword, but unlike Samarkand, it soon rose again from its ruins. Half a century later, in 1273, the Mongols from Persia again devastated the town.

The situation changed in 1500 when Bukhara fell into the hands of the Uzbeks. They made it their capital from the middle of the 16th century until the 1917 Revolution. During this period, Bukhara regained the greatness it had enjoyed and added to it were several further territories, as well as numerous public buildings, palaces, mosques and medreses.

When the revolution broke out, Bukhara became a refuge for the anti-Bolshevik forces of Turkestan and soon developed into one of the centres of the Basmach movement which found allies in the White Army, supported by the British. The Emir of Bukhara was overthrown in 1924 and Bukhara joined the Soviet People's Republic and became part of the new Soviet Republic of Uzbekistan.

Our group had only two days to explore this wonderful old town of small narrow streets, mostly unpaved, forming a labyrinth through which it is difficult to find one's way. At the corners of these streets there were often mosques and schools.

Bukhara has a large number of medreses (Moslem religious schools) which, in outward appearance, look brilliant, pompous and aggressive, but are dark, stuffy and fetid inside.

On our first sightseeing tour we saw the Balyand Mosque (Great Mosque) a 16th century building which is notable for the richness of its interior decoration, with its glazed tiles in gilded patterns, wall paintings and a handsome open gallery supported on wooden columns. Next, we visited the Registan Square to see the massive citadel or Ark, the walls of which tower some 20 metres above the square.

We were told that the foundations of this fortress no doubt dated back to the 9th century, but the present walls are much later. We entered it by a paved ramp and a fortified gateway. On each side of the entrance are dungeons and casements. Inside the fortress are a mosque, houses and a museum, and in the attic of the main building are some very fine gold brocaded fabrics, pottery and copper and silver vessels and an excellent view of the town.

Opposite the entrance to the Ark, we saw the Bola Khauz Mosque which was built about 1712, but its portico with wooden columns was copied and is of much more recent origin and together with its basin near it, and a minaret, is the work of a local craftsman. We were delighted and impressed by a display of singing and dancing in the Registan Square that evening.

Next morning, we were out early on another sightseeing day. We went to the Kirov Park to see the Mausoleum of Ismail Samani and the tomb of Chashma-Ayub.

The Mausoleum is the oldest building in Bukhara, and dates back to the 9th or 10th century and was built for members of the Samanid dynasty and is made of baked brick. It is a building of striking simplicity and harmony of form, cube shaped with a dome borne on eight arches clearly visible from the outside. On each side of the structure is an arched opening with a recessed bay. These walls are covered both inside and outside with various ornamental patterns in the brickwork itself as well as some alabaster panels.

When we left the Kirov Park on the last of our visits in Bukhara, we walked through crowded streets and covered markets and visited several further medresas and the Kaylan Mosque with its guest house. The Mosque is one of the most imposing in the Moslem world and is famous for its monumental portal and massive dome, enriched with turquoises over the central hall, and for its beautiful mihrab (minaret). The mosque was originally built in the 12th century, then rebuilt in 1514 and it could accommodate a congregation of 10,000.

Continuing eastwards along the main street, we visited the two medresas of Ulugh-Beg and Abdulaziz Khan on opposite sides of the street, both of them well known for their lovely proportions and richly carved decorations, and we ended the afternoon sightseeing by going through the Tiri Abdulla Klan market, full of flowers and vegetables.

I had read so much about Bukhara and the Sufis who have lived there that it was an uplifting experience to see where these wonderful people actually lived and worked.

En route for Tashkent, our next big city, we stopped to look at the old walled town of Khiva, another of the well known attractions of Uzbekistan, though more remote than Samarkand and Bukhara and consequently not so well known.

Khiva is situated in the Khorezm oasis to the west of the Amu-Darya River which reaches across the river into Turkmerstan. Khiva was founded in the 10th century, but only began to play an active role in the 16th century when the Khanate of Khiva (established in 1511) controlled the trade routes between Central Asia and the Volga region. It was then one of the leading slave markets of Central Asia, rivalling Bukhara in this respect. But its most brilliant period was in the 19th century, shortly before the Russian occupation (1873). Khiva has been part of Uzbekistan since 1924.

We were taken to visit the old walled town of Ichan-Kala with its flat-roofed houses of pise or sun-dried brick, which was a busy and colourful scene with crowds of Uzbek and Turkmenian peasants thronging the streets with their donkeys.

The market square was the central part of our visit. On the south we could see the minaret of the Said Bay Mosque (1842) said to have been built by the children of Khiva on the orders of the Khan and is still in use.

Then from here we entered the old town by way of the covered bazaar and we came to a narrow lane in which is the windowless wall of the Palace of Allakuli Khan or Tash-Khauli (Courtyard of Stone). The 163 rooms of the palace were formerly occupied by the women of the harem. Now part of this building is used to accommodate a historical and ethnographical museum.

A short distance away to the south are two medressas★; the best preserved is the medresa of Allakuli Khan which has a very beautiful facade and is in an excellent state of preservation. In 1970 this was made into a museum devoted to Avicenna, the great doctor, and one of its chief items of interest was a woman's skull dating from the Christian era which bears the mark of trepanning. The other Medresa★ of Kutlug Murad Inak bears the name of Allah-Kuli Khan's uncle, which some historians think is earlier, possibly dating from 1812. It, too, is well preserved and there is a well in its court-yard.

Finally, we saw the Islam-Khodzha Minaret whose slender silhouette is a characteristic feature of the Khiva skyline. It was built in 1908 by a well- known architect for the Vizier of Asfendiar Khan. It is decorated with magnificent glazed tiles in horizontal bands of ornament. Visitors can climb to the top, from which they can obtain fine views. We were also shown the remains of a fortified palace (Kunya-Ark) of the Khans of Khiva. The surviving rooms include the Throne Room and Prayer Hall, both with fine wooden columns and decorated wooden ceilings, and the Mint.

When we walked round the walls of old Khiva, we saw many circular brick built tombs and old houses made with daub and wattle.

★ Spelling varies – Medresa or Madrassa.

Khiva has grown considerably in size in recent years. A large cotton mill was built in the modern town and there is an Agricultural Institute, and an Institute of Medicine, an Educational Institute and a School of Music and its theatre enjoys a considerable reputation.

Our next visit was to Tashkent. an oasis town like Samarkand and Bukhara, but since the great earthquake of 1966 and the following hurricane, it was decided to rebuild the town, taking into account the lessons learnt from the earthquake. Help came from all parts of the Soviet Union – there were large blocks of flats built and the centre of Tashkent was completely cleared and replaced by wide avenues and intersections on two levels and underpasses were laid out with public gardens and ornamental ponds. The modern buildings were erected on piles, capable of withstanding intense earth tremors. The modern city thus built has lost a lot of colour of the Old Tashkent but the area of open space per head of the population which was 4 square inches before the earthquake has now arisen to 38 – and the plan of this town may still have further modifications. It is now the seat of the Academy of Sciences of Usbekistan and has a university and several institutes, an observatory, a theatre and a permanent circus in its own building to which we went and spent a very enjoyable evening doing so. There is a Russian Dramatic Theatre, an Uzbek Philarmonic Society and a well- known singing and dancing group and an opera house. All are connected with an excellent "underground" railway, which is the pride and joy of its people, as it is in Moscow.

Tashkent has also a leading part to play as a centre for cotton production and also particularly concerned with research and general teaching and there have been large scale irrigation schemes which have made an increase of production an outstanding success. We were taken to a cotton mill to see this for ourselves. We stayed near the Theatre Square in the centre of new Tashkent in Lenin Street, and near the new Lenin Museum and opposite the new opera and ballet theatre. The Lenin Square behind the hotel is the ultra-modern supreme Soviet. This is the real centre of Tashkent and the place where various popular celebrations are held. There on a pedestal of granite and labradoute is a bronze statue of Lenin and nearby is the Ankhor irrigation canal, which cuts across the wide and handsome Alisher Navoy Street.

One of our friends in our party was a learned professor of languages and he was constantly out with his little Russian dictionary trying to learn all he could in a short space of time, but he became very frustrated by the street signs, which were illuminated round the tops of buildings and constantly moving. They would tend to disappear before he could find their meaning in his dictionary!!

One evening, Keith and I with another couple set out on the famous "underground" to go to the circus. We were very impressed by the lovely clean atmosphere and the huge candelabras which lit the underground. The trains, also, were quick and quiet and much less "fussy" than ours in England. The circus, too was a delight to watch – very few performing animals, many wonderfully trained trapeze artists and very comfortable seating accommodation.

We decided to try and get a taxi for our return trip to our hotel, and while we were wandering along a footpath by the wide open road, we were accosted by a Russian policeman who obviously wanted to help us, and when we said "taxi", he was off and returned with one shortly. We thanked him profusely!!

Now, we had to get ready for the most exciting part of our trip – to fly near the Caucasus Mountains to Erevan and T'Blisi.

We were told to put most of our baggage ready outside our hotel doors and just keep what we needed for overnight with us. The plane was scheduled to leave in the early morning for Erevan, but there was some doubt as to whether it would "fly" then. So we were asked to go to bed in the usual way and we would be wakened by telephone if we were needed. I am a rather light sleeper at the best of times, and this information did not help. However, the telephone did ring in the early hours to tell us we would not be needed then. The next night we went to bed with the same instructions, but when we were again phoned in the early hours to be told that we would not be going that night. I took a sleeping tablet and prepared to have a good sleep. Alas and alack – the information turned out to be untrue, and at 4.30 am we were phoned up again to be told to be ready to 'take off' in half an hour. I was parading with the others in the lobby at the appropriate time, feeling rather triumphant!

We did, indeed, have wonderful views of the snow capped range of the Caucasus Mountains silhouetted in the rising sun, capped by Mount Ararat, but I was very exhausted when we reached our hotel at Erevan and had to miss one 'sightseeing' that morning.

Erevan, capital of Armenia, is one of the oldest towns in the U.S.S.R., if not in the world, and it lies at an altitude of 1,000 metres above the deep canyon of the Razdan, a tributary of the Araxes, and the town is dominated by the twin peaks of Mount Ararat (in Turkey). It was founded in 783 BC and had a population of about 30,000 people. Now, it has followed the usual pattern of wide avenues and spacious squares and large bridges and is full of industrial and cultural activities centralized in buildings of pink colour or ochre tufa, not usually more than four stories high, since this town is subject to earth tremors, but some blocks of buildings are now thirteen storeys high.

This capital of Armenia is a city of composers, writers, painters and students. There are many museums, chief of which is the 'Matenadaran', which looms over Erevan like a grey stone fortress and contains many manuscripts and documents in many languages and date from the 5th Century AD.

We spent some time in the Armenian Church of St. Sergius – there was some lovely singing within the Church and we were surprised to hear that it came from a group of Scandinavian students on a visit to the town and also a number of Russian soldiers who were sitting in the Church and enjoying the music and singing too. We joined them and were impressed by the cosmopolitan atmosphere.

We also drove out of Erevan to see some Armenian Christian churches. The cathedral at Echmiadzin was founded in 303 by St. Gregory and was built on the site of an ancient temple, the remains of which were discovered beneath the choir, but the original church was demolished and rebuilt several times. But the present cathedral has remained the main centre of Armenian Christianity in the 14th century and has remained so up to modern times. There are some tombs of important people at its entrance and the paintings inside the Cathedral are reminiscent of Persian art, but they are by a famous Armenian painter. A sacristy was added later and contains the treasury of the Cathedral. Around it are the remains of the monastic buildings, the seminary, printing press, offices and the episcopal palace.

Our next flight took us to Tbilsi, capital of Georgia, better known under its Persian name of Tiflis, which was in use up to 1917, then it was changed by the Russians to Tbilisi, which means the town of the hot springs, on account of the many sulphur springs found there.

Visitors have christened this town 'the Florence of the Caucasus'. It is now spread over the slopes of the red hills, in places standing 40 metres above the muddy but fast flowing river Kura. There are picturesque houses, with wide wooden balconies painted a delicate faded blue which nestle in old streets, reminiscent of the Orient and shaded by Caucasian plane trees. The city loses nothing of its charm by being a large modern town, a dynamic capital, and the heart of a nation with an ancient language and culture very much alive today.

Our group spent several very happy days here. Our hotel on

Rustaveli Avenue was centrally located. We were able to take the 'Motatsminda' cable railway from Rustaveli Square (opened in 1958). This railway ascends the 'Sacred' Mountain or David's Mountain. David was one of the Syriac Saints who built himself a cell and chapel on the terraces here and a church was later built on an upper plateau, and between the two plateaux the space was transformed in 1939 into a pantheon for the tombs of famous people and their inscriptions – very impressive.

There was a path leading from the Pantheon to the top of the Mtatsminda which is laid out as a park with gorgeous views of the snow capped peaks beyond.

There were also a number of museums and theatres to be visited and one evening we broke up into small groups to go to ballet, opera and puppet shows. Two of our friends recall their evening at the ballet – they were unable to read their librettos, but were helped by their dictionaries. However, it was a hilarious experience to try and keep up with the words and their meaning!

Keith and I were enthralled with the puppet show we chose to go to, and after a short time, the little figures became so real to us we forgot they were just puppets.

We were very happy in Tbilisi and we took the people of Georgia to our hearts in spite of the language difficulties and we enjoyed their museums of Georgian Art and Agricultural Machinery before we flew back to Moscow and home.

We were able to pay a brief visit to the Tretyakov Gallery in Moscow and were escorted by our lecturer. As it was on a weekend, the gallery was crowded with schoolchildren and visitors from all over the Soviet Union. We had a limited time at our disposal and so our guide deftly took us in a tight group around to the ikons and pictures that he knew and loved. While Keith went with a small group to the War Museum, where he was impressed by the huge paintings of scenes from the Russian Revolution, and especially vivid was a picture of a smiling girl about to be beheaded. We stayed again at our enormous ultra modern hotel of metal and glass where we required a "pass" to come and go from it, and when we were in the vicinity of the Kremlin, various individuals would come towards me offering me local money in exchange for American dollars – but I did not oblige them!

Our flight back to England by British Airways was uneventful, but we were sorry to have to part from the many good friends who had shared with us the many experiences of this unusual holiday.

Our Baltic Cruise, June 1989

Keith and I set out from Tilbury Docks on the Cruise Liner "Royal Princess" owned by the P & O Lines on June 26th. Our itinerary included stops at Copenhagen, Leningrad, Helsinki, Stockholm and Amsterdam before returning to Tilbury on July 8th.

Since my early trips to the Baltic and Scandinavia in the 1920s, I have always enjoyed the Scandinavian way of life, their lovely ports, new and fresh looking buildings and their lakes and waterfronts. Now we would be able to see a little of Leningrad as well, where my brother-in-law, George von Harten, was born and loved so much, and possibly catch a glimpse of the island of Osel in the Bay of Riga, where George and his family lived for some years before the Soviet Revolution in 1917.

The Royal Princess was quite the most comfortable cruise liner that we had ever been on. Our state room cabin was well equipped with two beds, a shower etc. and excellent furniture and a small deck instead of a porthole where we could sit out and have our breakfast each morning.

There were two sittings in the large dining hall where we were given a table with two other English ladies and a member of the ship's staff. We chose second sitting in order to enjoy our drinks in the large circular lounge in comfort before partaking. The ship contained all the usual facilities for our enjoyment, a swimming pool, of course, and deck chairs and sun loungers, a boutique, shipboard casino and video recordings, and I was able to take advantage of the sauna and massage provided and the Beauty Shop for my hair. There was, as always, an excellent small library.

There were excursions possible at all ports of call which we could sign up for beforehand. As we were older than many other passengers we always tried to go on excursions that did not require too much walking. So we went on a drive excursion in Copenhagen which took us to Christiansborg Palace, through the Royal Reception Rooms and the theatre museum. This was the third Palace which stands on the very spot where more than eight hundred years ago Bishop Absalom built his stronghold beside the village of Haver, and where in turn the first and second palaces of Christiansborg arose. Fire claimed the second palace, but the third palace was built of granite and is much more solid; the roof was sheathed in copper. The tower terminates in a crown five metres in diameter, carrying a weather vane shaft with two crowns and a vane and is very tall.

In the north section of the main building and in the wing along Prince Jorgen's Courtyard are the Royal Reception Rooms which we saw with Her Majesty's Library, the Audience Chambers, Supreme Court and the Prime Minister's Department. There are also the Royal Stables, coach house and the Theatre Museum round the riding grounds. We were very impressed with the position of the Royal Palace and its lovely dimensions.

Another favourite of mine – the lovely modern built Grundvigs Church on the outskirts of Copenhagen with its beautiful interior of modern polished wood and its classic organ loft.

Then we sailed north to Leningrad (St. Petersburg). We edged into her broad harbour, where every sort of ship and boat could be seen. We had opted for a canal excursion here and I wanted above all else to see some of the treasures of the "Hermitage" at least. We were only able to be in Leningrad for two days – so more was not possible.

The canal trip was an excellent introduction to this famous city, but we did not have a very good guide. What we saw were beautifully coloured palaces, little bridges exquisitely built and perfected filled both of us with delight, but much that we saw looked shabby, how wonderful it must have been in its heyday. Then we were taken to Palace Square, completed by the Italian architect, the great Carlo Rossi, who also built the Pushkin Theatre and, of course, the Mihailov Castle now known as Engineer's Castle, and other great works of art.

Here in Palace Square, he built an addition on the north side, facing the Winter Palace, of a splendid semi-circle-housing the Ministries of War, Finance and Foreign Affairs with, at its centre, the great double triumphal arch surmounted by a chariot and winged victory, which leads through to the Nevski Prospect, the famous central route in Leningrad. In the centre of this large square stands a tall, pink granite column to the memory of Alexander I, surrounded by the statue of a winged angel or archangel holding a cross. It was here in Palace Square that the big ceremonial parades were held for the Emperor and later demonstrations which led to the revolutions of 1905 and 1917 when the crowd burst into the Winter Palace. Standing on one side of this huge square one can see the mass of the St. Peter and St. Paul Fortress and two lovely small palaces painted in rose stucco and green stucco with the length of the Hermitage building between.

I'm afraid I stood there and wept. I was overcome with the sight of this enormous and beautiful Palace Square. Although I did not have the time on this visit to view the many museums listed in my guide book. I hoped to come again, possibly with George's younger brother Andreas von Harten, for another look.

There was, however, an excursion planned to the Hermitage Museum, and in spite of all sorts of prophecies of physical discomfort, I was determined to go and this proved a wonderful experience. The palace itself is so beautiful with its huge crystal chandeliers, lofty ceilings white and gold painted and beautiful dimensions, each room a picture in itself and with its treasures displayed around the walls and on tables in each room. I climbed up the lovely staircase to view some further pictures and art treasures on the first floor before leaving again through the entrance into Palace Square. I had only a glimpse of the treasures it contained in the early rooms – early Russian culture, Caucasian and Central Asian Arts and Ancient Egyptian, Chinese, Indian and Japanese exhibits. Some of the paintings of the Italian, Spanish and French Schools. I left regretfully and determined to come again.

Leningrad was full of dancing and music schools and much more – what a cultural centre, indeed, to be born into and to live in. I salute my brother in law and also my early teacher, Mr. Peter Ouspensky, who lived and worked here.

But our "home" was on the move again, and we had to leave this lovely city and go once more across the Baltic Sea to Helsinki, Finland, and what a change in atmosphere. The Finnish people were friendly, welcoming and entirely happy. They showed us their memorial to their great composer, Sibelius, and some of their works of art in their museums. We enjoyed their well filled shops and excellent food and drinks before embarking once more to continue our trip in the Baltic south to Stockholm. We were now, of course, in the land of the midnight sun, and I observed from my deck seat in my cabin one evening that it was already 11.30 pm and the sun was only then just beginning to set.

Passing the Gulf of Riga, we saw the little island of Osel where the von Harten family lived for some years before being driven out by the Soviet Revolution in 1917.

The von Harten family originally came from Poland, but in 1796 when Poland and the Polish State disappeared from the map, central Poland with its capital Warsaw was allocated to Russia and its citizens automatically became Russian nationals. (Father) Von Harten was by profession a mining engineer and so was able to go freely where he was needed and during the childhood and youth of his sons Alexander and Georg in St. Petersburg life was reasonably normal and even the German speaking minority could lead a peaceful life.

In 1909, the von Hartens bought a smallholding on the island of Osel in the Bay of Riga not far from Arensburg, the main town of the island, and this became the focal point of the family. Their grandfather, Hermann von Harten, who was born and brought up on this Island and had returned there after a long life and died in 1917. Three cousins who were living there were the same age as the older von Harten boys, and so became like brothers and sisters to them.

Unfortunately, all was not well with Russia and when the Russian Revolution broke out in 1917, the Soviet soldiers came across the ice in the winter to capture the island of Osel, but the inhabitants were ready for them and put up so much resistance, although the eldest son of von Harten was killed. The inhabitants found that the telephone had not been cut between the islands, and they managed to telephone for help and the Estonian troops were able to rescue them.

Meanwhile, we contined on our way south to Stockholm on our cruise.

Keith and I had again signed up to see Stockholm by boat and we were looking forward to this boat trip very much, but unfortunately the motor boat which was to take us, moored beside our own Royal Princess, suddenly caught fire and we were all evacuated in a hurry. At such short notice, no replacement could be found and so we were left to our own devices for the day. Some took taxis and explored the city, but we opted for a quiet day and bought some of the linen and other trinkets offered on the wharf.

Cruising on to Amsterdam, we drove to the Rijks Museum and enjoyed the lovely Rembrandt paintings before returning to England and Tilbury Docks.

CHAPTER 36

My Visit to Mother Meera, a Modern Avatar

"Mother Meera", daughter of farmer parents, grew up in India and was born on December 26th, 1960. She was not especially religious, and was not brought up in any traditional religion, but her contact with the Absolute was immediate and unmediated. From the age of two or three, she would go to different lights when she was in need of comfort.

At six years old, she had her first experience of Samadhi when she fell senseless for a whole day; an experience, which she tells us, taught her complete detachment from human relations." *

Mother Meera claims to be the living Incarnation of the Divine Mother and her work is the transformation of humanity into God, of time into Eternity, of matter into Divine Matter. Her work is a work of transformation and it has no end. Mother Meera has come to purify the consciousness of the earth so it may be ready for transformation. She is calling down onto the earth the light of the Supreme that makes Transformation certain. Her work in our time is to open all people to the power and radiance of this Light so the Divine Will may be done and the Divine Life established on earth.**

I was able to take "Darsham" with Mother Meera during the autumn of 1994. Mrs. Hadding, my Godchild, lives with her family in Hessen and had recently lost her mother and my great friend. After visiting her grave in Marburg, Lahn, we drove on by car to stay near the village of Dornburg, Thalheim where Mother Meera lives. At the appointed time, we drove there. We had been asked to assemble at the Town Hall where we would be given further instruc-

* The Mother by Adilakshmi, p.7.
** All and Everything by G. Gurdjieff, p. 1063.

tions about parking facilities and access to her home. Visitors were asked to sit on a bench outside her home until the front door was opened, and then visitors stepped inside and took off their shoes inside the passage. An Indian lady, Adirakshmi, seemed to be in charge of the seating, which was in three rooms of medium size, and the hall passage.

I was asked to sit in the hall passage where I had an excellent view of Mother Meera as she walked past me to take her seat in one of the main rooms to start "Darsham". Then each person in turn took a place kneeling in front of Mother Meera and was blessed by her. This routine went forward with clockwork regularity. Mother Meera would place her hands on each person's head and shoulders and then it was time for Mother Meera to look up and look deeply into the eyes of each visitor for several seconds.

As I was rather older than most of those present and walking with a stick, I decided to try to go last, and when my turn came, a helper signalled for a chair to be placed in front of Mother Meera and I sat there. The first time I came, I was rather nervous over these proceedings, but on the second evening when I took Darsham and I looked into Mother Meera's eyes, I saw a wide highway stretching into the distance with high poles on either side with lights on each of them. As always, it was a deep blessing to have been amongst others who had a similar spiritual goal and I gained much strength and happiness from the two evenings spent there.

CHAPTER 37

Finale

As I start my last chapter, I find it very difficult to sum up my feelings. I am now in my ninetieth year and so much is happening still in my life and around me. Our earth is indeed becoming a single world; so many barriers are now open.

The spiritual teachers that taught me so much and also my beloved companion and sister whose interest in things spiritual was shared by me and our Father, Sir Charles Marston are now gone. My father, who wrote so vividly from his experiences in Israel at Jerusalem, Jericho and Lackish, said in his book "The Bible Comes Alive" when talking about the prophecies made in the Bible, announcing the completion of the present age and the return of the Divine King of Kings, to set up his promised Kingdom on earth, may be rapidly ripening for fulfilment. "Howbeit when the Son of Man cometh, shall he find faith in the earth?" * (Luke XVII.8). Sir Charles ends his book "The dawn of a true science – the science of Men and of his God, which we find set up in the Bible, may yet save our civilisation from destruction and rescue us from the further pursuit of vain substitutes and the building of more Towers of Babel – but have we much more time to waste?**

Thanks to Mr. Ouspensky's current book "Tertium Organum" and its early translation into English (described by me in Ch.6) enabling it to be read widely in the U.S.A. and England, Lady Rothermere invited him to come to England. Accordingly, Mr. Ouspensky and his wife, having obtained an appropriate visa, and with a considerable command of the English language, one day in

* "The Bible Comes Alive" – by Sir Charles Marston, p. 188.
** "The Bible Comes Alive" – by Sir Charles Marston, p. 188.

1921 set out for London, while Mr. Gurdjieff and his party, including the de Hartmanns, left for Germany. Mr. Bennett became more and more engrossed with politics.*

My sister and I have felt all our lives that there exists a sort of golden thread which links us together at important times of change (see Ch.5). The "Movements" Display in New York City, U.S.A. for instance and the contact there with Mr. Orage - ostensibly for my sister so that she could learn to write and later this made it possible for her to meet Mr. Gurdjieff and begin work with the New York groups. As I was living at the time (in 1928/29) in New York with my sister, I was also part of the thread, although for some years I continued my own life and education.

It was not until 1936 on my return from a world trip that I asked my sister to put me in touch with Mr. Ouspensky's group which was very active in London. My sister felt that I was now older and mature enough to go and so I started hearing the lectures being read entitled "The Psychology of Man's Possible Evolution" and later the cosmological lectures. It was the beginning for me of the study of the "Science of Man"

Just now, with the millennium in sight, we have been given a great opportunity to raise ourselves to a higher level of spiritual attainment. Two *known* avatars** are working on earth to bring this about and to help mankind to correct those vices inherent in them. One of these avatars, Mother Meera, I have already discussed in the previous chapter.

On my return to England from my visit to Mother Meera, I was privileged to hear from my friends at Glastonbury about an Avatar living in south India known already throughout the world as Sathya Sai Baba – one memorable book written about Him by a husband and wife team called "Sai Baba – the Embodiment of Love". They are convinced that this extraordinary Saint, who has indeed performed every kind of miracle, is the One who will save our planet from self-destruction. Sai Baba has said: "The calamity which has come upon mankind will be averted and a new golden age will recur. The time will come when I will have to move across the sky and use the sky as an auditorium. Yes – that will happen – believe me.

I do believe that sometime in the 21st century Sai Baba will apport himself across the sky and, standing on a levitated rostrum, speak to perhaps ten million people on a campus of perhaps ten thousand

* "Witness" by J.G. Bennett - Ch. 6 (American Edition)
** Avatar – Divine Incarnation

acres. And that alone will make our politicians and our media stand in fear and trembling.

Sai Baba says: "When there is a small local disturbance, a police constable is enough to put it down, but when all mankind is threatened with moral ruin, the Inspector General has to come; that is the Lord." Surely it is up to every one of us to help him.*

★ Sai Baba -The Embodiment of Love by Peggy Mason and Ron Laing: p.259.